Language

Language

An Invitation to Cognitive Science

Volume 1

edited by Daniel N. Osherson and Howard Lasnik

A Bradford Book
The MIT Press
Cambridge, Massachusetts
London, England

Second Printing, 1990

This book was set in Palatino by Asco Trade Typesetting Ltd., Hong Kong and printed and bound by The Halliday Lithograph in the United States of America.

Library of Congress Cataloging-in-Publication Data

An Invitation to cognitive science / edited by Daniel N. Osherson and Howard Lasnik.

    p.   cm.
Includes index.
Contents: v. 1. Language
ISBN 0-262-15035-2 (v. 1).—ISBN 0-262-65033-9 (v. 1 : pbk.)
  1. Cognition. 2. Cognitive science. I. Osherson, Daniel N. II. Lasnik, Howard.
BF311.I68   1990
153—dc19
                                     89-30868
                                         CIP

Contents

List of Contributors

Kenneth I. Forster
Department of Psychology
University of Arizona

Merrill F. Garrett
Department of Psychology
University of Arizona

Morris Halle
Department of Linguistics and
Philosophy
Massachusetts Institute of
Technology

James Higginbotham
Department of Linguistics and
Philosophy
Massachusetts Institute of
Technology

Richard K. Larson
Department of Linguistics and
Philosophy
Massachusetts Institute of
Technology

Howard Lasnik
Department of Linguistics
University of Connecticut

Joanne L. Miller
Department of Psychology
Northeastern University

Daniel N. Osherson
Department of Brain and Cognitive
Sciences
Massachusetts Institute of
Technology

Steven Pinker
Department of Brain and Cognitive
Sciences
Massachusetts Institute of
Technology

Edgar B. Zurif
Department of Psychology
Brandeis University

Foreword

The book you are holding is the first of a three-volume introduction to contemporary cognitive science. The thirty chapters that make up the three volumes have been written by thirty-one authors, including linguists, psychologists, philosophers, computer scientists, biologists, and engineers. The topics range from arm trajectories to human rationality, from acoustic phonetics to mental imagery, from the cerebral locus of language to the categories that people use to organize experience. Topics as diverse as these require distinctive kinds of theories, tested against distinctive kinds of data, and this diversity is reflected in the style and content of the thirty chapters.

As the authors of these volumes, we are united by our fascination with the mechanisms and structure of biological intelligence, especially human intelligence. Indeed, our principal goal in this introductory work is to reveal the vitality of cognitive science, to share the excitement of its pursuit, and to help you reflect upon its interest and importance. You may think of these volumes, then, as an invitation—namely, our invitation to join the ongoing adventure of research into human cognition.

The topics that we explore fall into four parts: "Language," whose nine chapters are found in volume 1, along with an introductory chapter for the volumes as a whole; "Visual Cognition" and "Action," which make up volume 2; and "Thinking," whose seven chapters belong to volume 3, along with an epilogue devoted to three supplementary topics. Each volume ends with a listing of the chapters in the other two.

Since each part is self-contained, the four parts may be read in any order. On the other hand, it is easiest to read the chapters within a given part in the order indicated. Each chapter concludes with suggestions for further reading and questions for further thought.

The artwork at the beginning of each chapter was provided by Todd Siler. We hope that it enhances your enjoyment of the work.

Paul M. Churchland

K Dowler

Merrill F. Garrett

Innis Harn

John M. Hollerbach

Howard Gosink

Joanne L. Miller

Daniel N. Osherson

Mary C. Potter

Edward E. Smith

Stephen P. Kosslyn

Charles E. Wright

Edgar Zurif

Fred Dretske

H. L. Galiana

Alvin I. Goldman

James Higginbotham

Keith Holyoak

Richard K. Larson

Richard Lewontin

Ferdinand Verhulst

Steven Pinker

Paul Horn

Elizabeth Spelke

Shimon Ullmann

Al Yonille

The Study of Cognition

Cognitive science is the study of human intelligence in all of its forms, from perception and action to language and reasoning. The exercise of intelligence is called cognition. Under the rubric of cognition fall such diverse human activities as recognizing a friend's voice over the telephone, reading a novel, jumping from stone to stone in a creek, explaining an idea to a classmate, remembering the way home from work, and choosing a profession. Cognitive processes are essential to each of these activities; indeed, they are essential to everything we do.

Research on cognition has historical roots in antiquity and was already flourishing in the 1800s. The field drew new impetus in the 1950s, however, from theoretical innovations in linguistics (Chomsky 1956, 1957) and computer science (Minsky 1956, 1961; Newell and Simon 1956). The rapid development of these fields raised the possibility of genuine insight into the structure of human cognition and exerted a magnetic attraction on other disciplines concerned with intelligence, both human and artificial. These disciplines included parts of neurophysiology, psychology, philosophy, anthropology, mathematics, and economics. The result has been a vigorous dialogue among scientists working within diverse traditions, employing different methodologies, and starting from different assumptions. By the mid-1970s it was becoming clear that the different approaches were complementary and that the next generation of scientists would need to have a distinctive kind of training, drawing from several established disciplines. In response, undergraduate and postgraduate programs in cognitive science were started in many universities, both in North America and in Europe.

The new programs have created a need for new textbooks, especially introductory textbooks that open cognitive science to the beginning student. Such is the purpose of these three volumes. They provide a glimpse of the topics treated within the discipline, the methods used, and the theories produced so far.

Why Study Human Cognition?

Before looking at the contents of these volumes in more detail, let us consider some reasons for the scientific investigation of human cognition.

The Fascination of Cognitive Science

Think about your last conversation with a friend. From a certain point of view it went this way. Your friend had an idea or thought that she wanted to convey to you. For this purpose she sent volleys of commands to scores of muscles in her abdomen, chest, throat, tongue, and lips. The resulting oral gymnastics had the effect of vibrating the air molecules around her. Ultimately the vibrations in the air caused corresponding vibrations at your eardrum. These vibrations were passed along in attenuated form through bones, fluids, and tissues in your ear until they resulted in a volley of sensory discharges along the auditory nerve to your brain. The sensory discharges then acted in such a way as to cause some counterpart of your friend's idea to be formed in your brain. This idea gave rise to an idea of your own, so you sent volleys of commands to scores of muscles in your abdomen, chest, throat, tongue, and lips that had the effect ... and so forth. The intricacy of this process is astonishing. It allows the communication of ideas and thoughts of great originality and subtlety, yet operates at remarkable speed (producing comprehensible speech at several words a second) and requires no noticeable mental effort by the speaker and listener. This point is worth stressing. Speech and understanding are effortless and unconscious activities that go on while we think about the topic of the conversation (instead of having to think about the mechanism of communication). How does this marvelous communication system work? This is the subject of the part entitled "Language" (this volume).

Almost any human competence arouses the same sense of curiosity and wonder. Consider visual recognition. For you to know that it is your friend across the room, it suffices for light reflected from his face to flash across the retinas of your eyes for a fraction of a second. Within broad limits, it does not matter how much ambient light there is in the room, or whether the light reflected to the retinas comes from a profile or a frontal view of your friend's face. Typically, the central area of only one retina is enough for the job, which amounts to no more than 10 square millimeters of retinal surface (about 3 percent the size of a fingernail). As in the case of language, the nervous system relies on unconscious processes to transform successive flashes of light on the retina (which typically jumps from position to position several times per second) into the seamless visual scenery we experience. These processes are the subject of the part entitled "Visual Cognition" (volume 2).

In addition to the fascination engendered by their sheer intricacy and efficiency, human cognitive processes are of interest for another reason. To a large extent a person just *is* the ensemble of cognitive processes she harbors; the thoughts, perceptions, utterances, and actions created by these processes help define her as a person. As a result, cognitive science focuses on a fundamental question both for the individual and for the species, namely, What does it mean, from the cognitive point of view, to be human?

Technological Development

It is a commonplace that Western societies are being transformed by the introduction of computer technology. Every month we learn of progress in the speed and size of available computer hardware and in the development of software for new domains of modern life. It is easy to be dazzled by the pace of progress.

For this reason it is important not to lose sight of a sobering fact about modern computers and the programs that make them run. Years of effort have not succeeded in endowing computerized systems with even rudimentary abilities in areas where humans excel. An example is human tool use. No computer-driven, mechanical hand approaches the multipurpose dexterity of the human carpenter's hand, and no breakthroughs are in sight that will close the gap appreciably. The human advantage is even more pronounced with respect to perceptual-motor coordination between hand and eye. No existing or immediately foreseeable computerized system rivals the effortless partnership between visual processing and motor planning that underlies the carpenter's ability to drive a nail just where it is needed. (The complexities of human limb movement and control are discussed in the part entitled "Action" (volume 2).)

The same can be said for other human competences. In the case of language, computerized translation systems lag far behind the skill of bilingual humans. Even within a single language, although language comprehension systems continue to improve, there is as yet nothing close to a computerized system that could discuss airline reservations, for example, in normal speech. Even the elementary task of voice transcription—in which speech is converted to printed text—remains beyond current technology, whereas this ability amounts to little more than basic literacy in the human case. (For more on this topic, see chapters 4 and 5 of this volume.)

These considerations suggest that the investigation of human intelligence can play a useful role in the search for artificially intelligent systems. Study of the human case might suggest new design principles to be incorporated into computerized systems. For example, investigating how the human visual system processes and interprets light might aid computer scientists in attempting to build automated stystems with similar powers. Of course, there is no guarantee that investigating the human case will shed light on the artificial case. The human system might prove so difficult to understand that computer scientists would do better to look elsewhere for guidance. In addition, Nature may not have invented the only way to process visual information efficiently, to move a hand, to speak, and so on. (Analogously, bird and insect flight—involving the deformation and agitation of wings—did not turn out to be the only mechanism available for air travel.) Nonetheless, the tremendous powers of the human system provide good reason to study it, and collaboration between cognitive scientists and computer scientists has increased steadily over the years.

Preparation and Repair of the Cognitive System

The human cognitive apparatus may be thought of as a tool for interacting successfully with the environment. Like any complex instrument, this tool must be fine-tuned to the specific circumstances of its use and repaired if damaged. These activities correspond to education and medical treatment, respectively. Research in cognitive science can contribute to both domains.

Education. Designing a successful curriculum for a given field of knowledge (say, one of the sciences) requires two kinds of expertise on the part of the designer. First, he must be solidly competent in the field. Second, he must understand (if only implicitly) how the learner's cognitive apparatus is structured. The second kind of expertise guides the way lessons are built and organized, so as to maximize learning. It is reasonable to expect that progress in cognitive science will illuminate the cognitive structure of children and adults in such a way as to aid the design of effective curricula. Research relevant to this theme is presented in chapter 6 of the part entitled "Thinking" (volume 3).

Another kind of learning consists in better appreciating the strengths and weaknesses of one's cognitive apparatus. To illustrate the point, consider your own ability to assign probabilities to chance outcomes. In what kinds of situations do you assign probabilities correctly, and in what kinds of situations are you subject to illusions and systematic errors? Research in cognitive science raises and analyzes questions of this nature. By making us aware of potential pitfalls in our reasoning and perception, such research can help many people make better judgments. Some aspects of human judgment are discussed in these terms in chapters 3 and 4 of volume 3.

Medical treatment. The brain may lose its remarkable cognitive powers through traumatic injury, stroke, or diseases like schizophrenia and Alzheimer's syndrome. Advances in tissue grafts and in brain chemistry have brought treatment of such conditions into the realm of possibility. However, if new treatments are to be effective in restoring lost or threatened functions, much information will be needed about the cognitive role played by different neural structures. In fact, this is a primary area of research in cognitive science. (For discussion of the neurological basis of language, see chapter 7 of this volume.)

Cognitive science is also central to advances in the diagnosis of neural disease and damage. In light of detailed knowledge of the relation between brain and cognition, the fine grain of a patient's perceptual, linguistic, or motor behavior may assume diagnostic significance. The attempt to correlate such behavior with the onset of neural disease is another area of active research in cognitive science (see Posner et al. 1988; Kosslyn 1988).

Social Choices

How people decide to organize themselves when they are free to choose, as well as what social structures they find tolerable when their choices are constrained, is determined in part by their conception of themselves as human beings. Consider the following opposing views:

View 1: People are basically lazy, moved to activity and inquiry only under the pressure of organic need.

View 2: People are innately curious and industrious, becoming lazy only from stifled ambition and training for passivity.

A community that shared view 1 might well be led to different political choices than a community that shared view 2.

A scientifically sound theory of human cognition can be expected to throw light on questions such as these. It is not to be expected (or desired) that scientific information of this sort determine political choices by itself. Such choices are governed by more than scientific information (notably, by the values and aspirations of those concerned). Nonetheless, it may be hoped that greater understanding about this one component of human nature, namely, human cognition, can lead to more adaptive reflection on some of the choices that face contemporary society.

Organization

Next let us turn to some of the principles that underlie the organization of the three volumes.

The Parts of Cognitive Science

Human cognition is so complicated that only small pieces of it can be investigated at a time. However, it is not obvious how to divide up a cognitive activity into units that can be meaningfully studied in isolation. Consider, for example, a conversation between friends over coffee. Numerous cognitive capacities are implicated in this commonplace activity, each interwoven with the others. Linguistic ability is exercised in formulating and understanding the sentences traded back and forth. Auditory perception is involved in interpreting the speech produced by each participant. Visual perception is implicated, both in registering the reaction caused by an utterance (in the form of frowning, head shaking, eyebrow furrowing, and so on) and in "reading" features of the speech signal from the lips of the speaker. Motor control is presupposed in the act of talking, since each articulator in the mouth and throat must be sent into motion at just the right moment in order to create the desired speech sound. Finally, an underlying process of thinking and reasoning controls the selection and interpretation of the utterances produced. Thinking and reasoning of course embrace a multitude of cognitive capacities, from remembering old information and integrating new information to planning a course of action and anticipating its consequences. It is not immediately evident how to factor these cognitive prerequisites to a conversation in a way that favors understanding any one of them. Indeed, the factorization question can be theoretically controversial in its own right.

For this reason, the organization of these volumes does not represent a theory of the natural components of human cognition but instead reflects the informal understanding that most people have about their mental faculties. Among other abilities, people typically recognize competence in the areas of language, visual perception, motor control, and thinking. The four parts of this work are titled accordingly. Each part represents a selection of topics that are central to contemporary cognitive science and illustrates the kind of progress that has been made in the field as a whole. Although many topics are omitted, a healthy sample of contemporary concerns is represented. The three chapters forming the epilogue (volume 3) cover additional issues.

Levels of Analysis for Cognitive Faculties

The choice of chapters for each part has also been influenced by an important methodological principle. Since the appearance of an influential monograph by David Marr (1982), it has been widely appreciated that a given cognitive competence can be investigated at three levels of analysis. These levels are often given the names *level 1* (implementation), *level 2* (representation and algorithm), and *level 3* (computation). The following analogy explains these distinctions.

A computer engaged in a complex calculation may be approached at each of the three levels. At level 1, the level of implementation, the computer's hardware is described. At level 2, the level of representation and algorithm, a more abstract description of the computer is given, including a representational part and an algorithmic part. The representational part concerns both the form in which the computer stores data needed for its calculation and the form in which it writes its output and any intermediate results. The algorithmic part concerns the succession of decisions and operations carried out by the computer as it performs its calculation in real time (for instance, whether an input number is squared before it is added to some other input number, or whether the addition comes before the squaring). These kinds of facts about representation and algorithm are easily obscured at level 1 since the details of hardware do not allow the logic of the computer's behavior to shine through. This logic is captured at level 2, which abstracts from the physics of circuits and chips to describe how the hardware is being used. Level 3, the level of computation, abstracts even further. At this level computational analysis of the computer provides a mathematically transparent description of what it is doing by providing, for example, an equation for the function being calculated. Here as well, the efficiency of the computer is analyzed by characterizing the time and memory resources it requires to perform its calculation.

A central idea of modern cognitive science is that the human cognitive system can be understood as though it were a giant computer engaged in a complex calculation. As with the computer, it is assumed that we may approach human cognition at the same three levels of analysis. In the case of language, for example, the level of implementation corresponds to neurological analysis of the structures and connections in the brain that underlie the use of language. The level of representation and algorithm focuses on the processing of information by the system and on the format of linguistic knowledge stored in memory. It is at this level that cognitive scientists attempt to describe the information flow required by language use, that is, the successive psychological steps required to interpret or produce speech. At the level of computation language is analyzed grammatically and its structural properties are exposed. At this level as well, an attempt is made to understand the general properties of the procedures described at the second level, including their efficiency and reliability.

It is crucial for understanding contemporary cognitive science to see that the different levels of analysis are connected, in the sense that facts and principles discovered at one level contribute to analyses at other levels. For example, knowledge of the grammar of a language (described at level 3) informs us about the kind of algorithm that is needed to recognize and understand its sentences. Grammatical knowledge thus constrains our hypotheses at level 2 about the information processing that underlies language use, since an accurate theory of information processing must be consistent with the grammatical properties of language. Similarly, a level 1 theory of the brain imposes requirements on theories at level 2, inasmuch as the information flow described at level 2 must be capable of being implemented using the neural hardware described at the level of the brain.

The organization of these volumes has been greatly influenced by this approach. Each part includes chapters that focus on distinct levels of analysis: implementation, representation/algorithm, and computation. Where possible, information about theories at one level is brought to bear on theories at another. In addition, chapter 1 of the epilogue discusses a distinctive approach to cognitive science that attempts to exploit to the fullest the theoretical constraints that exist between levels.

Other Kinds of Analyses

We may add other kinds of analyses to the three proposed by Marr. One of these is *philosophical*. Philosophical analysis attempts to clarify the concepts and presuppositions that figure in theories of a given cognitive capacity. It also attempts to use scientific findings about the capacity to illuminate traditional philosophical issues. Each part concludes with a philosophical chapter that bears on the cognitive capacity discussed therein. A more general philosophical discussion occupies chapter 3 of the epilogue.

Another kind of analysis is *developmental* in character, tracing the origins of a cognitive capacity to infancy and childhood. It provides an inventory of the competences available to infants and children and attempts to uncover the mechanism responsible for the transformation of the child's competence into that of the adult. Insight into the adult competence can often be achieved by developmental analysis, much as the structure of a mature organ is better understood in light of its embryological development. Several chapters are devoted to developmental issues.

Finally, there are *comparative* and *evolutionary* analyses. Comparative analysis contrasts the cognitive abilities of different species. Aside from the intrinsic interest of such contrasts, investigators hope that they will shed light on important features of the human case. These volumes do not treat the comparative aspect of cognitive science, but comprehensive discussions may be found in Roitblat 1987 and Gallistell 1990. Evolutionary analysis attempts to trace a competence through its manifestations in hominids ancestral to man. Chapter 2 of the epilogue is devoted to this topic.

A final comment will set the stage for all that follows. We—the authors of these volumes—hope they will communicate our fascination with human cognition and our conviction that the abilities it comprises are among the great miracles of life. As much as an invitation to explore theories and data, then, these volumes are our invitation to you to share the intellectual excitement of cognitive science.

References

Chomsky, N. (1956). Three models for the description of language. *IRE Transactions on Information Theory*, IT-2(3), 113–124.

Chomsky, N. (1957). *Syntactic structures*. The Hague: Mouton.

Gallistell, C. R. (1990). *The organization of learning*. Cambridge, MA: MIT Press.

Kosslyn, S. (1988). Aspects of a cognitive neuroscience of mental imagery. *Science* 240, 1621–1626.

Marr, D. (1982). *Vision: A computational investigation into the human representation and processing of visual information*. San Francisco: W. H. Freeman.

Minsky, M. (1956). *Heuristic aspects of artificial intelligence*. Lincoln Laboratory, Technical Report 34–57, MIT, December 1956.

Minsky, M. (1961). Steps towards artificial intelligence. *Proceedings of the IRE* 49, 8–29.

Newell, A., and H. A. Simon (1956). The logic theory machine: A complex information processing system. *IRE Transactions on Information Theory*, IT-2(3), 61–79.

Posner, M. I., S. E. Petersen, P. T. Fox, and M. E. Raichle (1988). Localization of cognitive operations in the human brain. *Science* 240, 1627–1631.

Roitblat, H. (1987). *Introduction to comparative cognition*. New York: W. H. Freeman.

Language

Language: Introduction

Howard Lasnik

One of the most remarkable human cognitive capacities is that involved in the use and acquisition of language. A moment's thought is sufficient to establish the extraordinary richness of this system of knowledge. In particular, it allows the production and comprehension of novel sentences of essentially unlimited complexity. Further, this creative use of language is by no means an exotic talent. Rather, it is crucially involved in normal language use. For example, the probability is extremely low that you have ever before encountered the sentences of this paragraph. Nonetheless, you are able to recognize them as part of your language and comprehend them, whereas if the same sentences were read (or spoken) back-to-front, you would immediately reject them as not part of your language. Why is this so?

The foregoing question is one of the most profound in cognitive science. As a first step toward an answer, it will help to break the question into pieces: (1) What does a person who knows a language know? (2) How is the knowledge used in the process of speaking and understanding? (3) How does that person acquire that knowledge? The nine chapters that follow address these issues.

1

Syntax

Howard Lasnik

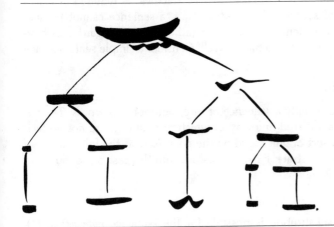

When we speak, the utterances we produce are normally framed in a particular language, and we expect to understand an utterance only if we happen to know the language in which it is framed. Knowledge of a language is thus of paramount importance in every speech event and must be the primary target of the scientific study of language.

In fact, mature mastery of a human language involves knowledge of several different kinds. As speakers of English, we know facts about its *semantics* or meaning structure (chapter 2), about its *phonology* or sound structure (chapter 3), and about its *syntax* or grammatical structure—the subject of this chapter.

Most obviously, as speakers of a language, we know a large number of words. In addition, we evidently have command of a productive system for the appropriate arrangement of words into sentences, the syntax of the language. Given the creative use of language—the fact that new sentences are routinely used and understood—it could not be true that the syntax of a language consisted merely of a list of sentences that are memorized in the course of language acquisition. Something more complex—hence, more interesting—must be involved. In this chapter, we will explore some central aspects of this complex and interesting system of knowledge.

1.1   Syntactic Structure

An initial assumption about syntactic structure might be that speech (like written English) is broken into sentences, and the sentences into words. This already involves a substantial degree of "abstractness," since, as will be discussed in chapter 3, there are few, if any, direct physical correlates of these divisions. But in fact, even further abstractness is required in a successful account of syntactic knowledge. Thus, a sentence cannot be analyzed as simply a sequence of words but rather must be regarded as having a certain hierarchical structure as well. Consider a simple sentence such as (1):

(1)   The man left.

Clearly, this is not simply a sequence of three autonomous words. *The* and *man* are closely associated in a way in which *man* and *left* are not. In fact, they constitute a sort of unit based on the noun *man*, as the following two syntactic tests demonstrate. First, a "pro-form" (in this case a pronoun) can substitute for *the man*:

(2)   He left.

No comparable substitution is possible for the sequence *man left* in (1). Second, an adverb modifying the sentence can easily be inserted between *man* and *left*, as in (3), but not between *the* and *man*, as in (4):

(3)   The man obviously left.

(4)   *The obviously man left.   [* indicates an ungrammatical sentence, a sequence of words that is not a sentence of the language under investigation.]

   This pattern of data strongly suggests that the sequence *the man* constitutes a unit, whereas the sequence *man left* does not. How can this fact be represented? Apparently, sentence (1) is divided into two major parts, or *constituents*. The first part is based on a noun, and the second part on a verb. Let us then designate the first part *noun phrase*, and the second, *verb phrase* (henceforth, *NP* and *VP*). We might now say that an English sentence (*S*) like (1) consists of an NP followed by a VP, roughly corresponding to the traditional subject-predicate division. (5) is a shorthand way of stating this property of English sentences:

(5)   S → NP VP

An NP, in turn, consists of a noun (N) optionally preceded by a determiner (Det), and a VP consists of a verb (V):

(6)a.   NP → (Det) N   [Parentheses indicate an optional item.]

   b.   VP → V

There are many other types of NPs and VPs. In a moment we will look at some of the further possibilities for VPs. (Chapter 2 will discuss another option for NP.)

The rules in (5) and (6) are *phrase structure rules* governing the structure of English sentences. They can be thought of as part of the system of knowledge underlying the procedures for the analysis of structures and for the production of structures. By hypothesis, then, a person who knows English knows these rules, in some sense, though the knowledge is not necessarily conscious. (This point will be given further attention in chapter 9.)

The structure that the rules in (5) and (6) determine for (1) can be represented by the *phrase structure tree* in figure 1.1. Another way of representing the same information is the *labeled bracketing* in (7):

(7)   [$_S$[$_{NP}$[$_{Det}$ The][$_N$ man]][$_{VP}$[$_V$ left]]]

In addition to very simple VPs containing only a verb, there are VPs that contain NPs, as in (8):

(8)   The man solved the problem.

This indicates that (6b) should be revised so as to allow an NP direct object for the verb:

(9)   VP → V (NP)

As in (6a), the parentheses are to be understood as allowing, but not demanding, that the enclosed material occur in a structure. Taken together, (5) and (9) correctly assert that exactly the same kinds of sequences of words that can appear as subjects of sentences can also appear as objects

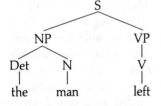

Figure 1.1
Phrase structure tree for sentence (1), *The man left.*

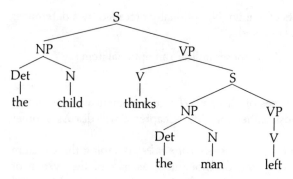

Figure 1.2
Phrase structure tree for sentence (10), *The child thinks the man left.*

of sentences, since the constituent NP occurs in both positions. Without analysis of sentences into constituents, this fact would remain entirely accidental.

We are now in a position to begin to answer the question with which this part opened, concerning the creative use of language. A major way of constructing longer and longer sentences is to embed one sentence inside another. We have already seen VPs of the form VP → V and VP → V NP. Another extremely important possibility exists as well. The material following V can be an entire sentence:

(10)   The child thinks the man left.

In (10) the direct object of the verb is our original sentence, (1). The structure of (10) is represented in figure 1.2. An additional VP phrase structure rule immediately allows for this possibility:

(11)   VP →V S

Now the structure in figure 1.2 can be produced by application of rule (5) followed by, among other things, application of rule (11), followed by another application of rule (5). Then the usual rules for expanding NP and VP can apply. This process can be continued indefinitely, with rule (11) introducing an S that, by rule (5), introduces (in addition to another NP) another VP, and so on. Phrase structure rules with this property are said to be *recursive*. It is important to note that the simplest possible rule for generating the structure in figure 1.2—namely, rule (11)—automatically gives the system of rules (the *grammar*) the recursive property. Thus, with just the rules we already have, (10) can be further embedded to produce an even more complex sentence such as (12), with the structure given in figure 1.3:

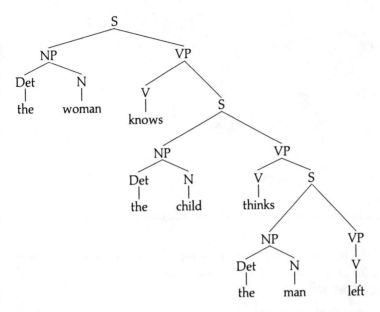

Figure 1.3
Phrase structure tree for sentence (12), *The woman knows the child thinks the man left.*

(12) The woman knows the child thinks the man left.

Recursive rules thus provide a finite means for generating an infinite number of sentences and thereby a crucial part of the answer to the fundamental question of the creative use of language—of how the human brain, with its finite storage capacity, is nevertheless capable of producing and comprehending an infinite number of novel, grammatical sentences of theoretically unbounded length.

1.2 A Case Study: Aspects of the Distribution of Pronouns

Another phenomenon that crucially involves constituent structure is illustrated in (13) and (14):

(13) John thinks he won.

(14) He thinks John won.

In (13) *he* can be used (though it need not be) to designate John: *John* and *he* can be *coreferential*. Curiously, though, in (14) *he* cannot be used to designate John: *John* and *he* are necessarily *noncoreferential* in this instance. We will use indices (numeral subscripts) to represent these possibilities;

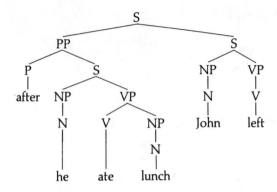

Figure 1.4
Phrase structure tree for sentence (18), *After he₁ ate lunch, John₁ left.*

coreference between two NPs will be represented by coindexing them (that is, by giving them the same index). Thus, (15) is grammatical and (16) ungrammatical:

(15)   John$_1$ thinks he$_1$ won.

(16)   *He$_1$ thinks John$_1$ won.   [Here * indicates ungrammaticality *on a particular interpretation.*]

Under certain circumstances, then, coreference between a pronoun and a "full" NP is prohibited. (17) is a first approximation of this condition, compatible with the facts of (15) and (16):

(17)   If a pronoun precedes a full NP, then the two expressions may not be coreferential.

However, it is not difficult to find counterexamples to (17), such as (18):

(18)   After he$_1$ ate lunch, John$_1$ left.

The structure of (18) is roughly as given in figure 1.4, where *after he ate lunch* is shown as a prepositional phrase (PP) consisting of the preposition *after* and its "object," the sentence *he ate lunch.* (Compare *After lunch, John left.*)

If (18) is grammatical, then why is (16) ungrammatical? The crucial difference is that in (18) the pronominal NP is more deeply embedded (that is, farther from the top of the tree) than the full NP. To state this property more precisely, some additional terminology will be necessary. Let us call S, NP, VP, and so on, (phrasal) *categories.* Further, let us use the term *domination* for the relationship in a given structure between, for example, S, on the one hand, and NP and VP, on the other. That is, in the structures

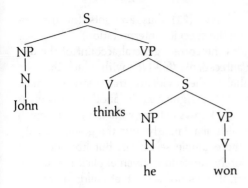

Figure 1.5
Phrase structure tree for sentence (15), *John₁ thinks he₁ won.*

we have considered so far, S dominates both NP and VP. Based on these notions, we define the structural relation *c(ategory)-command* as follows:

(19)   In a given structure a category X c-commands another category Y if every category that dominates X also dominates Y.

In particular, one NP in a given structure c-commands another NP if, in that structure, every category that dominates the former NP also dominates the latter NP. Consider the structure of (15) shown in figure 1.5. Here the NP *John* c-commands the NP *he*, since the "highest" S is the only category that dominates the former NP, and it also dominates the latter. On the other hand, the NP *he* does not c-command the NP *John* since there are two categories—the lower S and the higher VP—that dominate the former but not the latter. Note that in the ungrammatical (16) the pronoun c-commands the full NP, whereas this is not the case in the grammatical (15). Furthermore, in the unexpectedly grammatical (18) the pronoun does not c-command the full NP, since the former is dominated by an S (and a PP) that the latter is not dominated by. This suggests principle (21), based on definition (20):

(20)   One NP *binds* another NP if the former c-commands the latter and the two are coindexed.

(21)   A pronoun may not bind a full NP.

Consider the phrase structure tree in figure 1.5 again, in light of definition (20). If *John* and *he* are to be coreferential, they will be coindexed. Then *John* binds *he* in this structure, since *John* both c-commands *he* and is coindexed with it. This is allowed by (21), since the pronoun does not bind the full NP. If, on the other hand, the two NPs were reversed, as in (16), the pronoun *would* bind the full NP. (21) thus accounts for the ungrammaticality of that example (on the specified interpretation).

To the extent that (21) provides the correct general account of the distribution of pronouns and their antecedents (full NPs with which they are coreferential), we have substantial further evidence that sentences must have structural representations. (21) is significant in another respect as well. Every speaker of English tacitly knows (21) (or something very much like (21)). That is, speakers of English unanimously give the grammaticality judgments indicated above for the example sentences. But how do they come to have that knowledge? Surely, no child is given explicit instruction about these properties. Moreover, it does not seem that children are presented with relevant direct evidence in the form of sentences they might hear, since (21) in effect *prevents* certain sentences from occurring (by preventing them from being grammatical with certain meanings). (See chapter 8 for extensive further discussion of the kinds of evidence available to the language-learning child.) This strongly suggests that (21) is not, in fact, learned. But if children know it without learning, then it is reasonable to conjecture that it is "wired in" (that is, innately present in the structure of the brain) and even to ask whether it has any obvious counterpart in any other cognitive domain. If, as seems likely, it does not, then we have evidence for a "language faculty" as a discrete module of the human mind.

1.3   Deep and Surface Structure

We have seen a number of reasons for assuming that sentences have phrase structure, even if this phrase structure generally has no direct physical manifestation. Thus, knowledge of language involves, in part, mental computation of abstract representations. In this section we will ultimately see evidence for an even further degree of abstractness.

In section 1.1 we examined some of the forms that the VP can take in English sentences, illustrated in (1), (8), and (10), (repeated here):

(22)   The man left.   (VP → V)

(23)   The man solved the problem.   (VP → V NP)

(24)   The child thinks the man left.   (VP → V S)

Left unexpressed so far, however, is the fact that not just any verb can appear in any of these VP types. For example, the verb in (23) would be ungrammatical in the VP of (22):

(25)   *The man solved.

Similarly, the verb in (24) is incompatible with the VP in (23):

(26)   *The man thinks the problem.

Lexical properties—that is, properties of particular lexical items (words)—thus play a major role in determining syntactic well-formedness. In traditional terms, there are transitive verbs, such as *solve*, which require a direct object. Alongside these are intransitive verbs, such as *sleep*, which do not tolerate a direct object:

(27)   *Harry slept the bed.

Furthermore, some transitive verbs, such as *solve*, take an NP, but not an S, as their direct object:

(28)   *Mary solved Bill left.

Others, such as *think*, take an S, but not an NP, as direct object.

  The large lexical category V is thus divided into smaller lexical *subcategories*, each with its own special privileges of occurrence. We can express the properties of the subcategories in the following way:

(29)a.   sleep ⟨___⟩

   b.   solve ⟨___ NP⟩

   c.   think ⟨___ S⟩

(29a) is to be interpreted as the requirement that *sleep* can be inserted only into a VP that has no direct object, that is, a VP like the one shown in figure 1.6a. A verb with the requirement in (29b) could be inserted only into a VP like the one shown in figure 1.6b. And so on.

  Presumably, these syntactic properties of verbs follow, in large measure, from their semantic properties. Thus, in a sentence with *solve* there is a semantic function for a direct object to fulfill; in a sentence with *sleep* there is not. We would be surprised if the next language we investigated had a transitive verb meaning 'sleep' and an intransitive one meaning 'solve'. These semantic functions that direct objects (and subjects) fulfill are called *thematic (theta) roles*. We might then speculate that (25) is ungrammatical because a necessary semantic function has not been fulfilled—a theta role associated with the verb has not been assigned. Conversely, (27) is ungrammatical because it contains an NP, *the bed*, with

Figure 1.6
Phrase structure representation of the subcategorization requirement for (a) *sleep* (*sleep* ⟨___⟩) and (b) *solve* (*solve* ⟨___ NP⟩).

no theta role at all, since *sleep* has only a theta role to assign to a subject and none to assign to an object. (30), the *Theta Criterion*, is a statement of these paired requirements:

(30)a.   Every NP must have a theta role.

    b.   Every theta role must be assigned.

With this much in mind, let us consider (31), which is fully grammatical in some dialects of English and at least marginally acceptable in virtually all dialects:

(31)   This problem, the student solved.

Certainly it is far better than the completely ungrammatical (32):

(32)   *The student solved.

We already know what is wrong with (32): *solve* belongs to the sub-category of verbs that must be inserted into VPs of the form shown in figure 1.6b, since they have an object theta role that they must assign to a direct object—an NP in the VP. But then why is (31) acceptable? The VPs in the two examples appear to be identical. Even more curious is the fact that if (31) is modified so as to have the appropriate kind of VP, it becomes ungrammatical:

(33)   *This problem, the student solved that problem.

Strangely, it is (33), and not (31), that feels like a Theta Criterion violation. Put another way, in (31) (but not in (33)), even though *this problem* is at the front of the sentence, it functions just as though it were in the VP. Suppose, then, that (31) really has *two* representations, one determining the thematic relations of the sentence and the other the pronunciation. In the first representation, the *deep structure* of the sentence, the understood direct object will actually be in the VP. In the second, the *surface structure*, that NP will have been displaced leftward from the position that determines its thematic role. The deep structure of (31) will then be as shown in figure 1.7. This deep structure representation neatly accounts for the interpretation of (31) and is consistent with all of the principles and lexical requirements we have discussed so far. It does not, however, account for the structure of the sentence as immediately perceived. For that, we need an additional representation in which the direct object has been displaced to the front of the sentence, as shown in figure 1.8. An operation of this sort, relating one phrase structure representation to another, is known as a *transformation* (hence the name *transformational grammar* for this general approach to syntax). Let us call the transformation that relates the structure in figure 1.7 to the one in figure 1.8 *Topicalization*. (Note that no Topi-

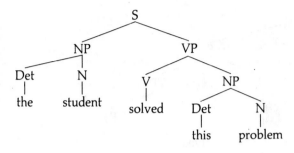

Figure 1.7
Deep structure representation for sentence (31), *This problem, the student solved.*

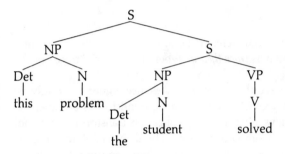

Figure 1.8
Surface structure representation for sentence (31), *This problem, the student solved.*

calization analysis is available for (33), since (33) has no vacant position from which *this problem* could have moved.)

Although the structure in figure 1.7 is straightforward, given the assumptions outlined earlier, two questions can be raised about the structure in figure 1.8. One concerns the attachment site of the displaced NP. We will assume without much discussion that that NP is attached to the front of the S by what is called (*Chomsky*) *adjunction*, a transformational process attaching a moved item (in this case, an NP) to another category (in this case an S) by creating a "higher" instance of the target category that dominates both the moved item and the target category. Figure 1.8 displays left adjunction (attachment on the left) of NP to S. Note, in passing, that figure 1.8 does capture one striking phonological property of sentence (31): there is a major pause between the fronted NP and the remainder of the sentence, corresponding to the major constituent break created between that NP and the residual S.

A second question concerns the position from which the NP moves. Is that position totally eliminated (as assumed in figure 1.8), or does some

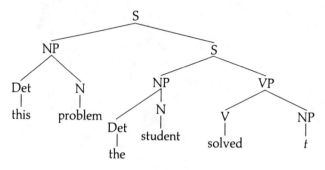

Figure 1.9
Surface structure representation for sentence (31), *This problem, the student solved*, with a trace.

trace of the previous inhabitant remain? Figure 1.9 represents this second possibility (which is known as *trace theory*), where *t* is a silent "trace" of the moved NP, *this problem*.

There is reason to believe that trace theory (hence, figure 1.9) might be correct. Three facts will provide relevant background for an argument in favor of this point of view. First, the Topicalization transformation is not limited to direct objects of simple sentences. The displaced item can even come from an embedded sentence, as in (34), where the topicalized NP is the direct object of the lower verb, or (35), where it is the subject of the lower verb:

(34)   This problem, Mary thinks the student solved *t*.

(35)   The student, Mary thinks *t* solved this problem.

Second, an embedded sentence need not be finite, with a verb in the past tense (like *solved*) or the present tense (like *thinks*). It can also be infinitival, as in (36):

(36)   You want [ₛ the student to solve this problem].

Third, colloquial English has a contraction process by which *want* and *to* become *wanna* when they are immediately adjacent:

(37)a.   You want to solve this problem.

   b.   You wanna solve this problem.

That this process demands adjacency between *want* and *to* is shown by the impossibility of (38), based on (36):

(38)   *You wanna the student solve this problem.

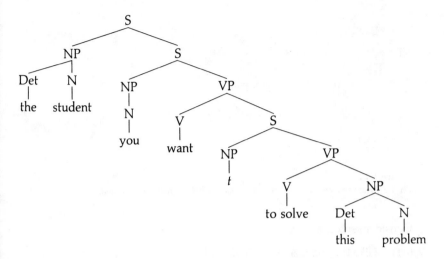

Figure 1.10
Surface structure representation for sentence (39a), *The student, you want to solve this problem,* with a trace.

The relevant (and surprising) property of *wanna* contraction is that even if *the student* in (38) is displaced by Topicalization, contraction is still blocked for most speakers:

(39)a.   The student, you want to solve this problem.

   b.   *The student, you wanna solve this problem.

Superficially, nothing appears to intervene between *want* and *to* in (39a); hence, there seems to be nothing to prevent contraction. But if we assume that Topicalization leaves a trace, then in fact something *does* intervene: the trace of *the student.* Figure 1.10 represents this hypothesis. Even though it is silent, the trace is evidently real, as far as the syntax is concerned.

1.4   Constraints on Transformations

As a result of the Topicalization transformation, an NP can move to the front of its clause, as in (31), and can also move out of its clause to the front of the next higher clause, as in (34), (35), and (39a). In fact, an NP can move still farther, as in (40):

(40)   This problem, Mary thinks John said Susan solved.

However, the operation of Topicalization is subject to certain constraints.

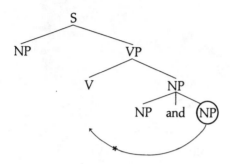

Figure 1.11
Phrase structure tree for sentence (44), *That book, I like this magazine and.*

Consider sentence (41):

(41) · I like this magazine and that book.

In this example the object NP is a *coordinate structure* consisting of two NPs joined by the coordinating conjunction *and*. We might posit phrase structure rule (42) to account for this type of NP:

(42)   NP → NP and NP

Now notice that although (43) is a good instance of Topicalization, (44) (illustrated in figure 1.11) is entirely ungrammatical:

(43)   This magazine and that book, I like.

(44)   *That book, I like this magazine and.

Apparently extraction out of a coordinate structure is prohibited. (45) is another example of the general prohibition (the underlined space marks the extraction site):

(45)   *This magazine, I think that book and ____ impressed Fred.

In an important respect, this Coordinate Structure Constraint is like the constraint on binding (21) discussed earlier. In neither case is it likely that the child learning English is presented with evidence for the constraint. Thus, in both cases it is reasonable to conjecture that the relevant bit of linguistic knowledge is innate. If that conjecture is correct, we should expect the constraints not to be particular to English, since any normal human child can learn any human language. (See chapter 8 for further discussion.) Hence, we should expect the constraints to show up in human languages in general. Overwhelmingly, this expectation is confirmed. Of the hundreds of languages that have been investigated under the sort of approach outlined in this chapter, no clear instances have emerged of languages different from English in these respects.

These constraints are thus examples of abstract properties that appear to be central to human language while playing no obvious role in other cognitive systems and that are evidently not logically necessary. We could imagine a perfectly useful communication system that lacked both the constraint on binding and the Coordinate Structure Constraint: for example, one that differed from English only in allowing sentences like (16) and (44). However, human beings seem not to be designed to make use of such systems as their native languages. As will be emphasized in chapter 9, the discovery of such biases represents a contribution to the investigation of the nature of the human mind.

Suggestions for Further Reading

For a detailed introduction to transformational grammar and some of the issues it raises for cognitive science, see Baker 1978. Van Riemsdijk and Williams 1986 provides an accessible comprehensive review of more recent work in syntactic theory. At a somewhat more advanced level, Lasnik and Uriagereka 1988 presents a detailed overview of one line of recent work in syntax.

The approach to syntax outlined in this chapter was introduced in Chomsky 1957 and modified in Chomsky 1965. It is in the latter work that the notion of deep structure, in essentially its current sense, was first presented. For extensive discussion of the philosophical and methodological foundations of linguistic theory (and especially syntactic theory), see chapter 1 of Chomsky 1965 and also Chomsky 1975.

The Coordinate Structure Constraint was proposed in Ross 1967, where indeed many syntactic phenomena were analyzed in terms of such constraints. An early version of the constraint on binding discussed in the text appears in Lasnik 1976. Both constraints on transformations and constraints on coreference continue to be the subject of a substantial amount of syntactic research; for an extremely useful introductory overview of these topics, again see Van Riemsdijk and Williams 1986.

Questions

1.1   Using the appropriate phrase structure rules from (5), (6), (9), and (11), draw the phrase structure tree for the following sentence:

(i)   The reporter claims the woman knows the child thinks the man saw the accident.

1.2   The structure in figure 1.4 requires two phrase structure rules in addition to those presented in the text. State the two rules, compose an additional sentence utilizing those rules, and draw the phrase structure tree for your sentence.

1.3   The following sentence requires one new rule (in addition to those you have already seen or proposed). State the rule, and draw the phrase structure tree for the sentence.

(i)   After lunch, John left.

1.4   State all the c-command relations that hold among the three NPs in figure 1.3. (For example: *The woman* c-commands *the man*. *The man* does not c-command *the woman*.)

1.5   In *John likes him*, *John* and *him* may not corefer; that is, *him* must refer to someone other than John. This fact might be stated as follows, given the notational conventions presented earlier:

(i)   *$John_1$ likes him_1

Is this accounted for by (21)? If so, show how. If not, show why it is not.

1.6   Using rules stated in the text (including (42)), draw a phrase structure tree for the following NP:

(i)   John and Bill and the dentist

1.7   The rules actually make two different structures available for example (i) in question 1.6. Draw an additional structure.

1.8   Draw the deep structure tree and the surface structure tree for the following sentence:

(i)   John, I think Mary likes.

1.9   In section 1.3 we briefly considered certain subcategories of the category V and conjectured that what subcategory a particular verb belongs to follows from semantic properties of the verb. If there truly are "optional" subcategorizations, as (i)–(ii) and (iii)–(iv) seem to suggest, what problems might this raise for the semantic approach to subcategories?

(i)   John left the party.

(ii)   John left.

(iii)   John ate a hamburger.

(iv)   John ate.

1.10   In the discussion of Topicalization we considered certain examples in which subcategorization properties superficially appeared to be violated. In particular, in example (31) the verb *solve*, which generally requires a direct object, seemed not to have one. In part based on this fact, we concluded that there exist not one but two levels of representation, one more abstract than the other, and a transformation relating the two. This general line of reasoning should not be limited to Topicalization structures but should in some sense be applicable whenever we find a sentence whose structure superficially violates lexical requirements. What might this line of reasoning indicate about each of the following examples?

(i)   The problem was solved by Mary.

(ii)   Which problem will you solve?

References

Baker, C. L. (1978). *Introduction to generative transformational syntax*. Englewood Cliffs, NJ: Prentice-Hall.

Chomsky, N. (1957). *Syntactic structures*. The Hague: Mouton.

Chomsky, N. (1965). *Aspects of the theory of syntax*. Cambridge, MA: MIT Press.

Chomsky, N. (1975). *Reflections on language*. New York: Pantheon.

Lasnik, H. (1976). Remarks on coreference. *Linguistic Analysis* 2, 1–22.

Lasnik, H., and J. Uriagereka (1988). *A course in GB syntax*. Cambridge, MA: MIT Press.

Riemsdijk, H. van, and E. Williams (1986). *Introduction to the theory of grammar*. Cambridge, MA: MIT Press.

Ross, J. R. (1967). Constraints on variables in syntax. Doctoral dissertation, MIT, Cambridge, MA. [Distributed by Indiana University Linguistics Club, Bloomington. Now also published as *Infinite syntax*. Norwood, NJ: Ablex.]

2

Semantics

Richard K. Larson

?

We have seen that, as speakers of English, we know facts about its *syntax*: that expressions divide into categories like verb, noun, and preposition, that verbs and prepositions typically precede their objects in English, that the words of a sentence cluster together into constituents. In addition, we know facts about its *semantics* or meaning structure: that sentences are related as synonymous or contradictory, that they are true under certain circumstances, that certain notions do or do not correspond to possible words.

2.1 Knowledge of Meaning: Semantic Relations and Truth

Like other kinds of linguistic knowledge, knowledge of semantics reveals itself clearly in the form of certain abilities we possess. One is the ability to judge that various relations hold among sentences. Consider the examples in (1) and (2):

(1)a. John believed that the Earth is flat.

   b. John doubted that the Earth is flat.

(2)a.   John claimed that the Earth is flat.

   b.   John denied that the Earth is flat.

As speakers of English, we know intuitively, and immediately, that a certain kind of relation holds within the pairs of (1) and (2)—the same one in both cases. Pretheoretically, we grasp it as a relation of "incompatibility" or "exclusion" of some kind.

This exclusion relation does not arise from the grammatical form of the sentences; we know this because other pairs with the same form (subject–verb–complement clause) fail to exhibit the relation:

(3)   John knew that the Earth is flat.
      John dreamed that the Earth is flat.

Likewise, it does not arise from the particular phonetic shapes of the words; this is clear because other languages—for instance, German—express the same relation with quite different words ((4) corresponds to (1)):

(4)   Hans glaubte, daß die Erde flach ist.
      Hans zweifelte, daß die Erde flach ist.

The relation we detect in (1) and (2) issues from another property of these sentences: their *meaning*. The members of the pairs "express contrary thoughts," "describe mutually exclusive situations," or "convey opposing information"; they "cannot both be true at the same time," and so on. It is in virtue of the meanings they have that the sentences in (1) and (2) exclude each other. And it is in virtue of knowing these meanings that we judge this relation to hold.

Exclusion is not the only kind of semantic relation we can recognize; (5)–(7) and (8)–(10) illustrate other, analogous forms:

(5)a.   John sold a car to Mary.

   b.   Mary bought a car from John.

(6)a.   John is in front of Mary.

   b.   Mary is behind John.

(7)a.   John saw Mary.

   b.   Mary was seen by John.

(8)a.   John is a human.

   b.   John is a mammal.

(9)a.   Mary was laughing and dancing.

   b.   Mary was dancing.

(10)a.   Necessarily, apples are Nature's toothbrush.

   b.   Apples are Nature's toothbrush.

In (5)–(7) we grasp an identity relation of some kind holding between the members of each pair—a dimension in which the two are fundamentally the same. Likewise, in (8)–(10) we detect a relation of "inclusion" or subordination, a respect in which the first member in some sense "implies" the second member. Here again the relevant dimension is that of meaning. The pairs in (5)–(7) are all (largely) identical in meaning or "synonymous," to use the common term. They "express the same thought," "convey the same information," "describe the same situation," and so on. Similarly, the meanings of the first members of (8)–(10) include those of the second members: the thought expressed by *Mary is laughing and dancing* includes that expressed by *Mary is dancing*, the meaning of *human* implies the meaning of *mammal*, and so on.

In each case we are able to judge a certain relation between sentences, one reducible neither to sound nor to form. To account for this ability, we must assume a certain body of knowledge in our possession: knowledge of meaning.

Besides revealing itself in our capacity to judge various kinds of relatedness between sentences, knowledge of linguistic meaning is apparent in our ability to judge relations between language and the world. Consider the example in (11):

(11)   The cat is on the mat.

As speakers of English, we recognize that a special relation holds between this sentence and the situation depicted in part (a) of figure 2.1—one that does not hold, for instance, between (11) and the situation depicted in part (b). One way of describing this relation is through the familiar notion of *truth*; sentence (11) is true in the (a)-situation but not in the (b)-situation.

Figure 2.1
Situations in which sentence (11) is (a) true and (b) not true.

What is it that effects this association between a sentence of English and the world? What is it that we as English speakers know about (11) that allows us to make judgments about its truth or falsity? Surely not its grammatical form; many sentences with the same grammatical form as (11) (for instance, *The cows are in the corn*) fail to be true in the (a)-situation. Not its phonetic properties; the German sentence *Die Katze ist auf der Matte* is also true in the (a)-situation, but it is pronounced quite differently. What links the sentence and the situation is meaning. It is in virtue of meaning what it does that (11) is true in the (a)-situation but not in the (b)-situation. And it is in virtue of knowing this meaning that we can judge its truth or falsity.

2.2   Knowledge of Meaning as Knowledge of Truth-Conditions

These points make clear the reality of our semantic knowledge by showing us various things that knowledge enables us to do. However, they do not establish what knowledge of meaning actually *is*. They do not show precisely what it is we have internalized in acquiring English, German, or any other natural language, which grounds our judgments of semantic relatedness or truth and falsity.

To get some insight into this question, consider a simple hypothetical situation. Suppose you are trying to discover whether a foreign friend X knows the meaning of a particular English sentence like (11). You possess a powerful video-display device capable of generating pictures of various conceivable situations, and by using it you find that for any situation presented to X about which you can also make a judgment, X is able to say correctly whether or not sentence (11) is true. That is, for basically the same pictorial situations in which you can give a judgment, X is able to say "true" whenever the cat is on the mat, and "false" when it is not. What would you say about X? Does he know the meaning of *The cat is on the mat*? Does this kind of evidence settle the matter? Think about this question for a moment.

Intuitively, we are strongly inclined to answer "yes." If X can correctly judge whether the sentence is true or false whenever you can, then X knows the meaning. The evidence seems convincing in the sense that it is difficult to see what further proof we could ever require of X, or what stronger proof X could ever provide, that would show that he understood the meaning of *The cat is on the mat*. It is hard to see what X could be "missing" that, when combined with this knowledge, would "add up" to knowledge of what (11) means.

This little "thought experiment" suggests a simple idea about what it is we know when we know the meaning of a sentence, an idea extensively pursued in modern linguistic semantics. It suggests that knowledge of meaning might fruitfully be viewed as knowledge of *truth-conditions*, that is, knowledge of something of the form shown in (12), where p gives what the world must be like in order for the sentence in question to be true:

(12)   *The cat is on the mat* is true if and only if p.

If X has internalized such a piece of knowledge (with p filled in), then X knows the conditions under which *The cat is on the mat* is true. If X knows this, he will be able to judge for any circumstance whether (11) is true or not. But we have already observed that if X can do this, then, intuitively, he knows the meaning of (11). Thus, given our thought experiment, "knowing the meaning" seems to be largely captured in terms of "knowing the truth-conditions."

If knowledge of meaning amounts to knowledge of truth-conditions, then we can give a direct account of the semantic abilities discussed above. Recall the examples (1) and (2):

(1)a.   John believed that the Earth is flat.

   b.   John doubted that the Earth is flat.

(2)a.   John claimed that the Earth is flat.

   b.   John denied that the Earth is flat.

We said that in virtue of our knowing the semantics of English, we know that the pairs in (1) and (2) bear a relation of "semantic incompatibility" or "meaning exclusion." Suppose we explicate this relation as follows: two sentences are incompatible if their truth-conditions, together with our real-world knowledge, forbid them from being simultaneously true. Then this will correctly predict incompatibility. (2a), for instance, will be true if and only if (iff) John claimed the Earth is flat, and (2b) will be true iff John denied the Earth is flat. Assuming that we are talking about the same assertion by John, we know that the two cannot be simultaneously true. Any denial of p is a claim that not-p, and hence not a claim that p. Thus, the two exclude each other.

The pretheoretic notions of *synonymy* ("meaning identity") and *hyponymy* ("meaning inclusion") can be treated analogously. We can say that two sentences are synonymous if their truth-conditions, taken together with our real-world knowledge, entail that they are true in the same circumstances. Likewise, we can say that one sentence implies another if any situation in which the first is true is also one in which the second is true.

Under these proposals the sentence pairs in (5)–(7) will be correctly identified as synonymous. For example, (5a) is true iff John sold a car to Mary, and (5b) is true iff Mary bought a car from John; and in virtue of how the world is, any circumstance of the former sort is also a circumstance of the latter sort. Hence the two are synonymous. Similarly, the (a)-sentence of each example (8)–(10) will imply the (b)-sentence. Any situation making (9a) true will make (9b) true as well, since any situation in which Mary is laughing and dancing is one in which Mary is dancing. And so on.

Finally, knowledge of truth-conditions will clearly account for our ability to judge that a sentence S is true or false in a given situation. If we know the truth-conditions of S, then knowing whether S is true or false is just a matter of knowing whether these conditions are or are not met.

2.3 Compositionality

Truth-conditions appear to offer a promising approach to sentence meaning and the abilities that flow from knowing them. Let us now consider some facts bearing on the *form* in which that knowledge is encoded in us. In our exploration of syntax in chapter 1, we saw that the class of well-formed sentences in English—or any other natural language—is essentially boundless. With their grammatical knowledge, human language speakers are able to construct infinite collections of well-formed sentences, such as the following (from Platts 1979):

(13)a.   The horse behind Pegasus is bald.

   b.   The horse behind the horse behind Pegasus is bald.

   c.   The horse behind the horse behind the horse behind Pegasus is bald.

Given this *creative* aspect of syntactic ability, we know that our knowledge of the well-formed sentences of English cannot take the form of a simple list. Since the list is infinite, a finite object with finite storage capacity like our brain simply could not accommodate it. On the basis of this we conclude that syntactic knowledge must be encoded within us in the form of a finite set of rules and principles that allow us to *generate* the sentences of English from smaller, subsentential elements such as words.

Similar issues arise with meaning and knowledge of truth-conditions. The expressions of (13) are not only well-formed sentences of English, they are all meaningful as well. More than that, (13a), (13b), (13c), and so on, all have *different* meanings—or different truth-conditions, as we now say. The first is true only in situations containing at least two horses, the second only in situations containing at least three horses, the third only in situations containing at least four horses, and so on. Since the collection of interpretations associated with (13a–...) is infinite in number, it is clear that our knowledge of truth-conditions for the sentences of English cannot

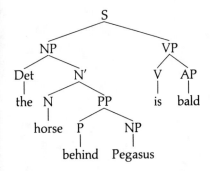

Figure 2.2
Phrase structure tree for sentence (13a), *The horse behind Pegasus is bald*.

take the form of a simple list like (14). Once again, such a list could not be accommodated in our finite brains.

(14)a.   *The horse behind Pegasus is bald* is true iff *p1*.

b.   *The horse behind the horse behind Pegasus is bald* is true iff *p2*.

c.   *The horse behind the horse behind the horse behind Pegasus is bald* is true iff *p3*.

Given this reasoning, it seems that our semantic knowledge must also take the form of a set of productive rules or principles that allow us to calculate truth-conditions for sentences from some "smaller" semantic contributions. That is, it appears that the truth-conditions matched with a given sentence of English must be *compositionally derived*.

How exactly might this be accomplished? How are the truth-conditions for a sentence composed, and from what? A plausible hypothesis is that they are calculated using internal syntactic structure. To illustrate, consider (13a), with syntax roughly as shown in figure 2.2, where N' is a nominal constituent intermediate between N and NP. (The phrase structure rules beyond those given in chapter 1 that are needed to generate this structure should be immediately clear.) Suppose we could assign some kind of semantic contribution or "value" to each of the "leaves" of this tree structure: a value to *bald*, a value to *Pegasus*, a value to *is*, and so on. Suppose further that we had a way of combining these values for each of the branches in figure 2.2 such that, at the top, they yielded the truth-conditions for the sentence: a general way of combining the values of nouns and PPs in the configuration [N' N PP], a general way of combining verbs and adjectives in the configuration [VP V AP], a general way of combining the values of NPs and VPs in the configuration [S NP VP] to yield the truth-conditions for S, and so on. Then we would in essence be using

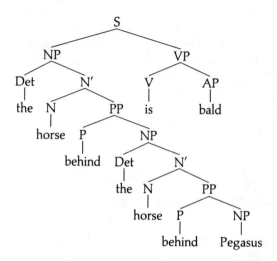

Figure 2.3
Phrase structure tree for sentence (13b), *The horse behind the horse behind Pegasus is bald.*

the "syntactic skeleton" of figure 2.2 as a guide to figuring out what it means. To borrow a phrase from Quine (1970), semantics would "chase truth up the tree of grammar."

If we could give such initial values and general combination schemes, then we could account very directly for our ability to assign truth-conditions to unbounded sequences of sentences like (13a–...). Consider the tree underlying (13b), depicted in figure 2.3. This tree differs from the one underlying (13a) in having extra [$_{NP}$ Det N'] and [$_{N'}$ N PP] branches involving the lexical items *the, behind,* and *horse.* Since all of these elements already occur in (13a), it follows that if we have the semantic resources for computing the truth-conditions of (13a), we will "automatically" have the resources for computing the truth-conditions of (13b). Our semantic values and rules will deliver truth-conditions for (13a), (13b), and indeed *all* the sentences in the sequence.

2.4   The Study of Meaning: Model-theoretic Semantics

Let us now attempt to implement one version of the account sketched above, giving elements of a theory that takes truth-conditions as the basis of our semantic knowledge and attempts to derive the truth-conditions for sentences in a compositional way. In doing this, we will adopt the basic perspective of *model theory.* As we have seen, truth-conditional theories take the view that meaning is fundamentally a relation between language and the world. Interpretation involves systematically correlating sentences with the world through the notion of truth. Model theory studies the relation between languages and worlds in a formal way. It does this by building mathematical models of worlds using the devices of set theory and by mapping expressions of language into them:

(15)   *Language*   *Model (of a World)*
       Lexical items   →   Set-theoretic objects
       Syntactic rules for   →   Rules for combining
       building up phrases   set-theoretic objects

As (15) shows, constructing a model-theoretic semantics for a language L involves correlating the basic expressions with appropriate set-theoretic objects and giving rules that state how these constructs combine for each of the syntactic configurations of L. This yields an interpretation—an object in our model—for each of the subsentential expressions of L, and a set of truth-conditions for every sentence.

We can see how a model-theoretic semantics operates by considering a small "sublanguage" of English, which we will call L*. L* contains the determiner elements *the, every,* and *some,* the common nouns *man* and *fish,* and the intransitive predicates *walks* and *drinks.* It also involves the syntactic configurations shown in figure 2.4 (where X is Det, N, or V and α is a lexical item). L* thus includes phrases like *some fish, the man,* and sentences like *Every fish walks, Some man drinks.*

To construct our model-theoretic semantics for L*, we start with some basic set A of individuals—intuitively, the set of entities in our model world M*—and establish a general correlation between the syntactic categories of L* and kinds of set-theoretic objects built out of A. We will adopt the following mapping:

(16)   *Language*   *Model*
       Ns, Vs   →   Subsets of A
       Dets   →   Binary relations on subsets of A

The categories of common noun and intransitive verb are associated with subsets of A. Intuitively, the common noun *fish* is associated with the subset of A that contains the fishes, the verb *walk* is associated with the subset of A that contains the walkers, and so on.

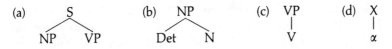

Figure 2.4
Syntactic configurations for language L*.

Determiners are matched up with binary relations on sets of As. In particular, we will associate the determiners *the, every,* and *some* with the following specific relations (where '$[\![\alpha]\!]$' is to be read 'the interpretation of α'):

(17)   Dets: $[\![every]\!]$ = EVERY, where for any sets X, Y
                                       EVERY(X)(Y) iff $X \subseteq Y$

                     $[\![some]\!]$ = SOME, where for any sets X, Y
                                         SOME(X)(Y) iff $X \cap Y \neq \emptyset$

                     $[\![the]\!]$ = THE,   where for any sets X, Y
                                         THE(X)(Y) iff $X \subseteq Y$ and
                                         $|X| = 1$

The idea behind these assignments derives ultimately from the philosopher Gottlob Frege, who suggested that determiners correspond to relations between properties or concepts. Thus, in examples like *Every whale is a mammal* or *Some whales are mammals* the determiner serves to relate the properties of whalehood and mammalhood.

In the case of *every* the relation is one of subordination. Every whale is a mammal if whalehood is a "species" of mammalhood. We have captured the notion of subordination here using the subset relation. In the case of *some* the relation is one of nonexclusion; some whales are mammals if whalehood and mammalhood are not mutually exclusive properties. Again we capture this using a set-theoretic relation: that of intersection. The relation expressed by *the* is essentially a subcase of the EVERY relation. THE holds between two properties like whalehood and mammalhood if the former is subordinate to the latter and furthermore only one individual falls under the former.

Having correlated the syntactic categories of L* with set-theoretic "interpretation spaces," we can construct semantic rules of combination for each of the syntactic configurations in L*. These are as follows:

(18)a. $[\![[_X \alpha]]\!] = [\![\alpha]\!]$, where X is Det, N, or V

    b. $[\![[_{VP} V]]\!] = [\![V]\!]$

    c. $[\![[_{NP} Det\ N]]\!] = \{Y : [\![Det]\!]([\![N]\!])(Y)\}$

    d. $[\![[_S NP\ VP]]\!]$ is true if $[\![VP]\!] \in [\![NP]\!]$ and false otherwise

(18a, b) give the (essentially trivial) interpretation rules for lexical nodes and intransitive VPs. (18c) gives the interpretation of NPs as families of sets—the family of sets that stand in the "Det-relation" to the set associated with the common noun head. (18d) states that a sentence is true (in our model M*) if and only if the set associated with the VP falls in the family of sets associated with the subject NP.

The initial assignments plus the rules just given determine an interpretation (a set-theoretic counterpart) for every subsentential expression of L*.

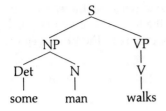

Figure 2.5
Phrase structure tree for the sentence *Some man walks* in language L*.

These in turn determine a set of truth-conditions for every sentence with respect to M*. As a brief example of how this works, consider the sentence *Some man walks*. In L* this sentence receives the syntax shown in figure 2.5. What will its truth-conditions be under our semantics? We compute them compositionally from the interpretations of the parts.

By (18a), the lexical nodes in figure 2.5 all receive the same interpretations as the lexical items they dominate. *Some* corresponds to the binary relations between sets given above:

(19) $[\![[_{Det} \text{ some}]]\!] = [\![some]\!] = \text{SOME}$

The common noun *man* is interpreted as a set of individuals (intuitively, the set of men in our model):

(20) $[\![[_{N} \text{ man}]]\!] = [\![man]\!] = \{x: x \text{ is a man in } M^*\}$

Likewise, the intransitive verb *walks* is also mapped to a set of individuals, the set of walkers in M*. Taking this result together with (18b), we thus have:

(21) $[\![[_{VP} \text{ walks}]]\!] = [\![[_{V} \text{ walks}]]\!] =$

   $[\![walks]\!] = \{x: x \text{ is a walker in } M^*\}$

Rule (18c) allows us to combine the results in (19) and (20) and compute the interpretation of NP. *Some man* will correspond to a family of sets—in particular, the family of sets bearing the "SOME-relation" to the set associated with *man*:

(22) $[\![[_{NP} \text{ some man}]]\!] = \{Y: \text{SOME}([\![man]\!])(Y)\}$

Given our earlier explication of the "SOME-relation," this amounts to the following:

(23) $[\![[_{NP} \text{ some man}]]\!] = \{Y: \{x: x \text{ is a man}\} \cap Y \neq \emptyset\}$

That is, *some man* corresponds to the family of sets having a nonempty intersection with the set of men. Or, more informally, *some man* maps to the family of sets containing at least one man.

Finally, rule (18d) establishes the truth-conditions for the whole sentence. It says that *Some man walks* is true iff the family of sets corresponding to the subject NP contains the set corresponding to the VP. Given the results in (21) and (23), this comes to (24),

(24)   [$_S$ Some man walks] is true if {walkers} ∈ {Y: {men} ∩ Y ≠ ∅},
and false otherwise

which is just to say:

(25)   [$_S$ Some man walks] is true if {men} ∩ {walkers} ≠ ∅,
and false otherwise

That is, *Some man walks* is true in M* if and only if there is at least one individual who is both a man and a walker in M*. This is intuitively the correct result.

The sample language L* is a very simple one, but it shows how the model-theoretic approach attempts to formalize the basic line of thinking sketched in section 2.3. Using some resources from set theory, we can assign semantic values to basic lexical items and give rules for calculating the values of complex expressions on the basis of their syntax. This ultimately yields truth-conditions for each sentence. To carry this analysis further, we would clearly wish to expand the class of lexical items and syntactic configurations in our language L*, but the basic procedure would remain the same.

2.5   Semantic Properties

The modeling of some domain by mathematical constructs has an important consequence, one that is exploited in all science: it allows us to study the properties of the domain through the mathematical properties of the constructs that model it. Since mathematical properties can be stated and manipulated precisely, our understanding gains depth and precision as a result.

These virtues hold in the domain of semantics as well. By modeling aspects of meaning formally, we can capture and study important linguistic properties in a precise way. We will consider this briefly by looking at two semantic properties for the category of natural language determiners: *directional entailingness* and *conservativity*.

2.5.1   Directional Entailingness

In the simple language L* we modeled determiner meanings with relations between sets and we associated English determiners with certain particular relations. These relations show a number of interesting differences. Consider the inference paradigms for *every* in (26) (where '#' indicates an invalid inference):

(26)a.   Every man runs.
         _____

         Every tall man runs.

    b.   Every tall man runs.
         _____

         # Every man runs.

    c.   Every man likes a green vegetable.
         _____

         # Every man likes spinach.

    d.   Every man likes spinach.
         _____

         Every man likes a green vegetable.

With sentences involving *every* we get a valid inference whenever we substitute a "more specific" common noun (*tall man*) for a "less specific" one (*man*), but not vice versa. On the other hand, we get a valid inference whenever we substitute a "less specific" VP (*likes a green vegetable*) for a "more specific" one (*likes spinach*), but again not vice versa.

Rather different patterns of inference emerge with the determiners *some* and *few*:

(27)a.   Some man runs.
         _____

         # Some tall man runs.

    b.   Some tall man runs.
         _____

         Some man runs.

    c.   Some man likes a green vegetable.
         _____

         # Some man likes spinach.

    d.   Some man likes spinach.
         _____

         Some man likes a green vegetable.

(28)a.   Few men run.
         _____

         Few tall men run.

b.   Few tall men run.

―――――

#Few men run.

c.   Few men like a green vegetable.

―――――

Few men like spinach.

d.   Few men like spinach.

―――――

#Few men like a green vegetable.

Evidently with *some* we must always infer from a more specific to a less specific phrase, whether it is the common noun or the VP that is involved. With *few* the situation is just the opposite: we must always infer from a less specific to a more specific phrase.

How can we state the semantic property behind these inference patterns? Taking determiners to correspond semantically to binary relations D between sets, where the common noun supplies the first argument of the relation X and the VP supplies the second argument Y, the relevant properties can be captured in terms of the notion of *directional entailingness*:

(29)   *Downward Entailingness*: A determiner relation D is
   a.   *downward entailing in its first argument* if for any X, Y, where
         $X' \subseteq X$, $D(X)(Y)$ only if $D(X')(Y)$

   b.   *downward entailing in its second argument* if for any X, Y, where
         $Y' \subseteq Y$, $D(X)(Y)$ only if $D(X)(Y')$

(30)   *Upward Entailingness*: A determiner relation D is
   a.   *upward entailing in its first argument* if for any X, Y, where
         $X \subseteq X'$, $D(X)(Y)$ only if $D(X')(Y)$

   b.   *upward entailing in its second argument* if for any X, Y, where
         $Y \subseteq Y'$, $D(X)(Y)$ only if $D(X)(Y')$

Thus, downwardly entailing environments are ones in which substituting a subset for a set (from "less specific" to "more specific") yields a valid inference, whereas upward entailing environments are ones in which substituting a superset for a set (from "more specific" to "less specific") yields a valid inference.

(26a–d) show that *every* is downward entailing in its first argument, the one corresponding to the common noun, but upward entailing in its second argument, the one corresponding to the VP. Similarly, (27a–d) and (28a–d) show (respectively) that *some* is upwardly entailing in both of its arguments and that *few* is downwardly entailing in both of its arguments.

Directional entailingness is a rather simple property of determiners but one that holds considerable interest for linguists: it seems to shed light on certain puzzling facts of English grammar. Consider the distribution of words like *ever* and *anyone*, and phrases like *give a damn* and *budge an inch*. These forms can occur smoothly only in certain rather restricted "environments"—typically the sort provided by a negative element (a word like *no, not,* or *never*):

(31)a. *John saw anything.

   b. John didn't see anything.

(32)a. *I believe that she will budge an inch.

   b. I don't believe that she will budge an inch.

(33)a. *Max said that he had ever been there.

   b. Max never said that he had ever been there.

   c. Max said that he hadn't ever been there.

Because of this property, expressions like *ever, anyone, anything, until, give a red cent,* and *lift a finger* are often referred to as *negative polarity items*.

One interesting question for the study of grammar is, What precisely are the environments in which negative polarity items are licensed? How are they to be characterized? The answer is not self-evident. Note that the licensing environments are not simply those involving negative words like *no, not,* or *nothing*. Negative polarity items are also sanctioned by *every* when they occur in its restrictive term (the bracketed portion in (34a)). They are not permitted in the VP, however (34b):

(34)a. Every [person who has *ever* visited Boston] has returned to it.

   b. *Every [person who has visited Boston] has *ever* returned to it.

This behavior contrasts with that of other determiners such as *few* and *some*:

(35)a. Few [persons who have *ever* visited Boston] have returned to it.

   b. Few [persons who have visited Boston] have *ever* returned to it.

(36)a. *Some [person who has *ever* visited Boston] has returned to it.

   b. *Some [person who has visited Boston] has *ever* returned to it.

The former licenses negative polarity items in both its restrictive term and the VP. The latter licenses negative polarity items in neither the restrictive term nor the VP.

What is the generalization here? If we consider the directional entailing-ness properties discussed above, a simple answer suggests itself. Recall that *every* is downward entailing in its first argument but upward entailing in its second argument. *Some* is upwardly entailing in both arguments, and *few* is downwardly entailing in both:

(37)   EVERY   (X)(Y)   ↓   ↑

      SOME   (X)(Y)   ↑   ↑

      FEW   (X)(Y)   ↓   ↓

Recall also that in sentences like (34)–(36), the restrictive term (the bracketed portion) corresponds to the X argument of Det and the VP corresponds to the Y argument. The generalization is clearly the following (from Ladusaw 1980):

(38)   A negative polarity item is licensed in a downward entailing environment.

That is, whenever the phrase containing *anyone*, *budge an inch*, and so on, corresponds to a downwardly entailed argument, the negative polarity item is licensed; otherwise, it is not.

These facts argue strongly that the semantic property of directional entailingness has reality for speakers of English. It is the property to which we are "attuned" in judging the acceptability of sentences containing negative polarity items.

2.5.2   Conservativity

Directional entailingness is a semantic property that distinguishes determiners like *every*, *some*, and *few* in different argument positions. It is of interest because it appears to shed light on specific facts about the grammar of English. These determiners also share other semantic properties, however—properties that are of interest because they seem to tell us something about human language generally. They appear to give insight into what constitutes a "possible human determiner concept."

One such property that has been studied in some detail is *conservativity*. Consider our three determiner relations again:

(39)a.   EVERY (X)(Y)   iff $X \subseteq Y$

    b.   SOME (X)(Y)   iff $X \cap Y \neq \emptyset$

    c.   FEW (X)(Y)   iff $|X \cap Y| \leq \alpha|X|$

According to (39a), to evaluate the truth of a sentence containing *every*, we must essentially "sort through" the set corresponding to the common noun (X), checking to see whether all of its members are in the set corresponding to the VP (Y). Similarly, with *some* (39b) we must sort through the common noun set, checking to see whether any of its members are in the VP set. Finally, with *few* (39c) we must sort through the common noun set, checking to see how many of its members are in the VP set ('$|X \cap Y|$'), and then determine whether this number is smaller than some understood proportion ('α') of the common noun set. There is an important regularity here: in each case we work always with members of the common noun set X in checking whether the given relation holds. The common noun uniformly "sets the scene"; it specifies the collection of individuals over which we range in the evaluation.

This regularity observed with *every*, *some*, and *few* is not found in all quantifierlike relations. Consider the relations expressed by *all-but* and *everyone-except* as they occur in examples like (40a, b):

(40)a.   *All but* boys received a prize.

b.   *Everyone except* mothers attended.

Intuitively, to evaluate whether (40a) is true, we do not sort through the set of boys, checking to see whether some quantity of them are prize recipients; rather, we must look precisely at nonboys. Similarly, we look not at mothers but at nonmothers in evaluating (40b).

This notion of "setting the scene" or "fixing the collection over which we quantify," which characterizes *every*, *some*, and *few* but not *all-but* and *everyone-except*, is, in essence, the property of *conservativity*. We may define it more precisely as follows:

(41)   A determiner relation D is *conservative* if for any X, Y, D(X)(Y) iff D(X)(X $\cap$ Y).

A conservative determiner relation is one that holds between two sets X, Y just in case it holds between the first and the intersection of the first with the second. Since X and X $\cap$ Y are both subsets of X, this means that we always range over members of the common noun denotation in evaluating whether a conservative determiner relation holds. X sets the scene.

Conservativity is a property that appears to characterize all human language determiner concepts—not just *every*, *some*, and *few*, but also *no*, *many*, *most*, *two*, *three*, *several*, and so on, and their many counterparts in languages around the world. It is what might be called a *semantic universal*. This result is quite surprising on reflection, since there is no clear a priori reason why things should be so. There is no sense in which nonconservative determiner relations are "conceptually inaccessible"; nor are they somehow "unnatural" or "unuseful." We have noted informally that *all-but* and *everyone-except* do not share the conservativity property because

Figure 2.6
Situation in which the sentence *Nall squares are striped* is true, where NALL (X)(Y) iff $(A - X) \subseteq Y$.

their common noun does not specify the range of quantification. Notice now that although these expressions are not themselves determiners in English (indeed, they are not even syntactic constituents), there is no difficulty in defining a hypothetical determiner relation *NALL* having exactly their semantics,

(42)   NALL(X)(Y)   iff $(A - X) \subseteq Y$

(where X and Y are subsets of A, our model's universe of things). Under this definition, a sentence like *Nall squares are striped* would be true, and presumably useful, in exactly the same situations as the sentences *All but squares are striped* or *Everything except squares is striped* (figure 2.6).

Nall is thus a perfectly reasonable candidate for a natural language determiner relation on general grounds. Nonetheless, no such relation occurs in English or in any other human language so far as we know. Nonconservative determiners like *nall* simply seem to be disallowed.

Why conservative determiners should be singled out by natural language is an interesting question that we cannot pursue in detail here. However, results by Keenan and Stavi (1986) suggest that this may arise from natural language determiner meanings being typically "composed" out of certain basic, "atomic" meanings. It can be shown formally that if one begins with elementary determiner concepts such as EVERY, THE (ONE), and POSS(essor) and augments this set with more complex determiner meanings constructed by elementary operations like intersection and complementation, then the result will include only conservative determiners. This is because the "atomic" determiners are all conservative and elementary set-theoretic operations preserve conservativity. The ubiquity of conservative determiners may thus reflect a deep fact about the way our space of determiner concepts is structured: that it forms a so-called Boolean algebra over certain elementary determiner meanings.

Suggestions for Further Reading

A good technical introduction to the model-theoretic framework discussed here is Dowty, Wall, and Peters 1981.

A classic paper that sets out a somewhat different version of truth-conditional semantics and the theory of meaning is Davidson 1967. Also valuable for its truth-conditional treatment of a variety of natural language phenomena is Platts 1979.

The relational analysis of natural language determiners is developed in the following works (the first largely nontechnical): Wiggins 1980, Barwise and Cooper 1981, and Keenan and Stavi 1986.

The phenomenon of negative polarity is discussed in the following two papers (the second of which argues against the analysis adopted here): Ladusaw 1980 and Linebarger 1987.

Questions

2.1   The language L* contains *every* and *some*. Consider extending it to include the determiners *no* and *two*. Which relations between sets should be associated with these elements?

2.2   Extending L* to include proper names like *John* and *Eunice* raises an interesting question. In our semantic theory for L*, NPs are interpreted as sets of sets. But intuitively, it seems the semantic value of *John* should be an individual j (a person). Can you see a way to interpret proper names that reconciles the view that NPs denote sets of sets with our intuition that *John* ought to be associated with an individual?

2.3   Consider the following determiners: *all, no, most, not many*. Determine their properties with respect to upward and downward entailingness, and check whether the distribution of negative polarity items conforms to these results.

2.4   In view of the definition of conservativity, one simple way to check whether a given determiner Det is conservative is to consider the validity of sentences of the following general form, for any common noun A and any VP B:

(i)   Det A B if and only if Det A is an A who B.

(For instance, *Both men run iff both men are men who run*.) If the scheme yields a true sentence, then the determiner is conservative. Using this scheme, show the conservativity of the determiners *every, some*, and *exactly two*.

2.5   The expression *only* appears determinerlike in sentences like *Only cats meow*. However, consider the following simple instance of the scheme in exercise 2.4:

(i)   Only men run iff only men are men who run.

Is this sentence always true, or are there situations in which it is false? If the latter, does this overthrow the claim that natural language determiners are conservative, or can you think of a way of defending the latter claim?

References

Barwise, J., and R. Cooper (1981). Generalized quantifiers and natural language. *Linguistics and Philosophy* 4, 159–219.

Davidson, D. (1967). Truth and meaning. In *Inquiries into truth and interpretation*. Oxford: Clarendon Press.

Dowty, D., R. Wall, and S. Peters (1981). *An introduction to Montague's semantic theory*. Dordrecht, Holland: Reidel.

Keenan, E., and Y. Stavi (1986). A semantic characterization of natural language determiners. *Linguistics and Philosophy* 9, 253–326.

Ladusaw, W. (1980). On the notion "affective" in the analysis of negative polarity items. *Journal of Linguistic Research* 1, 1–16.

Linebarger, M. (1987). Negative polarity and grammatical representation. *Linguistics and Philosophy* 10, 325–387.

Platts, M. (1979). *Ways of meaning*. London: Routledge and Kegan Paul.

Quine, W. V. O. (1970). *Philosophy of logic*. Englewood Cliffs, NJ: Prentice-Hall.

Wiggins, D. (1980). "Most" and "all": Some comments on a familiar program, and on the logical form of quantified sentences. In M. Platts, ed., *Reference, truth and reality*. London: Routledge and Kegan Paul.

3

Phonology

Morris Halle

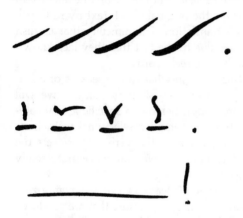

3.1 Speech as Strings of Discrete Sounds

A significant part of the knowledge that fluent speakers have of their language consists of the knowledge of its words. Normal fluent speakers of a language have little doubt that in producing an utterance they are producing a string of words. If pressed, they are likely to characterize words as temporally delimited sound sequences of which the letter sequences separated by blank spaces in our written or printed records of language are plausible representations. Unlike words on the printed page, however, the words in a spoken utterance are in reality not separated from one another (for instance, by little pauses). An utterance in which the speaker pauses briefly after each word sounds highly unnatural. Yet the fact that in speaking we do not separate words from one another affects our perception of utterances only rarely: in almost all cases we hear utterances in languages that we command (know) as sequences of words, and our understanding of an utterance is crucially based on our ability to segment the quasi-continuous acoustic signal into a sequence of discrete words.

The fact that words are not separated by pauses in an utterance does not give rise to serious conceptual problems. It is perfectly plausible that in learning a language we learn a large stock of words, which we then use to make up phrases and sentences. In pronouncing phrases and sentences, however, we no longer keep the words separate; rather, we pronounce one word after another as though the phrase consisted of just one very long "word." Knowing this fact enables hearers to segment the continuous utterance into its component words. In order to do this, however, hearers must know the language in which the utterance was framed. English speakers can readily segment into its component words an English sentence such as *adogneverplayswhenheisalone*, but they won't be able to do much with *pessinigdynehrajekdyžjesám*, the original Czech text by K. Capek of which the English sentence is a translation. The difficulty that English speakers encounter here is of course due to the fact that they lack knowledge of Czech and, most particularly, of Czech words.

It is reasonable to inquire at this point in what form speakers of a language store the words in their memory. (To simplify matters, we will ignore the fact that words have meanings, belong to specific lexical categories (such as noun, verb, adjective), and impose selectional restrictions on other words in the sequence (for instance, the verb *melts* selects the noun *sugar* but the verb *shaves* does not), and we will concentrate solely on words as phonic, auditory objects.)

A possible answer might be that when we learn a word, we memorize it as a purely acoustic event, as changes in the air pressure that are produced when the word is pronounced and that are sensed by our auditory system. There are reasons to doubt this answer. First, words have innumerable acoustic properties that speakers fail to remember. For example, we never remember the voice quality of the person from whom we learned a given word. Was the word spoken by a male voice or a female voice? Was it spoken slowly or rapidly, loudly or softly? And so on. All this information is obviously beside the point for the purpose of producing and understanding utterances in a particular language. So why should we remember it? Second, we are notoriously poor at identifying acoustic events. For example, few people can recognize more than a small number of sounds encountered in nature such as leaves rustling, the wind blowing, waves breaking, or one object hitting another, yet every normal speaker of a language has ready access to thousands of words.

Since there is nothing special about the sounds of speech from an acoustic point of view, and since we have a special propensity for memorizing words and no particular ability to memorize acoustic phenomena, it is plausible to suppose that we deal with words in a special way, radically different from our way of processing other acoustic signals that strike our ears. In fact, it has been assumed—more often tacitly than explicitly—that words are stored in memory as sequences of speech sounds—that is, as sequences of the sort of units that are at the base of alphabetic writing systems.

This proposal runs into immediate objections. First, words are obviously memorized by young children as well by others who lack all acquaintance with alphabetic writing. (The latter class is made up, on the one hand, by illiterates and, on the other hand, by people like the Chinese and the ancient Egyptians whose writing system is nonalphabetic.) One might wonder how speakers unacquainted with alphabetic writing would ever hit upon the idea of analyzing the quasi-continuous noises they hear into discrete sounds. Second, the fact that children learn the words of their native language with practically no overt teaching (of the relevant sort) implies that the knowledge children need in order to analyze words into sound sequences is acquired without benefit of teaching or even very extensive learning. This in turn raises the even more perplexing question of whether there can be knowledge that is not learned. (See chapters 8 and 9.) Third, since on this account memorizing words requires essentially the same processing of the speech signal as that involved in representing speech in an alphabetic writing system, we might wonder why great efforts have to be expended on teaching children to read and write, whereas they never need to be taught how to memorize the words of their native language. If these two processes are so similar, there should not be such a marked difference in the amount of training needed to acquire them.

Since the proposal that words are stored in memory as sequences of discrete speech sounds raises so many questions that lack obvious answers, it is necessary to remark at once that evidence in favor of the proposal is by no means lacking and that, as we will see, this evidence is quite persuasive.

Almost every language that has been studied supplements its basic stock of words via affixation. For example, in English we create agent nouns from verbs by suffixing -er to the verb stem (1a), we generate negative adjectives by prefixing un- (1b), and we make verbs by prefixing and/ or by suffixing (1c):

(1)a.   learn-er, work-er, teach-er, verbaliz-er, disestablishmentarianiz-er

   b.   un-clean, un-healthy, un-imaginable, un-original, un-otiose

   c.   em-power, en-rich, dark-en, hard-en, en-liv-en

We will use the term *morpheme* to refer to prefixes, suffixes, stems, and other meaning-bearing components of words. The processes of affixation do not always leave the component totally intact, as was the case in (1). In many instances affixation results in changes in the stems or the affixes or both. A simple illustration is provided by the formation of the feminine singular past tense and first person singular present tense forms of Russian verbs:

(2)a.		'crawl'	'can'	'bake'	'row'	'save'
	Past fem. sg.	polz-la	mog-la	pek-la	greb-la	spas-la
	Pres. 1 sg.	polz-u	mog-u	pek-u	greb-u	spas-u
b.		'stand'	'teach'	'sit'	'hold'	'bark'
	Past fem. sg.	stoya-la	uči-la	side-la	derža-la	laya-la
	Pres. 1 sg.	stoy-u	uč-u	siž-u	derž-u	lay-u
c.		'read'	'blow'	'live'	'know'	'sweat'
	Past fem. sg.	čita-la	du-la	ži-la	zna-la	pote-la
	Pres. 1 sg.	čitay-u	duy-u	živ-u	znay-u	potey-u

It is obvious from (2a) that the feminine singular past tense is signaled by the suffix -*la* and the first person singular present tense by the suffix -*u*. In (2a) the suffix has no effect on the stem; the examples in (2b, c) illustrate changes in the stem brought about by suffixation. The stems in (2b) end with a vowel in the past tense; yet this vowel is systematically eliminated in the present tense. (The *d* ∼ *ž* alternation in *side-la, siž-u* is due to a special rule that will not concern us here.) As shown by their present tense forms, the stems in (2c) end with [y] or [v], but the stem-final consonant is deleted before the past tense suffix -*la*. A Russian-speaking child aged three or four knows how to form the past tense and present tense of these verbs, or of verbs very much like them. (In fact, presented with the first person present tense forms of nonsense verbs such as *nurey-u, butay-u* and asked to use them in the context appropriate for the feminine singular past tense (*Yesterday my mother* ____), a Russian-speaking child would undoubtedly spontaneously generate the appropriate *nure-la, buta-la*. For an analogous experiment with English-speaking children, see Berko 1958, discussed in chapter 8.)

It has been shown (Jakobson 1948; Lightner 1972) that the examples in (2) as well as a great many others are manifestations of the rules in (3):

(3)a.   Delete a stem-final vowel before a vowel-initial suffix.

b.   Delete a stem-final [y] or [v] before a consonant-initial suffix.

Part of the knowledge that a fluent speaker of Russian has therefore consists of the rules in (3). Research carried out by linguists since the beginning of scientific interest in language has shown that every other human language exhibits analogous rules. Such rules therefore represent an essential aspect of the knowledge that is universally required to produce and process human utterances.

What is important for our purposes about the rules in (3) is that in order to apply them, speakers must be able to analyze the words of their language into sequences of discrete sounds. In particular, a speaker must determine whether a given stem ends with a vowel, with [y], with [v], or with any other speech sound, and whether the suffix begins with a vowel or with a consonant. If we now assume that words are stored in memory as sequences of discrete speech sounds, we can readily explain the fact that all languages have rules of the type illustrated in (3). If we do not make this assumption, this fact remains a mystery.

3.2   Phonetics

If words are represented as sequences of discrete sounds, then the same must be true of utterances since, at least to a first approximation, utterances are sequences of words strung together one after another. Physically an utterance is manifested as an acoustic signal produced by a particular gymnastics executed by certain anatomical structures in the upper portions of the respiratory and digestive tracts, specifically the lower lip, the tongue, the soft palate (velum), and the larynx. The cavities bordered by these structures are commonly referred to as the *vocal tract*, and the acoustic signal that strikes the ears during speech is produced by changes in the geometry of the vocal tract. An X-ray motion picture recording the behavior of the vocal tract in the course of producing a particular utterance bears a striking resemblance to a stylized dance performed by dancers of great skill. If utterances are regarded as "dances" performed by the lower lip, tongue, soft palate, and other movable portions of the vocal tract, then one must also suppose that underlying each utterance ("dance") there is a "score" in some "choreographic" notation that instructs each "dancer" what to do and when. The different phonetic transcriptions of utterances are such "choreographic" notations, and the subsections that follow are devoted to a discussion of one such notation.

Figure 3.1 illustrates the six anatomical structures that are involved in the production of speech. Each of these "dancers" is capable of only limited behaviors. For example, the soft palate, which has the most restricted range of behavior, is capable only of being lowered or raised: when the soft palate is lowered, air can flow through the nasal cavities, resulting in the characteristic acoustic effect of nasalization; when the soft palate is raised, no air flows through the nasal cavities and these remain acoustically inert. The other anatomical structures involved in speech have a greater repertoire of behaviors, which we will examine in the following subsections.

The actions of the different anatomical structures involved in speaking are independent of one another. Thus, the soft palate can carry out its movements without regard for the movements simultaneously being car-

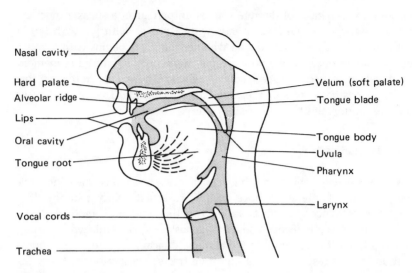

Figure 3.1
Midsagittal section through the human head and neck showing the articulators that make up the vocal tract. Adapted, by permission, from figure 4.5 of A. Akmajian, R. A. Demers, and R. M. Harnish (1984). *Linguistics: An introduction to language and communication.* Cambridge, MA: MIT Press.

ried out by the lower lip, the larynx, and/or the tongue. Viewed from the vantage point of articulatory independence, the tongue behaves not as a single entity but as three distinct agents: the blade, the body, and the root. We will use the term *articulator* to designate anatomical structures that function independently in the production of speech—namely, the six listed on the left in (4). The terms on the right are used to refer to these articulators in a number of recent studies and occasionally in this chapter as well:

(4) Larynx   = LARYNGEAL
     Velum   = SOFT PALATE
     Lower lip   = LABIAL
     Tongue blade = CORONAL
     Tongue body   = DORSAL
     Tongue root   = TR

3.2.1   The Production of the Vowels

What characterizes the articulation of vowels of all kinds is that in the center of its passage from the lungs up through the pharynx and the oral cavity the air flow encounters no obstacle sufficient to create turbulence or total blockage. The tongue body plays a central role in the production of all vowels. (The other articulators also take part in vowel production, but their role is subsidiary.) The tongue body is capable of being moved up and down in a direction parallel to the spinal column as well as back and front in a direction perpendicular to the spinal column, and different positions of the tongue body serve to differentiate one vowel from another. The positioning of the tongue body (and of the other articulators, as well) is of course in each case the result of forces exerted by muscles. Since the acoustic signal emitted by the vocal tract depends directly on the positions and behaviors of the articulators and only indirectly on the contractions and relaxations of the muscles, the phonetic notation focuses on the behavior of the articulators rather than on that of the individual muscles. (For some discussion of the muscular behavior underlying the production of speech, see Halle 1983.)

Although the tongue body has extraordinary freedom of movement and can assume many different positions relative to the stationary parts of the vocal tract—that is, relative to the roof of the mouth and the back wall of the pharynx—human languages use only a limited number of these positions to differentiate the vowels. In fact, only three vertical and two horizontal positions of the tongue body are used systematically to generate distinct vowels. The English short vowels in *bit, bet, bat* exhibit the three vertical positions of the tongue body. As speakers of English can readily establish by self-observation, the tongue body is lowest in *bat* and highest in *bit*. In producing each of these three vowels, the tongue is in a *forward* position. Retracting the tongue to a *back* position while pronouncing the vowel in *bat* produces the vowel in *cot* as it pronounced in most varieties of American English (though not in that of eastern Massachusetts or in many of the dialects spoken in Britain). Similarly, retracting the tongue to a back position while pronouncing the vowel in *bet* produces the vowel in *but*. English does not make systematic use of the backed counterpart of the vowel in *bit*. This sound is encountered in only a few words (for example, the adverb *just* in such expressions as *just a minute*).

In the phonetic alphabet in widest use, that of the International Phonetic Association (IPA), the vowels just described are symbolized as follows:

(5) [ɪ] bit   [ɯ] just
     [ɛ] bet   [ʌ] cut
     [æ] bat   [ɑ] cot

As noted earlier, only a limited number of articulator configurations play a role in language. Jakobson (1938) proposed—and linguists now widely (though not universally) accept—that for each independent articulator behavior, or *feature*, languages utilize exactly two configurations. Formally this fact is expressed by representing each feature with a coefficient—[xF]—where the coefficient x is understood as a variable ranging over the values $+$ and $-$.

In the horizontal plane the tongue body assumes exactly two relevant positions. We capture this fact with the binary feature [back]: in [+back] vowels (see (6)) the tongue body is retracted, whereas in [−back] vowels it is advanced. The featural description of the vertical position of the tongue body, where three positions are actually distinguished, is somewhat less straightforward. Since we have only binary features at our disposal, we must use two distinct features: [high] and [low]. Since each of these two features can assume two values, they provide the means for distinguishing four vowel types. It appears, however, that no language utilizes the feature complex [+high, +low]. We implement this universal restriction by imposing on feature complexes a formal constraint that disallows the complex [+high, +low]. The vowels in (5) will therefore be represented by means of the features [back], [high], and [low] as shown in (6):

(6)

	[ɪ]	[ɛ]	[æ]	[ɯ]	[ʌ]	[ɑ]
[back]	−	−	−	+	+	+
[high]	+	−	−	+	−	−
[low]	−	−	+	−	−	+

The feature complexes in the columns of (6) are partial definitions of the speech sounds represented by the alphabetic symbols in the topmost line. We thus have two ways of representing the speech sounds: by means of alphabetic symbols or as feature complexes. The representation in terms of alphabetic symbols implies that speech sounds are atomic entities—in other words, units that are not to be analyzed further into their constituent properties. By contrast, the representation in terms of feature complexes implies that speech sounds are composite entities made up of features. In section 3.3 we will see evidence suggesting that the latter rather than the former representation more accurately reflects what goes on in speakers' minds.

The three features in (6) represent the different capabilities of the tongue body articulator in producing vowels. They do not, of course, exhaust the capabilities of the human vocal tract as a generator of vowels. Languages often utilize the lips to distinguish different classes of vowels. The vowels in (6) are all generated with spread, rather than rounded, lip. In English, lip rounding is not admitted in the nonback vowels. In the back vowels, on the other hand, there are contrasts between rounded and unrounded cognates. Thus, parallel to [ɯ] as in *just* (*a minute*), American English has [ʊ] as in *put*; and parallel to [ɔ] as in *caught*, most American dialects have [a] as in *cot*. In addition, American English has the rounded [u] and [o] as in *shoe* and *show*, and the unrounded [ʌ] as in *cut*. The remaining rounded back vowels are of somewhat limited distributions in different dialects. For example, the rounded counterpart of the nonlow back vowel in *cut* is found in many British dialects in such words as *got, lock, Tom*, whereas the rounded counterpart of the low back vowel in *cot* is found primarily in the eastern Massachusetts dialect in the same words. By contrast with English, many French dialects exhibit rounding with both back and front vowels.

(7)   [−back, −round]   [−back, +round]   [+back, +round]
      [i] bise 'north wind'   [y] ruse   'ruse'   [u] rouge 'red'
      [e] thé   'tea'   [ø] creuse 'hollow'   [o] sauge 'sage'
      [ɛ] thèse 'thesis'   [œ] veuve 'widow'   [ɔ] loge   'box'

In addition, French has a [+back, −round, +low] vowel: [a] in *âme* 'soul'.

The tongue root articulator plays a crucial role in the distinction between the so-called long (diphthongized) and short (plain) vowels of English illustrated in (8). We will follow the suggestion made by Halle and Stevens (1969) in assuming that these pairs of vowels contrast as [+ATR] (advanced tongue root) versus [−ATR].

(8)   [−back, −round]   [+back, +round]   [+back, −round]
      [+ATR]   [−ATR]   [+ATR]   [−ATR]   [+ATR]   [−ATR]
      peel   bill   boom   bull   ——   ——
      pale   bell   bone   ——   ——   come
      ——   pal   call   ——   calm   bomb

In other treatments of English phonetics these distinctions are characterized by means of a contrast called *tense/lax* or *narrow/wide*.

The coronal or tongue blade articulator is active in English in signaling contrasts such as the one between the vowels in *cull–curl* and *bun–burn*.

The lowering and raising of the soft palate (velum) produce the contrast between nasal and oral vowels, a contrast systematically represented in languages such as French, Polish, and Portuguese, but not in English.

Laryngeal features affect the pitch of the vowels as well as properties of voice quality, sometimes referred to by terms such as *creaky voice* and *breathy voice*. The role of the laryngeal features in the production of consonants is discussed in the following section.

3.2.2   The Production of the Consonants

In the production of a vowel the air flowing from the lungs to the lips encounters no obstruction sufficient to create blockage or turbulence. By contrast, in the production of a consonant such an obstruction must always be present. To create this obstruction, one of the articulators makes full or virtual contact with the stationary part of the vocal tract (the roof of the mouth, the upper lip, or the rear wall of the pharynx). Of the six articulators, the lower lip, tongue blade, tongue body, and tongue root are capable of making this type of contact and therefore play a central role in the production of consonants. We will use the term *place articulators* to designate these four articulators.

The difference between the production of consonants and the production of vowels is perhaps manifested most strikingly in the pronunciation of syllables like English *kick* or *cook*, where most of the action involves the dorsal articulator. In the initial and final—consonantal—portions of the gesture by means of which these two words are produced the dorsal articulator makes contact with the roof of the mouth, whereas in the middle—vocalic—portion no such contact takes place.

This distinction between consonants and vowels is formally implemented by the feature [consonantal]: [+consonantal] sounds involve significant contact by a place articulator with a portion of the vocal tract, [−consonantal] sounds lack such contact.

There are differences among the consonants with respect to the type of contact involved in their production. The *stops* such as [p t k b d g] are produced with total blockage; they contrast with the *fricatives* such as [f v s z θ (as in *thin*) š (as in *shin*) ž (as in *usual*)], which are produced with a constriction narrow enough to generate turbulent air flow yet not narrow enough to block the flow of air. This distinction is formally implemented by the feature [continuant]: stops are [−continuant], fricatives are [+continuant].

Another distinction among consonants is implemented by a third feature, [strident], which contrasts [s z] (English *lease, ease*) and [θ ð] (*teeth, teethe*). Phonetically the former, noisier [+strident] consonants are produced by directing the air flow at right angles to a sharp obstacle, whereas their less noisy [−strident] counterparts are produced with an air flow that is parallel rather than perpendicular to the obstacle.

A fourth consonantal feature is connected with pressure buildup inside the vocal tract. In [+sonorant] consonants such as [m n l r] there is no significant pressure buildup inside the vocal tract; in [−sonorant] consonants such as [p t k b d g f s š v z ž] there is a noticeable increase in the pressure in the vocal tract.

These four features, which are known as the *stricture* features, participate in an important hierarchical relation: [continuant], [strident], and [sonorant] are used only for distinguishing among consonants and play no role whatsoever in the production of [−consonantal] sounds. The stricture features present yet another property that strikingly differentiates consonants from vowels. Each feature involved in the production of vowels—such as [back], [nasal], or [round]—is actualized by only one specific articulator: [back] by the tongue body, [nasal] by the soft palate, and [round] by the lower lip. By contrast, the stricture features [continuant], [strident], and [sonorant] are not articulator-bound; rather, they are realized by one of the four place articulators. As a result, when specifying a [+consonantal] sound, it is always necessary to indicate which of the four place articulators is the one that executes its stricture features.

These striking differences between vowels and consonants must not be allowed to obscure the obvious fact that for the production of both types of sounds, speakers have at their disposal only a single piece of anatomical machinery, the vocal tract with its six articulators. If the features discussed in section 3.2.1 correctly characterize the behaviors that each articulator is capable of, we should expect to encounter these features not only in the production of vowels but also in the production of consonants. And in fact we do.

The three features executed by the dorsal articulator, [back], [high], [low], distinguish the six classes of vowels in (6). But what role do they play in the production of consonants? Consider the difference in English between the [k] in *keel* and the [k] in *cool* (keeping in mind that here, and throughout this chapter, we will be concerned with the sounds rather than their—often idiosyncratic—orthographic representation). In the production of both words the tongue body touches the roof of the mouth, but contact occurs in different places: farther forward in the case of *keel* and farther back in the case of *cool*. This parallels precisely the position of the tongue body in the vowels of the two words. It is therefore said that the [k] in *keel* is [+high, −back], whereas the [k] in *cool* is [+high, +back]. Ladefoged and Maddieson (1986, 18ff.) indicate that in some languages the two different [k] sounds serve to distinguish otherwise identical words. Thus, the dorsal articulator serves to distinguish consonants in much the same way that it distinguishes vowels.

The parallelism between vowels and consonants is not restricted to the feature [back] but extends to the features [high] and [low]. In the vowels these two features implement three rather than four distinctions in the vertical position of the tongue body. Significantly, consonants too require three distinctions in the vertical position of the tongue. Thus, in addition to the *velar* [k]-type sounds discussed above, many languages have *uvular* consonants in which the obstruction produced by the tongue body is located at the level of the uvula (figure 3.1). Since the *velar* [k]-type sounds are [+high], these *uvular* consonants are [−high]. Among the languages that utilize the distinction between velar [+high] and uvular [−high] stops are many dialects of Arabic and other Semitic languages, as well as Quechua, one of the major languages spoken in Peru and adjacent areas, and Serer, a West African language (see Ladefoged 1964, 21–22).

We have seen that the feature [low] distinguishes two kinds of [−high] vowels. A parallel distinction is also found among the consonants, although it appears to be somewhat rare. A number of Arabic dialects have *pharyngeal* ([+back, −high, +low]) fricatives contrasting with uvular ([+back, −high, −low]) fricatives (Ladefoged and Maddieson 1986, 82).

Strikingly, no known language has consonantal counterparts to vowels that are [−back, −high]. The reason for this becomes obvious once we recall the fundamental distinction between vowels and consonants, namely, the requirement that the articulator make contact with a wall of the vocal tract in the production of consonants. Since the walls of the vocal tract are located above and in back of the tongue body, we can use the tongue body to produce consonantal contact only if it is [+high] and/ or [+back].

In making contact, the coronal articulator can choose between two points along the hard palate and can vary distinctively the extent of the contact area. The place of coronal (tongue blade) contact is controlled by the feature [anterior]. *Coronal* consonants like [t d s z θ ð] produced with contact in front of the alveolar (teeth) ridge on the upper palate are [+anterior]; sounds like [š ž r] produced with contact behind the alveolar ridge are [−anterior]. The extent of the contact area is determined by the feature [distributed]: [+distributed] sounds like [θ ð š ž] are produced with a flat tongue that for some distance parallels the roof of the mouth; [−distributed] sounds like English [t d s z] are produced by touching or approaching the hard palate with the tongue tip. In English only [r] is [−distributed, −anterior], but many languages of India, for example, have a whole complement of [−distributed, −anterior] (*retroflex*) sounds, often symbolized by a dot under the letter representing the corresponding [+anterior] sound: [ṭ ḍ ṣ ẓ]. (9) illustrates the feature composition of the coronal consonants:

(9)	[t d s z]	[θ ð]	[š ž]	[r ṣ ẓ ṭ ḍ]
[anterior]	+	+	−	−
[distributed]	−	+	+	−

In most languages only a single place articulator is involved in the production of the consonants, but consonants produced by the simultaneous operation of two place articulators are by no means unknown. The clicks of the southern African languages involve both the coronal and dorsal articulator. The widely spread *labiovelar* consonants [kp gb] encountered in the names of the African languages *Kpelle* and *Igbo* simultaneously involve the lips and the dorsal articulator. And there are even languages like Kinyarwanda (Sagey 1986) in which three place articulators participate in the production of a single consonant.

Unlike the four place articulators, the remaining two articulators—the soft palate and the larynx—participate freely in the production of consonants. When the soft palate is lowered, air is allowed to pass through the nose and the characteristic acoustic effect termed *nasal* is produced.

Sounds produced with the lowered soft palate are [+nasal]; sounds produced with the raised soft palate are [−nasal]. Since as a result of this lowering of the soft palate no pressure is built up in the vocal tract, [+nasal] consonants are always [+sonorant].

The primary role of the larynx in the production of consonants lies in the control of vocal cord vibrations (*voicing*) and aspiration. The presence versus absence of voicing distinguishes the two sets of consonants in (10):

(10) Voiced   [b d g v z ð ž]
      Voiceless [p t k f s θ š]

The vocal cords make up the edges of the slit (*glottis*) on the bottom of the vocal tract through which air from the lungs enters into the larynx and passes from there into the pharynx and the rest of the vocal tract. In order for air to flow upward from the lungs, the pressure in the lungs must exceed that in the cavities above. For small pressure drops across the glottis the vocal cords will or will not vibrate depending on their stiffness: if they are slack, they will vibrate; if they are stiff, they will not (Halle and Stevens 1971). At greater pressure drops, however, stiffness cannot prevent vocal cord vibration: in such cases greater stiffness results in more rapid vibrations, which are perceived as higher pitch, whereas lesser stiffness translates into slower vibrations and lower pitch.

Since air flows from the lungs upward during speech, the pressure of the air inside the lungs must be somewhat greater than that of the ambient (atmospheric) air. We have seen that when [−sonorant] sounds are produced, pressure builds up inside the vocal tract, but when [+sonorant] sounds are produced, no air is trapped in the vocal tract and no pressure is built up. This situation is illustrated schematically in figure 3.2. If we

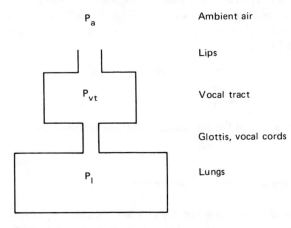

Figure 3.2
Schematic diagram of the air pressure relationships that obtain in the production of speech.

assume that during speech the lung pressure P_1 does not vary appreciably and since the atmospheric pressure P_a is constant during a given utterance, then it follows that the pressure drop across the glottis $P_1 - P_{vt}$ will be noticeably smaller in [− sonorant] sounds than in [+ sonorant] sounds. We already know that when the pressure drop across the glottis is small, differences in vocal cord stiffness will determine whether or not they vibrate, whereas when the pressure drop across the glottis is large, differences in stiffness correlate with the rate at which the vocal cords vibrate. In other words, in nonsonorant sounds vocal cord stiffness controls the presence or absence of vibrations (voicing), whereas in sonorant sounds—and most especially in vowels—which normally are voiced, the stiffness of the cords determines the rate of vibration and hence the perceived pitch of the sound. Thus, the variation in stiffness of the vocal cords has perceptually two rather distinct consequences: presence versus absence of voicing in one class of speech sounds, and variations in pitch in another class of speech sounds. In view of this, it is worth noting that in many languages voiceless consonants are related to high-pitched vowels and voiced consonants to low-pitched vowels.

In addition to controlling the stiffness of the edges of the glottis, a speaker can control the size of the glottal opening, by spreading or constricting (pressing together) the vocal cords. When the vocal cords are spread, a special [h]-like sound—known to phoneticians as *aspiration*—is produced. In English, aspiration differentiates the voiceless stops in word-initial position from their cognates in position after [s], as illustrated by the pairs in (11):

(11)   port − sport, till − still, core − score

In other languages, such as those of India, the aspiration distinction is much more widespread among the consonants. Thus, Hindi has the full complement of four stops allowed by the two binary features of [stiff vocal cords] and [spread glottis].

(12)

	[p t k]	[pʰ tʰ kʰ]	[b d g]	[bʰ dʰ gʰ]
[stiff vocal cords]	+	+	−	−
[spread glottis]	−	+	−	+

The features for consonants and the articulators for these features are summarized in figure 3.3.

3.3   On the Psychological Reality of the Features

We have seen that speech sounds are not the ultimate constituents of language but instead complexes of features that are themselves structured in

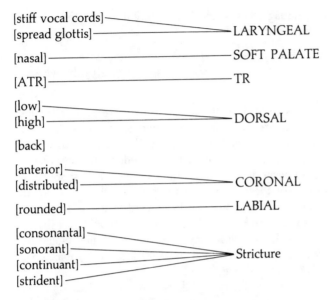

Figure 3.3
List of features and their articulators. The features in the *stricture* set are executed by one of the six articulators listed above, whose identity must be stipulated for each sound. For additional information on the internal organization of the features, see Sagey 1986.

a specific way. In this section we will see evidence that this elaborate structure not only is required by the way sounds are produced in the human vocal tract but also enters directly into the knowledge that speakers have of their language.

Three distinct suffixes are used to signal the regular plural of English nouns:

(13) [ɪz]   places, adzes, porches, cabbages, ambushes, camouflages
     [s]   lips, lists, maniacs, telegraphs, hundredths
     [z]   clubs, herds, colleagues, phonemes, terns, fangs, holes, gears,
            pies, apostrophes, avenues, cellos, violas

The choice of suffix is governed by the last sound in the word, as stated in rule (14):

(14) [ɪz]   if noun ends with [s z č ǰ š ž], otherwise
     [s]   if noun ends with [p t k f θ], otherwise
     [z]

Examination of the groups of consonants figuring in (14) reveals that the members of each group share features that distinguish the group from all other sounds in the language. Translated into feature notation, the rule for the English plural suffiix reads as follows:

(15)   [ɪz]   if noun ends with [+ coronal, + strident], otherwise
       [s]   if noun ends with [+ stiff vocal cords] ([− voice]), otherwise
       [z]

These two formulations predict different results with respect to nouns ending with sounds that are not part of the English sound system (L. Menn, personal communication). Rule (14) predicts that such words would invariably be given the suffix [z]. By contrast, (15) predicts that any one of the three suffixes could occur depending on the nature of the last sound in the word. A good test of these alternatives is provided by the German name *Bach*, which ends with the voiceless dorsal continuant, which is not found in English. If English speakers used rule (14), they would give [baxz], with [z], as the plural of this word; if they used rule (15), they would instead give [baxs], with [s]. Since the great majority indeed say [baxs], we must conclude that (15) is the rule employed.

This result implies that ordinary speakers have knowledge of the feature composition of the sounds of speech, including not only the sounds of their own language but also those of any other language. Thus, unless a more compelling interpretation of the results of our experiment is offered, we must accept the conclusion that *for the speaker words are made up of discrete speech sounds that are themselves complexes of features.* That the speaker might deny having this knowledge does not invalidate this conclusion; rather, it shows that we may know things without being aware of it. (See chapter 9.) The existence of such knowledge has been recognized almost since the beginnings of scientific concern with human knowledge. In the dialogues of Plato, for example, Socrates elicits many types of unconscious knowledge from his untutored interlocutors.

3.4   Rules and Rule Interaction

3.4.1   Plural Formation in Kasem

Affixation is one of the most common types of word modification (inflection and derivation) encountered among the languages of the world. A typical example is given by the singular and plural forms of Class C nouns in Kasem, a West African language, illustrated in (16). (For sources of data and additional discussion, see Halle 1978.)

(16)		'boy'	'granary'	'moon'	'shoulder'
	Singular	bakad-a	tul-a	čan-a	bakal-a
	Plural	bakad-i	tul-i	čan-i	bakal-i

As shown in (17), noun stems need not end in consonants: they may end in vowels as well. (Long vowels are represented by sequences of identical vowels.)

(17)

	'pot'	'yam'	'chameleon'	'slave'
Singular	kambi-a	pi-a	malaa	kabaa
Plural	kambi	pi	male	kabe

If the forms in (17) arose via suffixation alone, we would expect the forms in (18) instead:

(18)

Singular	kambi-a	pi-a	malaa-a	kabaa-a
Plural	kambi-i	pi-i	malaa-i	kabaa-i

Comparing the expected forms with the actual forms, we see that whenever the suffix vowel is identical with the stem vowel, one of the two vowels disappears. We will assume that the suffix is deleted. We therefore postulate rule (19), Truncation:

(19)   *Truncation*

$V_1 V_2 \rightarrow V_1$

Condition: V_2 is a word-final vowel and $V_1 = V_2$.

Truncation accounts for the singular forms in (17) as well as for the plural forms *kambi, pi*.

We still need to account for the plural forms [male] and [kabe] in place of the expected [malaa + i] and [kabaa + i]. These forms involve several rules. First, long vowels are shortened in prevocalic position by rule (20), Shortening:

(20)   *Shortening*

$VV \rightarrow V$ before V

Kasem vowels are also subject to rule (21), Contraction, which converts [ai] into [e] and [au] into [o]. The effect of Contraction is to monophthongize the diphthongs [ai] and [au] and replace each one with the nonhigh cognate of its second element—that is, [ai] → [e], [au] → [o] but [aa] → [a]:

(21)   *Contraction*

$$\begin{array}{ccc} V_1 & V_2 & \rightarrow & V_2 \\ | & | & & | \\ [+\text{low}] & [+\text{high}] & & [-\text{high}] \end{array}$$

As formalized in (21), Contraction will delete [a] only if it is short. In view of this, in order to obtain the correct outputs it is necessary that Shortening apply before Contraction and that Truncation apply before Shortening. In other words, the derivation must proceed as illustrated in (22):

(22)

	a.	b.
	malaa-a	malaa-i
Truncation	malaa	n.a.
Shortening	n.a.	mala-i
Contraction	n.a.	male

In applying the rules in (22), we follow the convention that rules apply in a linear order and that the input to a given rule R is the underlying sequence of sounds (the phonological analogue of the syntactic deep structure of chapter 2) as modified by all rules ordered before R. Thus, for example, if in derivation (22a) Shortening had applied before Truncation, we would have obtained the output *mala* with a word-final short [a] rather than the correct form with a long [aa].

This is not the only logically imaginable convention on rule application. For example, one might impose the convention that each rule applies to the underlying representation, rather than to the representation as modified by all rules ordered earlier than the rule in question. If this convention were imposed on the derivation (22b), Shortening and Contraction would produce, instead of [male], the output [malae]. Of course, we could generate the correct output [male] using this convention, but only at the cost of complicating the formulation of Shortening and Contraction. These complications would be gratuitous: they are forced upon us by the convention we are considering. We know that there is a simpler account of the facts, but this requires us to assume the convention on rule application exemplified in (22). Thus, unless we can establish the superiority of the alternative convention on rule application, we must adopt the convention of (22).

The forms in (23) show that in plural forms in Kasem, stem-final dorsal consonants [k g ŋ] are deleted, where [ŋ] represents the nasal cognate of [k g]. (The actual plural form of 'river' is [bwi], which is produced by the application of a rule of [u] desyllabification whose effect we will disregard here.)

(23)

	'river'	'room'	'song'	'leg'
Singular	bug-a	dig-a	laŋ-a	nag-a
Plural	bu-i	di	le	ne

We must therefore postulate the rule of Dorsal Consonant Deletion:

(24)   *Dorsal Consonant Deletion*

$$V \quad \underset{\mid}{C} \quad V \rightarrow V\,V$$

[+DORSAL]

Condition: in the plural

In order to obtain the output [di] from [dig-i], it is necessary to order Dorsal Consonant Deletion before Truncation. The form [ne] from underlying [nag-i] shows that Dorsal Consonant Deletion must also precede Contraction. We have no evidence for the relative order of Shortening and Dorsal Consonant Deletion, but we know that both must precede Contraction.

Finally, consider these singular and plural forms from Kasem:

(25)   'path'   'back'
       Singular   kog-a   čog-a
       Plural   kue   čue

(26)   'sheep'
       Singular   pi-a
       Plural   pe

The underlying forms of the stems in (25) are [kaug] and [čaug], respectively. This leads us to postulate for the plural the underlying strings [kaug-i] and [čaug-i]. Since these are subject to Dorsal Consonant Deletion, we obtain [kau-i] and [čau-i], which would give us the incorrect [koi] and [coi] as outputs by the rules proposed so far. To obtain the correct outputs, we would need the representations [kua-i] and [čua-i], which can be derived from [kau-i] and [čau-i] by rule (27), Metathesis:

(27) *Metathesis*

$V_1 V_2 V_3 \rightarrow V_2 V_1 V_3$

Condition: V_2 and V_3 are distinct

The forms in (26) show that Metathesis must be restricted so as not to apply when the second vowel in the sequence is identical with the third. We then postulate [pia-a] and [pia-i] as the underlying representations for *pia* and *pe* and derive the correct outputs as follows:

(28)   pia-a   pia-i
       Dorsal Consonant Deletion   n.a.   n.a.
       Metathesis   n.a.   pai-i
       Truncation   pia   pai
       Shortening   n.a.   n.a.
       Contraction   n.a.   pe

3.4.2   Velar Softening and [s]-Voicing in English

English has a large class of verbs composed of prefixes and stems of the sort illustrated in (29). (For additional discussion, see Halle and Mohanan 1985.)

(29) im-pel   ———   re-pel   com-pel   ———   ex-pel
      in-fer   de-fer   re-fer   con-fer   pre-fer ———
      im-port   de-port re-port com-port ———   ex-port
      in-cur   ———   re-cur   con-cur   ———   ———

Stem-initial [s] becomes [z] in cases where the prefix ends with a vowel and
the stem [s] itself is followed by a vowel:

(30) serve   con-serve de-serve re-serve pre-serve
      sign   con-sign   de-sign   re-sign   ———
      ———   con-sent   ———   re-sent   pre-sent

We will postulate that English is subject to the rule of [s]-Voicing, which is
informally stated in (31):

(31) [s]-*Voicing*

      [s] → [z] in the environment V ____ V

However, a number of stems do not undergo this rule. (Here again, recall
that in the standard orthography of English a given letter does not represent a unique sound. In particular, in certain contexts (for instance,
call, gall) the letters *c g* represent the sounds [k g], respectively, whereas
in other contexts (for instance, *cider/peace, ginger/cage*) they represent
the sounds [s ǰ]. In still other contexts (for instance, *delicious*) the letter
c can also represent the sound [š]. Bear in mind that we are concerned
with the sounds of the language rather than with their orthographic representations.)

(32) cite   in-cite ex-cite   ———   re-cite   ———
      cede   ———   ex-ceed   con-cede   re-cede   ———
      ———   ———   ———   con-ceive re-ceive de-ceive

Irregularities of all sorts are commonly encountered in language. For instance, the inflection of the verb *be* in English and its equivalent in many
other languages is totally unlike that of any other verb in the language
and must be given by special rules applicable only to this verb. It might
therefore appear at first sight that the irregularity in (32) is also to be accounted for by marking the stems *cite, cede,* and *ceive* as exceptions to [s]-
Voicing. This proposal is likely to be incorrect, for it fails to bring out the
fact that these very stems exhibit certain other apparent irregularities, all
of which together have a single explanation.

   A large part of the English vocabulary exhibits alternations between
[k]–[s] and [g]–[ǰ] of the sort illustrated in (33):

(33) electri[k]   –   electri[s]-ity   analo[g]   –   analo[ǰ]-ize
      Damas[k]us   –   Damas[s]-ene   collea[g]ue   –   colle[ǰ]-ial
      medi[k]   –   medi[s]-ine   tautolo[g]-ous –   tautolo[ǰ]-y

This replacement of [k g] by [s j], which traditionally has been referred to as Velar Softening, takes place before the syllable nuclei [I ɛ ay iy] (which are exemplified by the vowels in the words *ill, ell, aisle, eel*). The formal statement of this rule involves complexities that go beyond the scope of this chapter, but it can be stated informally in ordinary English as follows:

(34)   *Velar Softening*

The dorsal stops [k] and [g] are replaced by [s] and [j], respectively, before [I ɛ ay iy].

Since Velar Softening is part of the language, we now have a means of accounting for the absence of [s]-Voicing in the examples in (32). We postulate that in their underlying representations the stems in (32) begin with [k], which is turned into [s] by Velar Softening. If we assume further that Velar Softening is ordered after [s]-Voicing, we have explained the fact that the stems in (32) are not subject to [s]-Voicing. A modicum of support for this proposal comes from the fact that except for the verbs in (35), for which there is a special explanation, the stems of all verbs that are exceptions to [s]-Voicing have as their nucleus vowel [I ɛ ay iy]. If these stems were just irregular exceptions to [s]-Voicing, there would be no reason for them to be limited in this fashion.

The other class of exceptions to [s]-Voicing consists of stems that otherwise undergo the rule but fail to do so after certain prefixes such as *as-*:

(35)   sign   re-sign   as-sign
        ——   re-sent   as-sent
        ——   re-sume   as-sume

To account for this irregularity, we will assume that the prefix in the last column of (35) is subject to the special rule of Consonant Copy, which copies the initial consonant of the verb stem, applying only in verbs formed with this and a few other prefixes. As a consequence, verbs with these prefixes have phonological representations that are quite close to their representations in standard English orthography:

(36)   a-sign → a[s-s]ign   a-sent → a[s-s]ent   a-sume → a[s-s]ume
        a-fect → a[f-f]ect   a-cord → a[k-k]ord   a-tain → a[t-t]ain
        su-fuse → su[f-f]use   su-port → su[p-p]ort   su-round → su[r-r]ound

It is obvious that the representations in the first line of (36) cannot undergo [s]-Voicing, for [s]-Voicing applies only to a single [s] between vowels. The proposed representation thus accounts for the facts in (35). (Sequences of identical consonants in English are commonly pronounced like single consonants. Thus, [l] in the adverb *royally*, which is composed of the adjective *royal* and the adverbial suffix *-ly*, is pronounced exactly like the [l] in *royalist*, where the suffix added to *royal* begins with a vowel. To account formally for this fact, we must assume that English has a rule simplifying geminate (that is, double) consonants. It should be clear that this geminate simplification rule must be ordered after [s]-Voicing and Velar Softening; otherwise, the consonant created by Consonant Copy would be deleted, giving incorrect results.)

The forms in (37) provide additional evidence in favor of postulating the rule of Consonant Copy:

(37) cede   pre-cede   con-cede   ac-[s]ede   suc-[s]eed
      ——   ——   con-gest   ——   sug-[ǰ]est

Since the stem *cede* does not undergo [s]-Voicing in such verbs as *precede*, *proceed*, and *recede*, it must be represented underlyingly with a [k] that then undergoes Velar Softening, surfacing as [s]. We therefore postulate that the underlying representation for the verbs *accede* and *suggest* is as follows:

(38) a-[k]ede
      su-[g]est

If we now postulate further that these verbs are subject to the rule of Consonant Copy, we obtain the representations in (39),

(39) a[k-k]ede
      su[g-g]est

from which the required forms are readily derived by application of Velar Softening:

(40) su[g-ǰ]est
      a[k-s]ede

3.5 On the Innateness of Linguistic Knowledge

We have examined the manner in which speech sounds are produced in the human vocal tract and the role that the sounds play in the expression of various regularities and rules. Two results of this investigation are particularly significant: (1) sounds are complexes of features that reflect phonetic capabilities of the independently movable portions of the human vocal tract, and (2) certain phonological regularities must be expressed by means of rules whose method of interaction is best characterized by applying them in a linear order. Since these are crucial components of the knowledge that speakers have of their language, we may ask how speakers acquire this highly recondite type of knowledge. Since we cannot plausibly suppose that children could acquire essential aspects of this knowledge—for instance, that rules must be applied in a linear order—in the ordinary course of growing up in a normal speaking family or other social unit, we have no alternative but to assume that the knowledge in question is innate, that is, available to humans (either at birth or at some later time) as part of their genetic endowment. (A similar argument concerning aspects of syntactic knowledge is presented in chapter 1.) On this view, the ability of humans to acquire the language of their community is more like their ability to learn to walk upright and rather unlike the ability that dogs, cats, and elephants have to acquire the same behavior—in those special cases where the latter have been trained to perform this feat. If the difference between humans and other species with respect to the ability to acquire bipedal gait is due to the different genetic endowment of the species in question, then the difference between humans and other species with respect to the ability to acquire language is also likely to be due to genetic factors. This hypothesis implies that most of what is needed for learning a language is already present in normal human beings and that to acquire command of a language speakers must (and can) obtain from a speech community information only about fairly restricted (peripheral) aspects of their language. Although we have a fair picture of what aspects of language can be learned and what aspects must be innate, much more information in this domain remains to be discovered.

Suggestions for Further Reading

Halle and Clements 1983 contains an elementary survey of most of the issues discussed in this chapter.

Good systematic introductions to phonetics may be found in Ladefoged 1975 and Lieberman 1977. Lieberman 1977 is especially to be recommended for its clear discussion of the relation between acoustic properties of speech and their articulatory implementation.

Extensive technical discussions of many issues in phonology are found in Chomsky and Halle 1968 and in Kenstowicz and Kisseberth 1979, although both books are now somewhat out of date. Van der Hulst and Smith 1982 contains more up-to-date treatments of many of the same issues but may be more difficult for the beginner because the papers in the collection represent heterogeneous theoretical positions.

Questions

3.1   English uses three distinct suffixes for the regular past tense forms of the verb: [ɪd], [t], [d]. Find the principle governing the choice of suffix by a particular verb. (See the discussion of English plurals in section 3.3.)

3.2   Give examples of English monosyllabic words containing a vowel that is

(i)   [+high, −low, +back, +round]

(ii) [−high, −low, −back, −round, +ATR]

(iii) [−high, +low, +back]

3.3   What features are shared by the vowels in the following English words?

(i)   full, fill

(ii) foal, cull

(iii) bother, father, moth

3.4   a. Give examples of English words ending with consonants that are

(i)   [+nasal]

(ii) [+coronal] and [+strident]

b.   State the other features of the nasal consonants in the words you've given in answer to question (ai).

3.5   What features are shared by the consonant sounds in the following English words? (In some of the examples a sequence of letters stands for a single sound.)

(i)   pie, my, by

(ii) thigh, thy, sigh, xy(lophone)

(iii) key, tea, pea

3.6   Characterize in feature terms the differences among the [n] sounds in the following English words:

(i)   tenth, tense, trench

3.7   Consider the following Latvian nominal declensions (three masculine, three feminine):

	(i) Masculine	'father'	'swan'	'market'
Sg.	Nom.	tæævs	gulbis	tirgus
	Loc.	tæævaa	gulbii	tirguu
	Acc.	tæævu	gulbi	tirgu
	Dat.	tæævam	gulbim	tirgum
	Gen.	tææva	gulbya	tirgus*
Pl.	Nom.	tæævi	gulbyi	tirgi
	Loc.	tæævuɔs	gulbyuɔs	tirguɔs
	Acc.	tæævus	gulbyus	tirgus
	Dat.	tææviæm	gulbyiæm	tirgiæm
	Gen.	tæævu	gulbyu	tirgu

(ii) Feminine	'sister'	'land, earth'	'cow'
Sg. Nom.	maasa	zeme	guɔvs
Loc.	maasaa	zemee	guɔvii
Acc.	maasu	zemi	guɔvi
Dat.	maasay	zemey	guɔviy
Gen.	maasas	zemes	guɔvs*
Pl. Nom.	maasas	zemes	guɔvis
Loc.	maasaas	zemees	guɔviis
Acc.	maasas	zemes	guɔvis
Dat.	maasaam	zemeem	guɔviim
Gen.	maasu	zemyu	guɔvyu

*For the purposes of this exercise, ignore these two forms, which are exceptional.

a. Determine the underlying representation of each form, indicating morpheme divisions.

b. State the rules deriving the surface forms from the underlying forms.

3.8 Indefinite and definite adjectives in Latvian have separate declensions. These are given below for the root *lab-* 'good'.

(i)	M. Indef.	Fem. Indef.	M. Def.	Fem. Def.
Sg. Nom.	labs	laba	labays	labaa
Loc.	labaa	labaa	labayaa	labayaa
Acc.	labu	labu	labuɔ	labuɔ
Dat.	labam	labay	labayam	labayay
Gen.	laba	labas	labaa	labaas
Pl. Nom.	labi	labas	labiæ	labaas
Loc.	labuɔs	labaas	labayuɔs	labayaas
Acc.	labus	labas	labuɔs	labaas
Dat.	labiæm	labaam	labayiæm	labayaam
Gen.	labu	labu	labuɔ	labuɔ

In order to derive these forms, rules in addition to those postulated in question 3.7b will be required. State these rules and give the derivation of all the listed forms.

Questions 3.7 and 3.8 are adapted from M. Halle and G. N. Clements (1983). *Problem book in phonology*. Cambridge, MA: MIT Press.

References

Berko, J. (1958). The child's learning of English morphology. *Word* 14, 150–177.

Chomsky, N., and M. Halle (1968). *The sound pattern of English*. New York: Harper and Row.

Halle, M. (1978). Further thoughts on Kasem nominals. *Linguistic Analysis* 4, 167–185.

Halle, M. (1983). On distinctive features and their articulatory implementation. *Natural Language and Linguistic Theory* 1, 91–105.

Halle, M. (1985). Speculations about the representation of words in memory. In V. Fromkin, ed., *Phonetic linguistics*. Orlando, FL: Academic Press.

Halle, M., and G. N. Clements (1983). *Problem book in phonology*. Cambridge, MA: MIT Press.

Halle, M., and K. P. Mohanan (1985). Segmental phonology of Modern English. *Linguistic Inquiry* 16, 57–116.

Halle, M., and K. Stevens (1969). On the feature "advanced tongue root." In *RLE quarterly progress report* 94, MIT, Cambridge, MA.

Halle, M., and K. Stevens (1971). A note on laryngeal features. In *RLE quarterly progress report* 101, MIT, Cambridge, MA.

Jakobson, R. (1938). Observations sur le classement phonologique des consonnes. In *Selected writings*, vol. 1. The Hague and Berlin: Mouton.

Jakobson, R. (1948). The Russian conjugation. *Word* 4, 155–167.

Kenstowicz, M., and C. Kisseberth (1979). *Generative phonology: Description and theory*. New York: Academic Press.

Ladefoged, P. (1964). *A phonetic study of the West African languages*. Cambridge: Cambridge University Press.

Ladefoged, P. (1975). *A course in phonetics*. New York: Harcourt Brace Jovanovich.

Ladefoged, P., and I. Maddieson (1986). *Some of the sounds of the world's languages: Preliminary version*. UCLA Working Papers in Phonetics 64.

Lieberman, P. (1977). *Speech physiology and acoustic phonetics: An introduction*. New York: Collier-Macmillan.

Lightner, T. (1972). *Problems in the theory of phonology*. Edmonton, Alberta, Canada: Linguistic Research.

Sagey, E. W. (1986). The representation of features and relations in non-linear phonology. Doctoral dissertation, MIT, Cambridge, MA.

van der Hulst, H., and N. Smith, eds. (1982). *The structure of phonological representations*. Dordrecht, Holland: Foris.

4

Speech Perception

Joanne L. Miller

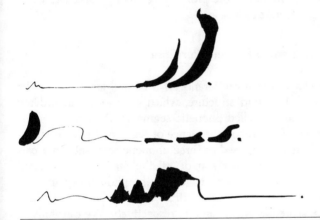

When we engage in conversation, we usually have little difficulty understanding the speech that is directed toward us. This is true even though we are often listening to unfamiliar voices, our surroundings are often quite noisy, and people talk at widely varying rates of speech. Moreover, the processes underlying language comprehension are largely unconscious, with the result that our impression as listeners is one of immediate, automatic recognition.

A question of primary concern to cognitive scientists is how this is accomplished—that is, what perceptual, cognitive, and linguistic mechanisms allow us, as listeners, to process speech in such an efficient, effortless manner? In this chapter we will examine this question with respect to one of the primary stages of the language recognition process: the recognition of the individual speech sounds (consonants and vowels) that form the words of the language.

Preparation of this chapter was supported by NIH grant NS 14394 and NIH BRSG RR 07143.

The study of this aspect of language comprehension, known as *speech perception*, draws from many disciplines. Major contributions have come from such diverse fields as linguistics, acoustics, speech science, psychology, and electrical engineering. Although a complete theory of speech perception is not at hand, much has been learned about both the physical properties of speech and the way in which these physical properties are processed by human listeners. One of the major findings has been that the recognition of speech sounds is far from being simple and straightforward. In this chapter we will examine what makes the problem of speech recognition so complex, and we will discuss possible ways in which the human processing system solves the problem, rendering speech recognition as effortless and accurate as it is.

4.1   Basic Characteristics of Speech Perception

As we learned in chapter 3, any utterance of a natural language can be analyzed in terms of its sound structure, which consists of an ordered sequence of speech sounds, called phonetic segments. Each word of the language is composed of a particular sequence of segments. Take as an example the word *suit*. It is composed of three phonetic segments, in a particular order: the initial consonant sound "s," the medial vowel sound "oo," and the final consonant sound "t." Using the phonetic symbols of the International Phonetic Association (IPA), this sequence of three sounds can be represented as [s], [u], and [t], respectively. We can think of the problem of speech perception as one of how the listener recognizes the particular sequence of segments that was produced by the speaker— for the word *suit*, the sequence [s], [u], [t].

This would be a relatively straightforward matter if the speech signal itself were composed of individual acoustic segments—patterns of physical energy—that corresponded in a one-to-one fashion to the distinct phonetic segments. To illustrate with the example [sut], this would mean that every time a speaker said the sound [s], a certain distinctive kind of acoustic energy pattern would be produced; every time the speaker said the sound [u], yet another distinctive acoustic pattern would be produced; and similarly for [t]. If speech worked in this way, then for every individual phonetic segment of the language—every distinct consonant and vowel that we perceive—there would be one and only one distinctive acoustic pattern of energy. The task of speech perception would be straightforward. In order to recognize the sequence of phonetic segments intended by the speaker (and hence the intended words), the listener would only have to recognize which of the distinctive energy patterns had been produced, and the order in which these had been produced.

But speech does not work like this (see Liberman, et al. 1967), in large part because of the way in which we produce speech. When uttering a given word, such as *suit*, we do not produce each sound—each segment—independently, that is, first [s], then [u], and then [t], with the next sound beginning only after the previous sound has been completed. This would in fact make speech production very slow and laborious—similar to spelling out loud. Instead, when we are producing the [s] sound, we are already shaping our articulators (tongue, jaw, lips, and so forth) in preparation for the [u] sound—and we are even preparing to produce the final [t] sound. This means that the articulatory movements for the different sounds within a word overlap one another in time. That is, the phonetic segments are not individually articulated but are instead coarticulated. Because of this coarticulation, individual phonetic segments do not correspond in a simple way to single, distinctive acoustic segments or properties in the speech signal.

There are two basic ways in which coarticulation complicates the mapping between the phonetic segments intended by the speaker and the speech signal. These have to do with *segmentation* and *invariance*.

4.1.1   Segmentation

A major tool in the study of speech perception is the *sound spectrograph*, a device that provides a visual representation of speech, called a *spectrogram*. In a spectrogram the frequency composition of the sound is displayed across time; frequency is represented on the ordinate (y-axis) and time on the abscissa (x-axis). As an example, a spectrogram of the consonant-vowel syllable [su], produced by a male speaker of English, is shown in the left panel of figure 4.1. This display clearly illustrates the change in energy pattern across the duration of the syllable. What is most striking is that there are two quite distinct acoustic segments, labeled on the figure as A and B. It is tempting to think that these two acoustic segments correspond in a straightforward way to the two phonetic segments, [s] and [u], respectively. But they do not—the relation between the acoustic segments A and B and the phonetic segments [s] and [u] is more complicated, and more subtle.

This can be shown experimentally in the following way (see Yeni-Komshian and Soli 1981). Using modern computer-editing techniques, an experimenter can make a cut in the speech signal at the acoustic break between segments A and B and play the segments individually for a listener. Upon hearing segment A, the listener will identify the consonant [s] with high accuracy, as we would expect. And, upon hearing segment B, the listener will easily identify the vowel [u]. However, upon hearing segment A and being asked to identify the *vowel* rather than the consonant, the lis-

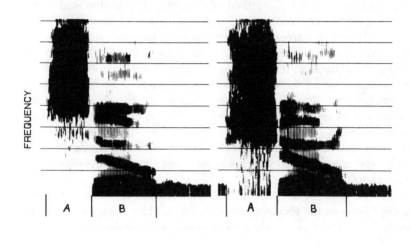

Figure 4.1
Spectrogram of [su] and [šu], produced by a male speaker of English.

tener can also answer quite accurately. This demonstrates that segment A contains information not only about which consonant was produced but also about which vowel was produced—vowel information is not limited to segment B. In other words, information about the consonant and vowel can be transmitted in parallel, by the same segment of the acoustic signal (in this case segment A). It is important to emphasize that such parallel transmission of information, which results from coarticulation of the consonant with the upcoming vowel, is the rule rather than the exception in speech. And because information about different phonetic segments is transmitted in parallel by the same acoustic segment, the listener must have a way of "unpacking" each acoustic segment in terms of the information it provides about multiple phonetic segments. This means that speech perception cannot simply be a matter of recognizing each acoustic segment and matching it to a single phonetic segment, one by one, from the beginning to the end of the word.

4.1.2   Invariance

A closely related complication that coarticulation introduces into the mapping between phonetic segments and acoustic segments is that there is no single, invariant property in the acoustic signal—no single, consistent pattern of acoustic energy—that corresponds uniquely to a given phonetic segment of the language. Because of coarticulation, the precise form of an acoustic property that is important for the recognition of a particular consonant or vowel changes according to the phonetic context in which the segment is produced.

As an illustration of this context-dependency, consider the distinction between [s] and [š] (the "sh" sound in *ship*). These two consonants are both fricatives, which are produced with a constriction of the vocal tract that is sufficiently narrow to generate turbulent air flow. They differ from each other in the precise placement of the articulators during their production. This difference causes the energy composition of the frication noise that is generated by the turbulent air flow to differ. In particular, the frication noise for [s] has its concentration of energy at relatively higher frequencies than does the frication noise for [š]. This is illustrated by the spectrograms of [su] and [šu] in figure 4.1, which were produced by the same speaker. If you compare the frication noises (labeled segment A) on the two spectrograms, you will notice that the energy for the [s]-noise is shifted upward along the frequency scale (y-axis), compared to the energy for the [š]-noise.

So far, there is no problem. The frication noise for [s] is concentrated at a higher frequency region than that for [š], so that the listener could identify whether [s] or [š] had been spoken simply by noting the frequency region of the frication noise. However, context complicates the matter, in the following way. The precise frequency composition of the frication noise of [s] and [š] is not invariant; instead, it changes, depending on which vowel follows the fricative during production (Mann and Repp 1980). We can see this context-dependency by considering what happens when [s] and [š] are produced in the context of two different vowels, [a] and [u], yielding the syllables [sa], [ša], [su], and [šu]. Because of coarticulation with the upcoming vowel, the placement of the articulators during the production of the fricatives [s] and [š] is itself different before [a] and [u]. This has the effect of changing the energy concentration of the frication noises. Specifically, for both [s] and [š], the energy of the frication noise is concentrated at a relatively higher frequency region before [a] than before [u]. Thus, the precise region in which the frication energy is concentrated depends not only on which fricative was produced, [s] or [š], but also on the vowel context in which it was produced, [a] or [u]. The consequence for perception is that in order to correctly identify whether the speaker produced [s] or [š], the listener must somehow take into account not only the frequency region of the frication noise itself but also the identity of the following vowel. This means that information *after* the frication noise is relevant to the identification of the fricative consonant. Thus, speech perception cannot simply be a matter of recognizing each acoustic segment and matching it to a single phonetic segment, in order, one by one, from the beginning to the end of the word.

4.2   Possible Mechanisms of Speech Perception

We have seen that the relation between the phonetic segments of the language—the consonants and vowels that we perceive when we listen to speech—and the acoustic properties of the speech signal is far from simple. Yet listeners have no trouble recognizing speech during ordinary conversation. The intriguing question is how the human processing system accomplishes this. Over the years two quite different proposals have been offered, and each has been subjected to a variety of experimental tests. In the following sections we will examine these proposals and the kinds of data considered relevant in trying to choose between them.

4.2.1   The Theories

One prominent theoretical position, most closely identified with Liberman and his colleagues at Haskins Laboratories, is that phonetic perception is accomplished by a processing system that is specialized for the perception of speech. Listeners possess this specialized system by virtue of their biological status as humans, just as, for example, bats possess specialized systems for echolocation and owls possess specialized systems for localizing sound in space. This view, which has been called the *motor theory of speech perception*, has three major components.

1.   Perception is based on production. The first and most basic component of the theory is that there is an intimate link between the system responsible for perceiving speech and the system responsible for producing speech—hence the "motor" in "motor theory." This special link permits the listener, upon hearing the speech signal, to determine which articulatory gestures the speaker has made and, by doing so, to determine which phonetic segments (consonants and vowels) have been produced. The main idea is that we perceive speech by virtue of our tacit (unconscious) knowledge of how speech is produced. We tacitly know how coarticulation complicates the mapping between the phonetic segments intended by the speaker and the speech signal, and we use this knowledge in processing the speech signal when recognizing the intended phonetic segments.

2.   Perception is species-specific. The second major component of the theory follows directly from the first: since only humans produce speech and have knowledge about how articulation works, and since perception operates in terms of this knowledge of articulation, only humans can actually perceive the phonetic structure of an utterance. Nonhuman animals

will hear speech as a series of "noises" of some sort; since they do not possess the specialized speech-processing system, they will not perceive speech as a structured series of consonants and vowels.

3. Perception is innate. The third major component of the theory is that this specialized processing system is innately given—it is part of our biological heritage as humans. It is further proposed that this innately given processing system is operative early in infancy. According to the theory, infants come to the world with tacit knowledge of articulation and the production-perception link. This allows them to perceive the phonetic structure of an utterance (the sequences of consonants and vowels) long before they can actually produce speech, and long before language acquisition occurs. In other words, we do not have to "learn" to perceive the sounds of speech.

In striking contrast to the motor theory of speech perception is what we will call the *auditory theory of speech perception*. Unlike the motor theory, this view is not identified with any single researcher or laboratory. We will consider the basic components of the auditory theory by contrasting it with the motor theory on the three points outlined above.

1. Perception is not based on production. According to the auditory theory, we do not perceive speech via a specialized system that refers to tacit knowledge of articulation. Instead, the auditory system itself does the job. Somehow, because of the way in which our auditory system processes sound—all types of sound, speech and nonspeech—the complications caused by coarticulation are "automatically" unraveled, such that we are able to perceive the ordered sequences of phonetic segments intended by the speaker.

2. Perception is not species-specific. Since the human auditory system is very similar to the auditory systems of many other animals, these animals should perceive speech in much the same way we do. Thus, according to the auditory theory, the ability to perceive speech is not a unique accomplishment of the human species.

3. Perception could be innate. To the extent that the auditory system is well developed in infancy (which it is), this view proposes that speech perception abilities should be operative early in infancy. Thus, the auditory theory and the motor theory can both accommodate early speech-processing abilities in infancy, though for very different reasons.

4.2.2   Some Evidence

Over the years a vast amount of research has been aimed at determining which of the two major theories can best account for the facts of speech perception. Let us examine some examples of how the theories have been submitted to experimental test, organizing the discussion around the three major points on which the theories have been contrasted.

Is speech perception accomplished by a specialized, articulatory-based system?

As noted earlier, because of coarticulation, the acoustic properties important for recognizing a given consonant or vowel vary according to the context in which that consonant or vowel is produced. For example, [s] and [š] are distinguished from one another primarily by the energy concentration of their frication noises, with the energy concentrated at higher frequencies for [s] than [š]. However, for both consonants, the exact region of energy concentration varies with vowel context; the energy is concentrated at lower frequencies before [u] than [a]. Despite this, listeners have no trouble correctly recognizing which fricative, [s] or [š], has been produced. According to the motor theory, this is because listeners have tacit knowledge of the complications caused by coarticulation—for this example, of precisely how the following vowel alters the frequency composition of the preceding frication noise—and they use this knowledge to recognize which fricative had been produced.

How could this explanation be tested? One way would be to look at the perception of fricatives and determine whether listeners do indeed alter their perception according to the vowel context, as the motor theory predicts. Just such an experiment was conducted by Mann and Repp (1980).

To test perception, these investigators used a computer-based system to generate (synthesize) artificial speech, known in the literature as *synthetic speech*. The advantage of using synthetic speech to test perception is that with synthetic speech the experimenter can precisely control the exact acoustic properties of the speech signal. The speech synthesis procedures involved two main steps. The first step was to synthesize a series of frication noises that varied, in equal acoustic steps, from a noise with a relatively low frequency concentration appropriate for [š] to one with a relatively high frequency concentration appropriate for [s]. When these noises were presented in isolation, listeners reported hearing the frication noises near the [š]-end of the series as [š] and those near the [s]-end as [s], with a rather sharp break in perception between [š] and [s] at a given location along the series. This location, which corresponds to 50 percent [š] and [s] responses, is called the *phonetic category boundary*. The second step was to generate two new series by appending each of the frication noises in the original series to vowel segments—in one series, the vowel [a], and in the other series, the vowel [u]. This resulted in two consonant-vowel series, one ranging from [ša] to [sa], and the other ranging from [šu] to [su]. The stimuli from these two series were randomized and presented to listeners, who were asked to identify the initial consonant of each stimulus.

If listeners do not take account of the following vowel, then the identification functions for the two series, [ša]-[sa] and [šu]-[su], should be the same. That is, the [š]-[s] phonetic boundary should be located at the same

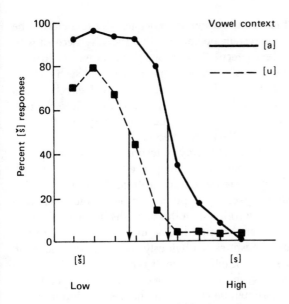

Figure 4.2
Identification functions for a [š]-[s] series in the context of [a] and [u]. Arrows indicate location of phonetic category boundary on each series. Adapted from V. A. Mann and B. H. Repp (1980). Influence of vocalic context on perception of the [ʃ]-[s] distinction. *Perception and Psychophysics* 28, 213–228. Reprinted by permission of Psychonomic Society, Inc.

frication noise along the series—after all, the frication noises in the two series are identical. However, if, as the motor theory predicts, listeners identify the frication segments in relation to the following vowel, compensating for the fact that the frication energy is concentrated at lower frequencies before [u] than [a], then listeners should start hearing [s], as opposed to [š], at a lower frequency noise on the [šu]-[su] series than on the [ša]-[sa] series. In other words, the [š]-[s] phonetic boundary should be located at a lower frequency noise before [u] than before [a]. Figure 4.2 shows the identification functions for the two series, [šu]-[su] and [ša]-[sa]. Clearly, the same frication noises were identified differently when they preceded the two vowels, in just the way necessary to overcome the effects of coarticulation.

This perceptual context effect (and many others like it are reported in the literature) provides clear support for the first component of the motor theory, namely, that speech perception is accomplished by a specialized perceptual mechanism that operates in terms of tacit articulatory knowledge. But does it rule out the auditory theory of speech perception? Not really. This is because there is no reason, in principle, why it could not be the case that our auditory system operates in just the way necessary to yield the perceptual context effects. At the same time, however, there is no reason why the auditory system should operate to yield such context effects—there is no obvious way to predict such context effects, given our current knowledge of how the auditory system works. Thus, the perceptual context effects do not rule out the auditory theory, but they are much more readily explained by the motor theory.

Let us now look at a very different way of testing the first claim of the motor theory, that speech perception is accomplished by a system specialized to process speech in reference to articulation. According to the theory, the real task during speech perception is to determine which articulatory gestures the speaker produced; in this way, the listener will know which phonetic segments were produced. One major source of information about the articulatory gestures is obviously the speech signal itself. But this is not the only source of information. It is also the case that some articulatory movements are visible on the speaker's face. According to the motor theory, the listener should be able to use this visual information, in conjunction with the information provided by the speech signal, to determine what was said. In other words, the motor theory predicts that the perceiver will integrate relevant information across the traditional modalities of audition and vision when perceiving speech.

Is there any evidence that speech perception does make use of such visual information? The answer is yes. We will examine this use of visual information by considering a study conducted by Massaro and Cohen (1983) (see McGurk and MacDonald 1976). They focused on the distinction between the stop consonants [b] and [d]. Stop consonants are produced with a full occlusion (or stop) at some place in the vocal tract during the production of the sound. [b] and [d] differ from each other in the place in the vocal tract where the occlusion occurs, that is, in their place of articulation. [b] is produced with the occlusion at the lips and is called a labial consonant, whereas [d] is produced with the occlusion at the alveolar ridge behind the teeth and is called an alveolar consonant.

Massaro and Cohen investigated whether the perceiver makes use of available visual information from the speaker's face about the place of articulation of the consonant—that is, whether the consonant is labial ([b]) or alveolar ([d])—when trying to identify it. Their basic strategy was first to examine the perception of ordinary auditory syllables that differed in place of articulation, [b] versus [d], and then to see whether the listener's identification of these syllables could be influenced by having the listener watch the speaker's face while the sounds were being produced.

To generate the ordinary auditory syllables, Massaro and Cohen used a computer-based speech synthesizer. They created a series of syllables (nine in all) that ranged, in small steps of the relevant acoustic properties that distinguish [b] and [d], from a good clear [ba] to a good clear [da]. These syllables were presented to listeners for identification as [ba] or [da] in three different conditions, all randomized together.

In the neutral condition the syllables were presented alone, with no accompanying visual information. A typical identification function for a speech series was obtained, as shown by the function labeled NONE in figure 4.3. As the figure illustrates, the syllables near the [ba]-end of the series were identified as [ba] nearly all of the time, those near the [da]-end of the series were identified as [da] nearly all of the time, and there was a sharp break at the point where perception changed from predominantly [ba] to [da].

In the other two conditions the syllables from the same auditory series were presented in synchrony with a silent videotape showing a speaker producing a list of syllables. In one of these conditions the syllable being produced by the speaker on the videotape was always [ba], and in the other condition it was always [da]. With this way of presenting the syllables, on some trials the auditory syllable and the visual syllable match, as when an auditory syllable at the [ba]-end of the series is presented in synchrony with a visual [ba], but on some trials there is a discrepancy between the auditory and visual information, as when an auditory syllable at the [ba]-end of the series is presented in synchrony with a visual [da]. However, the perceiver is not aware of these discrepancies! On any given trial the subject reports perceiving a single, unitary syllable; there is no awareness of any mismatch between auditory and visual information. Somehow, the perceptual system integrates the information from the auditory and visual modalities to yield the conscious experience of one syllable, one articulatory event, on each trial. This integration of information is clearly in accord with the predictions of motor theory.

But the theory can be subjected to an even stronger test. According to the motor theory, the visual information about place of articulation from the speaker's face should influence how the auditory syllable is identified on any given trial. That is, the perceived syllable should be jointly determined by the visual and auditory information—it should not depend on the auditory information alone. The following prediction can thus be made. When the auditory syllables along the series are presented in synchrony with the visual [ba], listeners should report hearing [ba] more often. And this is just what happened, as shown by the graph labeled BA in figure 4.3. As in the neutral condition, syllables near the [ba]-end of the auditory series were usually identified as [ba] and those near the [da]-end were usually identified as [da] but, overall, there were many more [ba] responses in this condition compared to the neutral condition. The converse should also hold. That is, when the auditory syllables from the series are

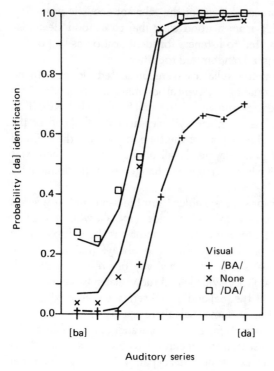

Figure 4.3
Identification functions for auditory [ba]-[da] series with no accompanying visual information (NONE), in the presence of visual [ba] (BA), and in the presence of visual [da] (DA). (The individual points represent the observed data, and the lines represent theoretical curves predicting the data.) Adapted from D. W. Massaro and M. M. Cohen (1983). Evaluation and integration of visual and auditory information in speech perception. *Journal of Experimental Psychology: Human Perception and Performance* 9, 753–771. © 1983 by the American Psychological Association.

presented in synchrony with the visual [da], subjects should report hearing [da] relatively often, compared to the neutral condition. This also occurred, as shown by the graph labeled DA in figure 4.3.

This pattern of results provides strong support for the motor theory. According to this theory, the perception of speech is accomplished by a specialized mechanism that refers to tacit knowledge of articulation. Any relevant information about articulation—be it auditory or visual—can be used by the system to identify the intended gestures of the speaker, and thus the phonetic structure of the utterance. But can the findings of cross-modal (auditory-visual) speech perception also be accommodated by the auditory theory of speech perception? The answer is no. This is because the auditory theory proposes that speech perception is accomplished by the operation of the auditory system itself. There is no way, within the theory, to explain just how (or why) the system would integrate auditory and visual information in the precise way that it does. Thus, data on auditory-visual speech perception provide strong evidence that the auditory theory alone cannot fully explain the facts of speech perception.

So far, it looks as though the evidence favors the motor theory over the auditory theory. But the situation is more complex, as we will see when we consider experimental tests of the second major claim of the motor theory.

Is speech perception species-specific?

The second major component of the motor theory involves the claim that the articulatory-based mechanism for speech perception is species-specific. The argument is simple: if speech perception is accomplished by a specialized mechanism based on articulatory principles, then nonhuman animals, who would not have such a mechanism, should perceive speech quite differently from humans. On the other hand, if speech perception is accomplished by the auditory system itself, as the auditory theory of speech perception claims, then nonhuman animals should show very similar processing to that of humans—especially if their basic auditory systems are comparable to those of human listeners. A way to test the claim that speech perception is species-specific becomes obvious: examine speech perception in nonhuman animals whose basic auditory systems are similar to those of humans, and see whether these animals process speech in the same way humans do.

Many such studies have been conducted, most notably by Kuhl and her colleagues. We will explore the basic procedures and findings by looking at a study that examined how chinchillas perceive speech (Kuhl and J. D. Miller 1978). Chinchillas were chosen because, as far as we know, their basic auditory sensitivity is very similar to that of humans.

The study focused on the perception of two consonants, [b] and [p]. Both are stop consonants and both are produced with occlusion at the lips; that is, they have a labial place of articulation. They differ from each other in that [b] is a voiced consonant whereas [p] is a voiceless consonant; the vocal folds vibrate during the production of the former but not the latter. For the voiced consonant [b], just as the consonant is released following the period of occlusion at the lips, the vocal folds start vibrating and they remain vibrating as the [b] is fully articulated. For the voiceless consonant [p], on the other hand, there is a delay between the initial release of the consonant and the beginning of vocal fold vibration. The time interval between the release of the consonant and the onset of vocal fold vibration is called *voice onset time*, or *VOT*. VOT turns out to be a very important property used by listeners in identifying whether a stop consonant is voiced or voiceless. If the VOT value is relatively short, listeners hear the consonant as voiced, and if it is relatively long, they hear it as voiceless.

One way to investigate the perception of consonants varying in VOT is to use a computer-based synthesizer to create a series of stimuli that range in small increments of VOT from a short value appropriate for [b]—say, 0 milliseconds, to a long value appropriate for [p]—say, 80 milliseconds. (One millisecond is .001 second.) For this experiment the synthetically generated stimuli ranged from [ba] to [pa] in 10-millisecond steps VOT. Spectrograms of three stimuli from the series, those with VOT values of 0, 40, and 80 milliseconds, are shown in figure 4.4. On each spectrogram the VOT interval is marked as the time between the release burst of the consonant (marked B) and the onset of vocal fold vibration, or voicing (marked V). As the spectrograms illustrate, during the VOT interval there is "noisy" energy in the high-frequency regions and no energy in the low-frequency regions.

The phenomenon tested on the chinchillas concerns the way in which listeners divide—or categorize—the stimuli in the [ba]-[pa] series. Many studies on human listeners have demonstrated that when stimuli from such a series are randomized and presented for identification, the following occurs. Humans perceive stimuli with low VOT values as [ba] and those with high VOT values as [pa], with a rather sharp break, or phonetic boundary, between categories at approximately 25 milliseconds VOT. The critical question is why the stimuli are categorized in this way. According to the motor theory, the location of the phonetic category boundary is a consequence of the operation of a species-specific perceptual mechanism that takes account of the fact that, in production, [b] is typically produced with VOT values less than 25 milliseconds, whereas [p] is typically produced with VOT values greater than 25 milliseconds. Since chinchillas do not have such a species-specific mechanism, they should not categorize the stimuli in this way. Alternatively, according to the auditory

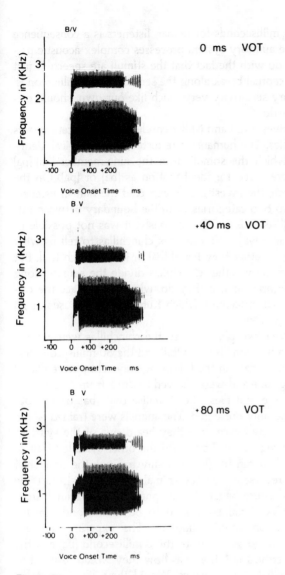

Figure 4.4
Stimuli from a voiced-voiceless series varying in voice onset time (VOT). Humans perceive
the 0-millisecond VOT stimulus as [ba] and the + 40- and + 80-millisecond VOT stimuli as
[pa]. The onset of voicing (V) and the onset of the burst (B) are marked. From P. K. Kuhl
(1986). Theoretical contributions of tests on animals to the special-mechanisms debate in
speech. *Experimental Biology* 45, 233–265. © 1986 by Springer-Verlag.

theory, the break at 25 milliseconds for human listeners is a consequence of the way in which the auditory system processes complex acoustic patterns; it has nothing to do with the fact that the stimuli are speech. It just so happens that the perceptual break along the series is at 25 milliseconds. Chinchillas, with auditory sensitivity very much like our own, should categorize the stimuli as we do.

To test these alternatives, Kuhl and Miller conducted identification tests on humans and chinchillas. The humans were tested with a typical identification procedure, in which the stimuli from the nine-member [ba]-[pa] series were randomly presented for identification as [ba] or [pa]. On the basis of previous research, the investigators expected the human listeners to divide the stimuli into two categories, with the boundary between categories at about 25 milliseconds VOT. Obviously, it was not possible to test chinchillas in the same way. We can't ask chinchillas to tell us what they hear—in this case, whether they heard [ba] or [pa] on each trial. But there are ways to determine whether chinchillas divide the sounds along the series into two categories and, if they do, where they place the category boundary. One such procedure, which Kuhl and Miller used, is an avoidance-conditioning procedure.

The procedure involved two phases. First, the chinchillas were trained to respond differently to the 0-millisecond [ba] and the 80-millisecond [pa] (the two endpoints of the series), in the following way. They were placed in a cage with a drinking tube and were allowed to drink from it. Every 10 to 15 seconds one of the syllables, the 0-millisecond [ba] or the 80-millisecond [pa], was randomly presented. The animals were trained to run to the other side of the cage every time they heard one of the syllables but to remain drinking every time they heard the other syllable. (Half of the animals were trained to run for [ba] and stay for [pa]; the other half were trained to do the reverse.) After the animals learned this setup, the second phase of the procedure began. In this phase all nine stimuli from the series—ranging in VOT values from 0 to 80 milliseconds, in 10-millisecond steps—were presented randomly. The experimenters expected the animals to respond as before to the 0-millisecond [ba] and the 80-millisecond [pa]; the critical question was how they would respond to the stimuli with intermediate VOT values. Would they, like human listeners, treat all stimuli with VOT values less than 25 milliseconds like [ba] and all stimuli with VOT values greater than 25 milliseconds like [pa]? If the human categorization data are due to the operation of a species-specific mechanism, the answer will be no. If the human data are instead due to the operation of the auditory system, the answer will be yes.

The human and chinchilla identification functions are presented together in figure 4.5. The two identification functions are remarkably similar, indicating that the chinchillas categorized the stimuli in much the

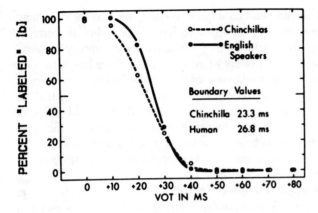

Figure 4.5
Identification functions for chinchillas and humans for stimuli on a series ranging from [ba] to [pa]. From P. K. Kuhl and J. D. Miller (1978). Speech perception by the chinchilla: Identification functions for synthetic VOT stimuli. *Journal of the Acoustical Society of America* 63, 905–917. © 1978 by American Institute of Physics.

same way as the humans. This is a clear problem for the motor theory. The findings suggest that at least some aspects of speech perception do not require the operation of a species-specific mechanism. Categorization of stimuli along a series seems to be the result of the operation of the auditory system itself. Of course, the demonstration that visual as well as auditory information is important for speech perception clearly indicates that speech perception involves more than just auditory processing. It thus seems that a more complicated theory, one that involves aspects of the auditory and motor theories, might be required to fully explain the facts of speech perception.

Is speech perception innately given, operative in early infancy?

Let us now turn to the final component of the motor theory, the claim that the proposed specialized, species-specific mechanism responsible for speech perception is innately given and, moreover, is operative in early infancy—long before language acquisition occurs. Given this claim, the theory predicts that young infants will show evidence of highly developed abilities to process speech. Such behavior would also be consistent with the auditory theory of speech perception, since the human auditory system is highly developed at birth. Thus, both theories predict that infants can process the speech signal very early in life, although they make this prediction for very different reasons.

At the turn of the century the prominent psychologist William James wrote that the world of the infant is one of "blooming, buzzing confusion"

(James 1890). At that time, and until quite recently, this was the prevailing view of infancy; infants were assumed to have little ability to perceive coherent patterns in the world, be they visual patterns, auditory patterns, or speech. But over the past twenty-five years or so there has been a remarkable change in the scientific view of how infants relate to the world. Using newly developed methodologies, researchers have learned that far from being a "blooming, buzzing confusion," the infant's world is one of coherence and structure. In fact, the change in how the scientific community thinks of infancy has been so striking that it has been picked up by the popular media; *Time* (August 15, 1983) even ran a cover story focusing on how "smart" babies really are.

Let us look at the case for speech. A considerable research effort over the past twenty-five years has revealed much about speech processing in early infancy. The major finding of this research is that young infants come to the task of language acquisition with a highly sophisticated processing system for speech. One phenomenon that illustrates this early, sophisticated processing concerns the categorization of speech. In the classic study initially demonstrating the categorization abilities of young infants, Eimas et al. (1971) examined how 1- and 4-month-old infants perceive the distinction between the stop consonants [b] and [p].

The stimuli were six syllables from a [ba]-[pa] series that had been synthesized on a computer—in fact, from a series very much like the one that was used to test categorization abilities in chinchillas. The VOT values of the six syllables used in the infant study were − 20, 0, 20, 40, 60, and 80 milliseconds. Thus, for the 0-millisecond stimulus, voicing began simultaneously with the release of the consonant, and for the 20-, 40-, 60-, and 80-millisecond stimuli, voicing was delayed by 20, 40, 60, and 80 milliseconds, respectively. For the − 20-millisecond VOT stimulus, voicing actually preceded the release of the consonant by 20 milliseconds. Since the phonetic category boundary for adults for this type of [ba]-[pa] series is located at approximately 25 milliseconds VOT, adults perceive the − 20-, 0-, and 20-millisecond syllables as [ba], and the 40-, 60-, and 80-millisecond syllables as [pa].

The most interesting question is whether infants also divide the syllables into two categories, with a boundary at approximately 25 milliseconds VOT. Since the chinchillas did show such categorization, we know that it does not require a species-specific perceptual mechanism. But is the underlying mechanism, whatever its nature, operative in early infancy, thereby providing the young infant with the ability to perceive speech in terms of categories? Unfortunately, just as with the chinchillas, it isn't possible to ask the infants to tell us what they hear. Moreover, it is very difficult to train infants as young as 1 month of age to respond differently to two different stimuli, so that the type of indirect identification

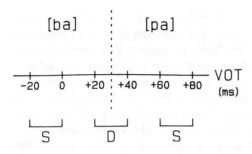

Figure 4.6
Experimental design of infant discrimination study. Based on P. D. Eimas, E. R. Siqueland, P. W. Jusczyk, and J. Vigorito (1971). Speech perception in infants. *Science* 171, 303–306. © 1971 by the AAAS.

procedure used to test chinchillas is not appropriate for infants. But there is another way to test indirectly how infants perceive these syllables, a procedure that is based on how infants discriminate syllables from the series.

This procedure is based on the finding that the ability of adults to discriminate syllables along a VOT series such as this one is strongly influenced by how the syllables are categorized. If the syllables are from two different categories, that is, one is [ba] and one is [pa], they are easy to distinguish. However, if the two syllables are from the same category, either both [ba] or both [pa], they are much more difficult to distinguish. If we could demonstrate that infants showed the same pattern of discrimination performance, we would have evidence—although indirect—that they did divide the syllables along the series into two categories, just like the adults.

Eimas and his colleagues used this strategy to test infant categorization of stimuli along the [ba]-[pa] series. The design of their study is shown in figure 4.6. The infants were tested on their ability to discriminate pairs of stimuli from the series that differed from each other by 20 milliseconds VOT. Two types of pairs were tested. For the "different" (D) pair, the 20-millisecond difference signified for adults a change in phonetic category. The tokens for this pair had VOT values of 20 and 40 milliseconds, which straddle the category boundary; adults hear these stimuli as [ba] and [pa], respectively. For the "same" (S) pairs, the 20-millisecond difference did not signify a change in phonetic category. Two sets of "same" tokens were used, one with VOT values of −20 and 0 milliseconds (both heard by adults as [ba]), and one with VOT values of 60 and 80 milliseconds (both heard by adults as [pa]).

If infants can perceive an acoustic difference as small as 20 milliseconds VOT but, unlike adults, do not perceive speech in terms of categories, then they should show evidence of discriminating both the "different" and the "same" pairs; in both cases a 20-millisecond acoustic difference is involved. This outcome would indicate that although the infant's perceptual system is highly sensitive to the kinds of acoustic differences that will come to be important for speech perception—in itself, rather remarkable—the system does not yet perceive speech in terms of categories. The ability to categorize would come later in life. However, if infants, like adults, perceive speech in terms of categories, then the "different" pair should be considerably easier to discriminate than the "same" pairs.

Note that the experimental design hinges on being able to assess discrimination in very young infants. How can this be done? Eimas and his colleagues adapted a technique for use with speech, which has come to be known as the *high-amplitude sucking* (HAS) procedure. The technique is based on the young infant's proclivity to seek novel stimulation, and works as follows. The infant is placed in an infant seat in front of a loudspeaker and given a pacifier to suck on. Once a baseline reading of high-amplitude sucking responses is measured, one stimulus from the pair to be tested is presented to the infant, contingent upon sucking—whenever the infant sucks, the speech sound is presented. Typically, infants respond to the contingency by increasing their rate of sucking. After some period of time, however, the sound loses its reinforcing properties and the rate of sucking declines. When a predetermined criterion of decline has been reached, the second stimulus of the pair is introduced, with no break in procedure. A renewed increase in sucking behavior to the new sound, compared to no increase in control infants who receive the first sound throughout testing, is taken as evidence of discrimination.

In the experiment, three groups of infants were tested. One group was tested on the "different" pair as described above, one was tested on the "same" pairs, and one was a control group. The results were very similar for both age groups; the data from the older infants are shown in figure 4.7. The infants showed clear evidence of discriminating the "different" pair but not the "same" pairs. Thus, infants could distinguish stimuli that differed by as little as 20 milliseconds VOT, but only if the stimuli were drawn from two different (adult) categories.

These data provide strong evidence that the young infant is highly sensitive to acoustic properties of speech (such as VOT) and, furthermore, that very early on infants perceive speech in terms of categories (such as those corresponding to [b] and [p]). And this phenomenon is not limited to the voicing distinction. Subsequent research on numerous phonetic contrasts (for example, contrasts in place of articulation) has demonstrated that such categorization by infants is the rule, not the exception. Thus, the basic phonetic categorization abilities required for language are something the infant brings to the task of language acquisition—not something that is learned in the course of language acquisition.

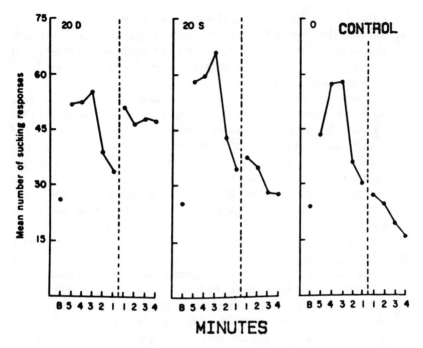

Figure 4.7
Mean number of sucking responses for 4-month-old infants as a function of time and experimental condition. The dashed line indicates the occurrence of the stimulus shift, or, in the case of the control group, the time at which the shift would have occurred. Adapted from P. D. Eimas, E. R. Siqueland, P. W. Jusczyk, and J. Vigorito (1971). Speech perception in infants. *Science* 171, 303–306. © 1971 by the AAAS.

The existence of such highly developed abilities in early infancy accords with both the motor theory and the auditory theory of speech perception, but the two theories account for these abilities in very different ways. According to the motor theory, the infant's abilities are due to the operation of a specialized, articulatory-based mechanism; according to the auditory theory, they are due to the operation of the auditory system itself, which is well developed at birth. Is there any aspect of infant speech perception that could, in principle, provide a test to decide between the two theories?

The answer is yes. In our earlier discussion of the adult's use of visual information from the speaker's face during speech perception, we saw that speech perception in adults is not entirely an auditory phenomenon. Adults appear to integrate relevant auditory information from the speech signal with relevant visual information from the speaker's face when identifying the phonetic structure of an utterance. This phenomenon is fully in accord with the motor theory but is problematic for the auditory theory. If we had data showing that infants also integrate relevant visual and auditory information during speech perception, we would have evidence that for infants, as for adults, the auditory theory alone is not sufficient to account for speech perception.

As of now, such direct evidence is not available. However, two very provocative studies suggest that young infants do have knowledge of the correspondences between articulatory movements on a speaker's face and the speech signal that is produced—knowledge that is necessary for visual information to play a role in speech perception. As early as 4 to 5 months of age, infants seem to be aware of the relation between how the articulators move and the sounds they produce (Kuhl and Meltzoff 1982; MacKain et al. 1983). This, of course, is just the kind of articulatory-based knowledge that infants should have, according to the motor theory.

Kuhl and Meltzoff's experiment illustrates the basic phenomenon. This study investigated whether infants are aware of the relation between the visual and auditory consequences of the production of two vowels, [i] and [a]. The procedure is schematized in figure 4.8. It involved two phases, familiarization and test. During familiarization, infants first saw a face articulating a repeating sequence of one of the vowels ([i] or [a]) and then saw a face articulating a repeating sequence of the other vowel. No sound was presented during this time, only the visual information. The purpose of this phase was simply to familiarize the infants with a face articulating the two different vowels. During the subsequent test phase, both faces were shown simultaneously, side by side, articulating their respective vowels. A synchronized soundtrack of one of the vowels was played over a loudspeaker during this time; for half of the infants the vowel was [i] and for the other half it was [a]. Thus, the sound matched one of the faces but not the other. We can predict that if infants detect the correspondence between the vowel sound and the articulatory movements on the face producing that sound, they might look longer at the face that matches the sound than at the other, mismatched face. And that is precisely what happened—the infants who heard [i] looked longer at the face producing [i], and the infants who heard [a] looked longer at the face producing [a]. This finding provides strong evidence that young infants have tacit knowledge of the relation between the auditory and visual consequences of articulation.

Where do the infant findings leave us in terms of the two alternative theories of speech perception? The infant's abilities to categorize speech can be accounted for by both the motor theory and the auditory theory. And since chinchillas can also categorize speech, this aspect of speech perception may well be due to the way in which the auditory system itself works. However, only the motor theory can readily account for the in-

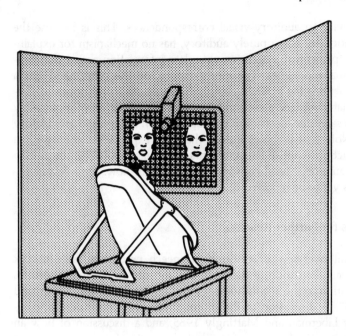

	Familiarization		Midline gaze	Test	
Visual stimuli	Face 1	Face 2		Both faces	
Auditory stimuli	...	...		/a/.../a/.../a/.../a/	
Time	10 seconds	10 seconds		2 minutes	

Figure 4.8
Top: schematic arrangement of infant placed in an infant seat, in front of viewing screen. Bottom: Experimental design of study. From P. K. Kuhl and A. N. Meltzoff (1982). The bimodal perception of speech in infancy. *Science* 218, 1138–1141. © 1982 by the AAAS.

fant's sensitivity to auditory-visual correspondences. This is because the auditory theory, by being purely auditory, has no mechanism for explaining how the perceptual system would relate information across the auditory and visual modalities. The motor theory, on the other hand, has a ready explanation: the infant's ability to detect the correspondence between the matching face and sound is due to the operation of an innately given, species-specific mechanism that operates on the basis of articulatory principles. Note that if this is indeed the right explanation, then we can make a prediction—unlike human infants, chinchillas should not be able to detect such auditory-visual correspondences! As of now, the relevant experiment has yet to be reported.

Suggestions for Further Reading

For a general overview of research in speech perception, see Jusczyk 1986, and for a discussion of the infant's early speech perception abilities and their relation to the acquisition of language, see Eimas, J. L. Miller, and Jusczyk 1987. A discussion of the motor theory of speech perception is provided by Liberman and Mattingly 1985, and a discussion of how an auditory theory might account for selected aspects of speech perception can be found in Pastore 1981. For a view of the basic problem of speech perception that is somewhat different from the one provided in this chapter, see Stevens and Blumstein 1981. Finally, a discussion of the relation between speech perception and other levels of language processing, especially word recognition, can be found in Pisoni and Luce 1987.

Questions

4.1   As we saw in this chapter, one of the major findings of research on speech perception is that the recognition of speech sounds is far from a simple, straightforward matter. Do you suspect that the complexity that exists for the perception of speech sounds also exists for reading? See Liberman, in press, and Liberman et al. 1967.

4.2   What kinds of parallels do you think might exist between the perception of speech by humans and the communication systems of animals, for example, birdsong? See Marler and Peters 1981.

4.3   In this chapter we saw that young infants perceive the sounds of speech in terms of categories. But we know that all languages of the world do not use exactly the same speech categories. How do you think the initial, universal speech categories of infancy might become modified as a particular language is learned? See Eimas, Miller, and Jusczyk 1987 and MacKain 1982.

References

Eimas, P. D., J. L. Miller, and P. W. Jusczyk (1987). On infant speech perception and the acquisition of language. In S. Harnad, ed., *Categorical perception*. Cambridge: Cambridge University Press.

Eimas, P. D., E. R. Siqueland, P. W. Jusczyk, J. Vigorito (1971). Speech perception in infants. *Science* 171, 303–306.

James, W. (1890).*The principles of psychology*. New York: Henry Holt.

Jusczyk, P. W. (1986). Speech perception. In K. R. Boff, L. Kaufman, and J. P. Thomas, eds., *Handbook of perception and human performance*. New York: Wiley.

Kuhl, P. K. (1986). Theoretical contributions of tests on animals to the special-mechanisms debate in speech. *Experimental Biology* 45, 233–265.

Kuhl, P. K., and A. N. Meltzoff (1982). The bimodal perception of speech in infancy. *Science* 218, 1138–1141.

Kuhl, P. K., and J. D. Miller (1978). Speech perception by the chinchilla: Identification functions for synthetic VOT stimuli. *Journal of the Acoustical Society of America* 63, 905–917.

Liberman, A. M. (in press). Reading is hard just because listening is easy. In C. von Euler, ed., *Wenner-Gren International Symposium Series: Brain and reading*. Hampshire, England: Macmillan.

Liberman, A. M., F. S. Cooper, D. P. Shankweiler, and M. Studdert-Kennedy (1967). Perception of the speech code. *Psychological Review* 74, 431–461.

Liberman, A. M., and I. G. Mattingly (1985). The motor theory of speech perception revised. *Cognition* 21, 1–36.

McGurk, H., and J. MacDonald (1976). Hearing lips and seeing voices. *Nature* 264, 746–748.

MacKain, K. S. (1982). Assessing the role of experience on infants' speech discrimination. *Journal of Child Language* 9, 527–542.

MacKain, K. S., M. Studdert-Kennedy, S. Spieker, and D. Stern (1983). Infant intermodal speech perception is a left-hemisphere function. *Science* 219, 1347–1349.

Mann, V. A., and B. H. Repp (1980). Influence of vocalic context on perception of the [ʃ]-[s] distinction. *Perception and Psychophysics* 28, 213–228.

Marler, P., and S. Peters (1981). Birdsong and speech: Evidence for special processing. In P. D. Eimas and J. L. Miller, eds., *Perspectives on the study of speech*. Hillsdale, NJ: L. Erlbaum Associates.

Massaro, D. W., and M. M. Cohen, (1983). Evaluation and integration of visual and auditory information in speech perception. *Journal of Experimental Psychology: Human Perception and Performance* 9, 753–771.

Pastore, R. E. (1981). Possible psychoacoustic factors in speech perception. In P. D. Eimas and J. L. Miller, eds., *Perspectives on the study of speech*. Hillsdale, NJ: L. Erlbaum Associates.

Pisoni, D. B., and P. A. Luce (1987). Acoustic-phonetic representations in word recognition. *Cognition* 25, 21–52.

Stevens, K. N., and S.E. Blumstein (1981). The search for invariant acoustic correlates of phonetic features. In P. D. Eimas and J. L. Miller, eds., *Perspectives on the study of speech*. Hillsdale, NJ: L. Erlbaum Associates.

Yeni-Komshian, G. H., and S. D. Soli (1981). Recognition of vowels from information in fricatives: Perceptual evidence of fricative-vowel coarticulation. *Journal of the Acoustical Society of America* 70, 966–975.

5

Lexical Processing

Kenneth I. Forster

Much of what happens when we comprehend sentences in our native language seems to take place completely automatically, and we have no awareness of having to "do" anything. The meaning of a sentence somehow just emerges as the words flow past. The same passive attitude applies in the case of understanding the meanings of individual words. Given the spelling or the pronunciation of a word, the meaning just occurs to us, or is "elicited," to phrase it in the language of classical conditioning. This is the essence of the concept of "associationism." We say that the stimulus "dog" is associated with the idea or the concept of a dog, and each time the stimulus occurs, it automatically "elicits" the appropriate ideas.

The purpose of this chapter is to consider *how* that associative process works. How is brain activity organized so that when a particular sequence of letters occurs, a particular set of memory traces is automatically selected? According to one line of argument, the process is analogous to the way we look up the meaning of a word in a dictionary, or the way a computer might look up the meaning of a word. According to another view, recognizing the meaning of a word is performed by quite primitive detector systems, neural circuits designed so that whenever a particular set of letters is presented, the correct output is automatically provided. As we will see, we have a long way to go before we can even begin to decide between these views. But one thing should be kept clearly in mind: we could scarcely be asking a more fundamental question about the nature of the brain's capacities, since the capacity to recognize words is just a special case of pattern recognition. And *that* capacity is absolutely vital to nearly every aspect of perception and cognition.

5.1   Measuring Association Time

The kinds of observational techniques available to the casual observer tell us very little about how stimuli get attached to their mental representations. If we watch someone reading, there is very little in the person's observable behavior that would provide useful information. So the experimental psychologist has been forced to invent special observational techniques. Because it is taken for granted that the basic associative mechanisms are the same in audition and vision, most of the research that we will discuss uses printed rather than spoken stimuli.

5.1.1   Tachistoscopic Identification

The first of these techniques was developed at the turn of the century. It involved presenting the letters of a word for a very short period of time and then asking the subjects of the experiment to report what they had seen. The optical device used for this purpose, which involved two viewing chambers separated by a half-silvered mirror, was called a *tachistoscope* (meaning "a device for presenting a swift view"). Today the same effect is achieved using a computer-controlled graphics display.

The rationale behind this procedure was as follows. If the stimulus is flashed for only one-hundredth of a second (10 milliseconds), then whatever the subject can tell us about the stimulus must have been established during that time. So, if the subject tells us that the stimulus word begins with B and has about five letters, then we would infer that these properties were established during the first 10 milliseconds of exposure. If we now double the exposure time to 20 milliseconds, and the subject now tells us that the stimulus word ends in N and that the second letter was R, then we would infer that these properties were established during the second 10 milliseconds of exposure. By successively increasing the exposure, we could learn something about the time required to establish each property of the stimulus, and this in turn might tell us something about the mechanism of association. We can also present different types of words and ask how long we need to expose each word before the subject can say what word it was. Finding out which types of words are recognized most quickly might also provide valuable clues to the nature of the associative mechanism.

But there is a problem with this procedure. When we ask the subject to respond, there is no particular time pressure to respond immediately. Subjects are free to take as much time as they need. Indeed, subjects may feel that it takes some appreciable time to sort out their various impressions of the stimulus, and hence a rapid response is pointless. But in "sorting out" these impressions, powerful cognitive operations may be called into play, whose purpose is to convert vague, fleeting impressions of the stimulus into something more concrete, like "It begins with B."

The problem is that these operations need not be very fast-acting at all. If the subject is able to place the results of the first 20 milliseconds of stimulus analysis into some kind of short-term buffer storage, then processes that normally take much longer to initiate can now be used to process the information further. For example, the subject may try to find a five-letter word that begins with BR and ends with N, such as BRAIN. On the assumption that the stimulus was in fact a word, then there is a fairly high probability that the stimulus was in fact BRAIN, since there are very few other words that match this description. If the subject guesses correctly, we will make the inference that 20 milliseconds of exposure was sufficient to produce a full identification of the stimulus, when in fact it was not.

We would also be making the assumption that this process of reconstructing the stimulus from fragments (that is, guessing) was a vital part of normal perceptual processing. But the truth of this proposition is one of the things we would hope to discover, not simply assume. If it is true, then the tachistoscopic procedure probably gives a useful picture of how perception of a word develops. But if it is not true, then it would be a mistake to rely on this technique alone.

5.1.2   The Lexical Decision Task

A quite different approach to the problem of measuring association time is based on the concept of reaction time. This technique was developed in 1970 by Herbert Rubenstein and is known as the *lexical decision task*. The subject of a lexical decision experiment is exposed to a sequence of letters (say, for 500 milliseconds) and is asked to decide as rapidly as possible whether or not it is a familiar English word. Half of the items in the experiment are familiar words, such as *horse*, and half are "nonwords" such as *porse* (these are also sometimes termed "pseudowords"). These are letter sequences that could perfectly well be English words but happen not to be. The subject presses one button for words and another for nonwords. The experimenter records how long it takes to make each decision.

Table 5.1
A lexical decision task. The subject must scan the list as rapidly as possible, marking all the nonwords.

HEAVEN	GOAT	CANTEEN	CLOSP
FRABLE	INJECT	WHICHER	TEMBER
KEERIN	HOBEL	RYE	BOOZE
CAVES	INVALID	FLENT	FAREND
CLERIC	DIZZLED	STATELY	TREER
DOLEMAN	DAMP	HASTLE	ENLIST
CASHEW	DIGEST	RAFT	DECORATE
FORGET	HATHER	SPREE	BLAWS
QUENT	SEMTER	JOUD	GRADIENT
FOOBLE	OPERA	SPROOD	DACKS

Normally, just one item at a time is presented. By averaging over the decision times for many different words, we can get a good estimate of the typical "association time." This turns out to be about 550 milliseconds, that is, a little over half a second. A somewhat cruder way to do the experiment is to present a list of randomly intermixed words and nonwords, as in table 5.1. Your task is to rapidly scan the list, marking all the items that are not words.

A good subject would complete this task in about 25 seconds—in other words, more than 550 milliseconds per item. This is because the nonwords always take longer to classify than the words (the disadvantage of this list-search technique is that it can only provide an average time for the positive and negative items).

The idea behind this technique is that the only way to tell whether a given letter sequence is a word or not is by seeing whether that sequence is associated with a previously stored representation. Hence, the time required to make the lexical decision must give us an approximate idea at least of the association time. It has to be approximate, because what we are measuring is the time required for the subject to become aware that this stimulus is associated with a previously stored representation, plus the time required to make a decision about the appropriate response to make, plus the time required to initiate that response, and this is not quite the same thing as the association time itself.

This technique is thought to be an improvement over the tachistoscopic technique because it limits the range of mechanisms that might be involved. For example, if the subject responds in a lexical decision experiment within 500 milliseconds, then obviously no process that takes longer than 500 milliseconds to begin operations could possibly exert any effect at all. It also seems to limit the contribution of guesswork, because the stimulus is presented not briefly but for as long as the subject needs to make an accurate response. Hence, there is not the same need to guess.

However, if guessing really is an important part of perception, even when the stimulus is clearly presented, then the lexical decision task still permits us to examine such effects. For example, one of the most reliably obtained phenomena in word recognition is the fact that commonly occurring words are better perceived than rare words. In a tachistoscopic task we are uncertain how to interpret this result, since it might just mean that people are better at guessing common words than rare words. But in a lexical decision task we could test whether this was the case by manipulating the nonwords.

This is done by varying the *similarity* of the nonwords to real words. For example, nonwords such as *vegteable, tigar,* and *cigraette* have a very high degree of resemblance to words, whereas nonwords such as *chistox, flaagi,* and *astoque* have a very low degree of resemblance to words. The procedure is to carry out the experiment twice. Each experiment involves the same words, but in the first experiment all the nonwords are very similar to words, whereas in the second they are all very dissimilar to words. To make a correct word-nonword discrimination in the first experiment with nonwords such as *vegteable,* very accurate information about each letter and its position is required, and there is no way one could afford to base a judgment on, say, just the first three letters and the last two (unless) one is prepared to make a huge number of errors). But in the second experiment with very distinctive nonwords, such as *chistox,* we could easily make quite accurate judgments on the basis of just a few of the letters.

Having completed these two experiments, we now look at the lexical decision times for rare and common words. If guessing plays a key role in producing the advantage for common words, then the difference between rare and common words should be smaller (or nonexistent) when we use nonwords like *vegteable,* which discourage the subject from guessing, larger when we use nonwords like *chistox,* which encourage the subject to guess.

Actual experiments designed in this way suggest that guesswork does not play a very important role in the lexical decision task, since the data show very similar results with both types of nonwords (see, for example, Antos 1979; O'Connor and Forster 1981).

5.1.3   The Naming Task

Obviously, the lexical decision task is open to the criticism that *decision* processes may play too great a role. What we want to measure is just the association time, but instead we are measuring a number of additional processes as well. The only way to avoid this problem is to use another task that also has association time as a prime determinant of response time but differs in the additional processes that are being tapped.

One such task is the *naming task*. In this case the subject is presented with a word and is asked to pronounce it aloud as quickly as possible. By using a voice-operated relay, we can measure the amount of time elapsing between presentation of the stimulus and the onset of the subject's vocalization. This task has the advantage that it does not require the subject to make any overt decision about the stimulus. Nor, in fact, is it even necessary that the subject be explicitly aware that the stimulus is a word. All that is required is that the subject pronounce it correctly. Because of the well-known difficulty of trying to pronounce English words by rule (for instance, *rough, cough, dough,* and *bough*), it seems that the only safe way to establish the correct pronunciation is to first determine whether the item has a lexical representation and, if it does, to then retrieve the information stored within that representation. This means that the time required to begin naming a word must include the association time as one of its components.

This hypothesis was first confirmed by Forster and Chambers (1973) and later by Frederiksen and Kroll (1976). Both sets of investigators found that words were named faster than nonwords, which of course is an essential requirement if we are to think of naming time as an index of the association time, or *access time*, as it is better known.

5.1.4   Eye Movements

If a subject is given connected text to read, then something can be learned from the time it takes the subject to switch attention from one word to the next. Careful measurement of eye movements during reading can provide an index of this process, and the last ten years have seen a resurgence of interest in this technique (Rayner and Pollatsek 1987). However, there is very little to be observed in the way of eye movements if only a single word is presented on each trial, so it is necessary to present more words than can be apprehended in a single glance. This raises the possibility that the time spent fixating each word may be more influenced by the global complexity of the sentence and only partly influenced by the time required to recognize each word. However, as we shall see, the eye movements technique is by no means alone in this respect. Perhaps the most attractive feature of the technique is that, like the naming task, it does not rely on explicit decision making. However, it would be wrong to claim that no decisions are involved at all. There must be a control mechanism that decides when sufficient information has been extracted from the stimulus to move from one fixation point to the next, so in a sense a kind of decision making is still involved. However, this need not be a conscious process—the subject may be quite unaware of the reasons for slowing down at a given point, or even that a slowing down has occurred. But in the lexical decision task the information on which the decision is based must reach the highest levels of awareness.

5.2   Determinants of Access Time

Whaley (1978) tested a large sample of words with the lexical decision task with the aim of determining which properties of words had the strongest influence on speed of response. Some of the variables discovered to have a measurable effect were properties having to do with the *form* of the word (number of letters and number of syllables) and, somewhat surprisingly, aspects of the *meaning* of the word, such as imagery value (a rating of how easily the word called some image to mind) and meaningfulness (as indexed by the number of different associations that could be made to the word within 30 seconds). However, very little attention has been paid to these kinds of factors in subsequent research, perhaps because the effects are difficult to replicate or to disentangle from other factors, or perhaps because these results failed to lead to any interesting speculation about the underlying causes. But one factor has received considerable attention, and that is the relative frequency with which we encounter a word.

5.2.1   Word Frequency

Whaley concluded that frequency of occurrence was by far the most important variable, with high-frequency (commonly used) words producing shorter decision times than low-frequency (rare) words. Fortunately, comprehensive records are available that document the relative frequency of occurrence of printed words in English (for instance, Thorndike and Lorge 1944; Kucera and Francis 1967; Carroll, Davies, and Richman 1971), and this makes it possible to design quite sophisticated experiments.

The first point to realize about the frequency effect in lexical decision experiments is that the words in the low-frequency category are not very rare words like *yttrium*. It would not be surprising if such a word produced longer decision times, since many subjects may be uncertain whether it really is a word, or whether it is spelled in this way, and hence might be less confident of their "Yes" response. Instead, we try to make sure that the low-frequency words are perfectly *familiar* words—like *puddle*, for example. Almost certainly every native speaker of English is quite confident that *puddle* is a word, and the reason that it is a low-frequency word is just that we don't spend very much time talking or writing about puddles.

In other words, it must be emphasized that the lexical decision task is not intended to be a measure of the extensiveness of a person's vocabulary. That is why the instructions in this task often stress that subjects should only respond "Yes" if the presented letter sequence spells a word with which they are familiar.

It should also be noted that this effect has nothing to do with the frequency of the individual letters making up the word, since it has been found that the average frequency of the individual letters of a word bears no relationship at all to lexical decision times (Whaley 1978).

Forster and Chambers (1973) also showed that word frequency had quite a strong effect on naming time (although not as strong as its effect on lexical decision times) and that there was a reasonably strong correlation between lexical decision times and naming times for the same set of words (that is, words having very long lexical decision times also had long naming times, and conversely). But this was so only if word frequency was allowed to vary. If frequency was held absolutely constant, then there was no correlation between the two measures at all. The implication is that frequency has its major effect on access time, and that this is all the two tasks have in common.

The word frequency effect is an inverse logarithmic function, which is to say that lexical decision times decrease as log frequency increases. Thus, increasing the frequency of a word from 1 per million to 10 per million has about the same effect on lexical decision time as increasing it from 10 per million to 100 per million, and probably there is not much further improvement beyond this. It is sometimes suggested that the frequency effect is really an *age-of-acquisition* effect (Carroll and White 1973), since most high-frequency words would be learned at an earlier age than most low-frequency words. Unfortunately, estimates of the age at which words are learned are very highly correlated with frequency, so it is very hard to distinguish between these possibilities. To do so, one is forced to look just at the very special cases where this relationship breaks down, such as words occurring fairly often in children's stories but not so often in adult reading material, such as *fairies* and *dragons*. The evidence currently suggests that both variables play a role in determining lexical decision time.

5.2.2   Priming Effects

Other factors that influence lexical decision time have mainly to do with circumstances of the presentation of the stimuli, rather than with properties of the words themselves. For example, if a word is presented for lexical decision a second time during the experiment, it produces a faster and more accurate response (Scarborough, Cortese, and Scarborough 1977). This is termed a *repetition effect*, and it too has been proposed as the basis for the frequency effect. If recently encountered words are accessed faster, then there should be a frequency effect, since a high-frequency word is more likely than a low-frequency word to have been recently encountered. However, this view predicts no frequency effect at all for recently encountered words, which is not the case (Scarborough, Cortese, and Scarborough 1977), so recency and frequency must have independent effects.

The repetition effect belongs to a class of effects called *priming effects*. The notion is that some set of circumstances changes the accessibility of a word for a brief period of time, as if the lexical processor has been "primed" to detect that word. The other major examples of priming effects are produced by a manipulation of the *context* in which the test stimulus occurs (repetition priming itself can also be seen in this way, the context being the prior presentation of the word during the experiment).

The most celebrated example of a context effect is the so-called *semantic priming effect*. Meyer and Schvaneveldt (1971) demonstrated that lexical decision times for a target word like *nurse* were faster if this word followed another word that was related to it in meaning, such as *doctor*, compared with a control condition in which it followed a completely unrelated word, such as *table*. This effect is very strong (around 80 milliseconds) and very reliable. One way to interpret this effect is in terms of selective access. Somehow, when a context word is supplied, the access system is able to exploit this information, so that it gains access selectively to just those words that are related in some way to the context word. Thus, not only would *nurse* be facilitated in the context of *doctor*, but also words such as *hospital*, *medical*, *operation*, and *scalpel* would receive similar benefit.

A second type of context effect is produced not by a single word but by an incomplete sentence, the target word being a possible completion of the sentence. This is referred to as a *sentence context effect*. Thus, if the subject is shown the sentence fragment *It is important to brush your teeth every* _____ and then is presented with the word DAY for lexical decision, responses are much faster than if the target for lexical decision had been the word YEAR. Notice that in this example DAY is not related to any of the other words in the context, so it is not possible to reduce this effect to a semantic priming effect.

5.2.3   Access and Postaccess Effects

Much of the current debate in lexical access theory concerns whether *any* of the variables we have just discussed actually determine access time, or whether they control some *postaccess* process, that is, a process that takes place well after the mental representation of a word has been contacted.

Table 5.2
Lexical decision with illegal nonwords. The task is to scan the list as rapidly as possible, marking all the nonwords.

TRANSPORT	YMEUA	THICK	OLFRD
OBQLUV	TMSIA	SWAY	COAXED
HLEA	BLEAK	GSLA	ACHED
BARGAIN	WHIM	OORGDR	LCITP
SPRAWL	HOVEL	LISTENS	REPORT
PERFUME	PKEN	KAAPI	FIHSG
NOEALR	QUICKER	TEMPEST	SROGGRE
XAMPQR	HHLOR	TSENJ	PQENTW
POWER	LPETR	TOWEL	PRETEND
ZHEMR	PEARL	PKIKC	IMPURE

As an example, consider the following case. Suppose we carry out a lexical decision experiment in which the nonwords are composed of letter sequences that are not characteristic of English at all, for example, FTRXL, GHIJME, EHRTG. These could never be English words, since they do not conform to normal English spelling patterns, and for this reason they are called orthographically "illegal" sequences.

Under these circumstances we find that lexical decision times for *both* the words and the nonwords are much faster (Shulman and Davison 1977). You can test this for yourself with the items in table 5.2, where the nonwords are all orthographically illegal letter sequences (whereas in table 5.1 they were all orthographically legal sequences). As before, the task is to work through the list as rapidly as possible, marking all the nonwords. You should find that this list is much easier than the previous one.

It is perhaps not surprising that illegal nonwords take less time to classify than legal nonwords. In the latter case one needs to establish that the letter sequence does not correspond to any word; in the former case it is sufficient merely to establish that the sequence is illegal, from which it follows that it could not possibly correspond to any word. But why are the *words* so much faster? Should we infer that access time has been decreased?

If we did, then we would have to explain why access time for a word depended on the sort of nonwords we were using. Obviously, this would very difficult, because normally nonwords are not encountered in reading, and it is only in artificial experiments devised by psychologists that procedures for dealing with nonwords are required. A much more sensible proposal is that the legality of the nonwords has its effects on the *decision* component of the lexical decision time, rather than on the access component. If we can tell very quickly whether the spelling pattern is legal or not, then we don't have to wait to find out whether contact with a previously stored mental representation will be made. We can make our decision on the basis of legality alone—provided that all the nonwords are illegal. In other words, on a high proportion of occasions, the subject is initiating a "Yes" response to a word without knowing what word it was. This implies that making lexical decisions must be a relatively time-consuming process and that subjects are therefore alert to any opportunity of decreasing this component of their reaction time.

If we accept this line of argument, then, we would conclude that the legality of the nonwords has no impact on access time. Once we take this step, we have to allow for the possibility that almost *any* systematic property of either the words or the nonwords might decrease decision times. For example, suppose that all of the words in the experiment began with B and ended with E, but none of the nonwords did. It seems very likely that this would *also* decrease lexical decision times for both words and nonwords—but does this necessarily mean that we can selectively access words beginning with B and ending with E?

We can list other possibilities. Suppose, for example, that all of the words in the experiment referred to edible fruits. From what we know, it seems very likely that this property would also decrease lexical decision times. If it did, then this result *might* mean that there is some special access path that can examine all (and only) the words referring to edible fruits. This kind of explanation would be described as an *access* interpretation. But it might also mean that we can make a word-nonword decision faster merely by keeping in mind the fact that all the words in the experiment are likely to refer to edible fruits.

Since decision making is a relatively conscious process (whereas lexical access is not), we presumably have to become *aware* of some change in our internal state. What kinds of things might we become aware of? One possibility is that we might try to decide whether some kind of *image* was produced. This might explain the effects of imagery that were mentioned earlier. Or in the case of an item presented in context, we might become aware of the fact that the target item cannot be sensibly integrated with the context, which might predispose us to believe that we had accessed the wrong entry.

How can these questions be answered? One way is to use more than one measure of access time. For example, suppose we could show that words referring to concrete objects could be *named* faster than words that referred to abstract objects. This would tend to be more persuasive evidence for an access effect, since there seems to be absolutely no reason why the *pronunciation* of a concrete word should become available more rapidly than that of an abstract word, unless the mental representations of concrete words can be contacted faster.

As noted earlier, the naming task has the advantage that it does not require any conscious awareness of having accessed an entry in the mental lexicon. Also, the response that must be made can never be inferred from circumstantial properties of the experiment. Thus, consider the semantic priming case. From the fact that the target item can be meaningfully related to the context, we can infer that the correct response in a lexical decision task must be "Yes," because only words can have this property. So our confidence in reaching a "Yes" decision might be increased if the target word fits its context, and this may produce an apparent priming effect, having nothing to do with access at all. But in the naming task no such bonus is obtained. The fact that the target word is meaningfully related to the context tells us nothing about how to pronounce it. Hence, there is a special value in using the naming task in studies of context.

It is therefore of some interest to know that semantic priming effects have been obtained with the naming task by numerous investigators, whereas the same cannot be said for sentence context effects (for more extensive discussion of these issues, see Seidenberg et al. 1984 and Tanenhaus and Lucas 1987).

5.3   Theoretical Models of Access

Merely listing the variables that might affect access time takes us only so far. It is not until we begin to consider how these variables have their effects that we begin to get some idea of the problems involved. To see this, we must consider the kinds of computational systems that have been proposed as models of the access process.

5.3.1   Word-Detector Circuits

It may be useful to begin by considering how we might design a simple circuit that could perform the lexical decision task. Suppose we had six switches, a battery, and 32 light bulbs. The light bulbs correspond to word detectors, and the switches correspond to letters (for instance, switch 1 being ON means the letter A is present). With six switches, we have 64 possible combinations, of which only 32 correspond to actual words. The task is to design the circuit so that a different bulb lights up whenever one of the 32 "permissible" combinations of switches is selected; otherwise, nothing happens. This system could now be used for lexical decision. We observe which letters are present in the target stimulus, we press the appropriate switches, and if a bulb lights up, we say "Yes," and if no bulb lights up, we say "No."

The obvious first step in solving this problem is to construct AND gates for each bulb so that they are connected to the battery only when their particular combination of switches is ON. But what happens if some other switches are also ON? The AND gate will ignore this information, and the bulb will still light up. This does not seem to be an appropriate outcome for a real word recognizer, since it would mean that the input BEARD would light the bulb not only for the word *beard*, but also for the word *bear*. Similarly, the *bear* bulb would be lit by the nonword input BEARF. We must therefore complicate the circuit and connect all switches that should be OFF to the bulb so that if any one of them is ON, the circuit connecting the bulb with the battery is broken. These could be described as having an *inhibitory* effect on the lighting of the bulb.

Another factor that needs to be taken into account is letter position. In the example just given the *bear* bulb would also be lit by the stimulus AREB, since the switches code only for the presence of a letter and ignore its position. We must therefore distinguish between "B-in-first-position" and "B-in-fourth-position," which means having separate switches. To be able to recognize words up to 10 letters in length, then, we need 260 switches (26 letters × 10 positions).

As specified, the circuit cannot really do the lexical decision task by itself, since it depends on a human operator to press the right switches and also to decide whether any bulb was lit. To get the right switches pressed, we would of course require a set of letter-detecting circuits that can process visual inputs. Getting a decision output is a little more difficult. A positive decision can be obtained simply enough by connecting each of the bulbs with a "Yes" output, but a "No" decision creates problems. We could construct AND gates for the 32 switch combinations that do not correspond to any word, and connect all of these to a "No" output line. In effect, this system is built to recognize all of the nonwords as well.

But this solution to the "No" decision problem becomes less workable if we increase the number of possible letter positions. For example, for 10-letter words there are 26^{10} possible combinations, of which only a very small proportion are words. Providing for a "No" decision in this case would involve constructing billions and billions of AND gates. This does not seem very realistic, especially since we do not normally encounter nonwords; nor is the lexical decision task something that we are normally required to do.

Probably the only way to avoid this problem is to set up an additional timing circuit that is switched on whenever a letter input is detected. This circuit will automatically activate the "No" output line after a specified time interval, provided the "Yes" line has not been activated. Once it has, this timing circuit is automatically switched off. This default procedure is generally referred to in the lexical access literature as a *deadline* mechanism.

5.3.2   Activation Models

Two influential models of word recognition use word-detector circuits similar to the example we have just discussed: the *logogen* model of Morton (1970) and the network approach of McClelland and Rumelhart (1986), which is now perhaps better known as a *connectionist* model.

In Morton's theory, logogens are word detectors, just like the bulbs in our example, except that they do not use AND gates. Instead, they sum the activation received from letter detectors, and if the sum of the activation exceeds the threshold for that logogen, it fires. Logogens also receive activation from other systems. For example, in order to explain the effect of a sentence context on word recognition (see section 5.2.2), Morton proposes that the cognitive system (which is responsible for comprehension) is able to direct activation back to the logogen system, so that words appropriate to the context receive activation and hence are detected more readily. Similar accounts can be offered for semantic priming effects of the *doctor-nurse* variety.

Very similar assumptions are involved in the connectionist models of word recognition (see McClelland and Rumelhart 1986 for a general survey of network models). The network consists of a series of layers, each layer in turn consisting of a bank of neuronlike detector units. Each unit in the network is connected to each unit in the adjacent layers, and also to each other unit within its layer. These connections vary in strength, and they are of two types. Connections *between* layers are excitatory, whereas connections *within* a level are inhibitory (see figure 5.1).

For word recognition, four layers are appropriate: one layer each for detecting visual features, letters, words, and semantic features. As the network gradually learns to recognize printed words, the connections change strength. Initially, then, the unit for "letter-A-in-first-position" might be connected with equal strength to all word units. After learning has been completed, however, most of these connections would be very weak, leaving only the connections with word units spelled with an initial "A."

The major feature of this model that distinguishes it from the logogen model (and the circuit model) is this assumption of varying strengths of connection. A further feature is the existence of inhibitory connections between units within a layer. These inhibitory connections allow the total network to approach a state of equilibrium. Basically, the units within a layer compete with each other. Thus, at the word level units receive activation from both the letter level and the semantic level, but they also receive inhibitory inputs from neighboring word units.

When a word is initially presented, the activation pattern is relatively diffuse, since there is a great deal of *cross-activation*. With an initial input B-E-A-R, for example, the units corresponding to these letters will be most

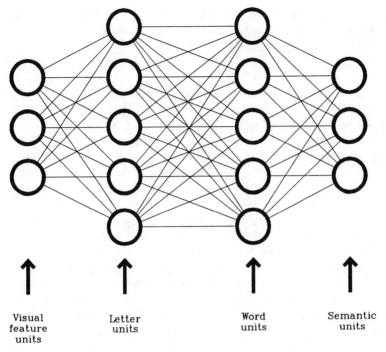

Visual	Letter	Word	Semantic
feature	units	units	units
units			

Figure 5.1
Connectionist network for word recognition. Units at each level have inhibitory connections (not shown here), which vary in strength. Connections between levels are excitatory. Initially every unit is connected to every unit at the next level, but as a function of experience some of these connections are weakened and others are strengthened.

strongly activated, but units corresponding to other letters will also be activated. Thus, in addition to the "B1" unit (that is, the unit for "B-in-first-position"), the "B2" unit is activated as well (although not as strongly), because the environmental conditions to which these units are tuned overlap to some degree. The "P1" unit will also be activated, because "B" and "P" resemble each other. All of these cross-activation effects will be passed on to the next highest level. At the word level, then, the unit for the word *fear* will receive strong activation because it shares three letters with the input, as will the unit for *pear*. The latter unit, however, might receive a higher amount of activation because of the extra effect of the similarity of its first letter to B.

These cross-activation effects are also passed on to the semantic level, so that the semantic features of *pear* are activated along with those of *bear*. However, the spread of activation continues still further. Activation from the word units is also directed back down to the letter units, thus starting a new cycle of activation back up to the word units. Also, the semantic units activate word units, so that the units for words sharing semantic features with *bear* (and *pear*) will be activated.

If this process were allowed to continue unchecked, eventually every unit in the network would become active. This is where the inhibitory connections play an important role. For example, if the unit for *bear* has strong inhibitory connections to the unit for *pear*, then the more strongly *bear* is activated, the more effectively it suppresses activation in the *pear* unit. Thus, competition between units reduces the amount of cross-activation, making the activation pattern sharper and less diffuse. Hence, it might be the case that activation in the *pear* unit is never transmitted to the semantic level when BEAR is input, because it is suppressed before it has a chance to be transmitted.

Returning to the examples discussed in connection with our circuit model, we can see that the BEAR-BEARD problem is handled differently in the network model. Our original solution was to connect the "D5" connector so that it would turn off the *bear* bulb (and the bulb for any other word not having D in fifth position). The same technique in the network model would mean having inhibitory connections *between* layers, which is not permitted. Hence, the input BEARD will inevitably activate the unit for *bear*, but this problem gets sorted out by competition between the units.

With such a network, deciding what word has been presented involves waiting until the network reaches a state of equilibrium, with just one word unit being strongly activated. If no unit remains active, then the input most likely was a nonword. Thus, making a lexical decision would involve somehow monitoring the distribution of activation across all word units, waiting until some statistical criterion of equilibrium is reached. If, after a preset interval of time, this criterion is not met, then the deadline mechanism discussed earlier would become effective, and a "No" decision would be reached.

Frequency effects are readily explained in the network model in terms of connection strengths. Each time a word is recognized, it is assumed that the strengths of the active connections are all incremented slightly. Thus, immediately after presentation of BEARD, the strength of connection between the "B1" unit and the *beard* unit is increased relative to other connection strengths, which means of course that the strength of the connection between "B1" and the *bear* unit decreases. If the frequency of occurrence of BEARD suddenly increases, then so will the strengths of the letter-word connections for this word, at the expense of the other connections. Inevitably, the unit for a word that has not been seen for a long time must have very weak connections to its constituent letter units.

This contrasts with the logogen account of frequency, where it is assumed that repeated exposure of a word gradually decreases the threshold for firing, so that the activation level reaches discharge levels much faster. In this case we do not assume that high-frequency words are more strongly activated than low-frequency words, just that they need less activation to reach threshold. This is referred to as a *criterion-bias* account, the criterion in question being the amount of evidence required to classify the input as being a particular word.

Both types of explanation of the frequency effect run into interesting problems when we consider the case of two words with substantial graphemic overlap but marked difference in frequency. For example, take the relatively high-frequency word *bright* and its low-frequency competitor *blight*. When the stimulus input is actually the low-frequency alternative BLIGHT, substantial activation is going to be produced in the unit for *bright*. But because of the frequency difference, the "B1" detector is more strongly connected to the *bright* detector than to the *blight* detector, and similarly for the "I3," "G4," "H5," and "T6" units. Hence, it is entirely possible that the *bright* unit will be activated more strongly than the *blight* unit, in which case the wrong word will be perceived, since there is no way that the *blight* unit can compete with the *bright* unit unless it is more strongly activated. If all connections were of the same strength, then activation from the "L2" unit would be enough to tip the scales in favor of *blight*, but once frequency is taken into account, this result is not guaranteed.

To be sure, there will be some occasions where this is the correct result. For example, if we flash BLIGHT onto a screen very briefly, it might be misread as BRIGHT. But what about the occasions where it is correctly perceived, as for instance in the preceding sentence? How is it guaranteed that the changes in connection strengths induced by frequency are never sufficiently large to prevent a low-frequency word from being perceived?

The problem here is that frequency is assumed to produce changes that are indistinguishable from those produced by stimulus properties—as if high-frequency words were somehow more intensely projected onto the retina. A network theory has little choice, however, since its only commodity is strength of activation, and every feature of performance must be explained in these terms (very similar arguments have been made concerning the logogen model; see Forster 1976). Hence, we need some principle that limits the influence of frequency so that this type of problem does not arise.

In the preceding sections we have been considering how we might design extremely primitive circuits to perform word recognition. Essentially, we attempted to build the word recognition system directly into the hardware, so to speak. In the next section we consider another approach that tackles the problem from a purely computational standpoint.

5.3.3   Lexical Search Theory

Rather than trying to describe the operations of the lexical processor in terms of simple network circuits, lexical search theory moves to a more abstract level and defines the operations of the lexical processor in terms of information retrieval algorithms. The basic assumption is that information about words is stored in a way comparable to that of a random-access mass storage device in a digital computer.

Each word is associated with a lexical entry, which is like a data file that specifies all the necessary linguistic properties of the word, such as its pronunciation, spelling, part of speech, and meaning. The collection of all such entries defines the mental lexicon for a given person. Lexical access involves comparing the letter pattern of the stimulus with the orthographic specification of each lexical entry in turn, until an exact match is found. Variation in lexical access time across different words is explained in terms of the way in which information is stored and the search methods used to locate and retrieve that information.

The most important difference between this kind of model and the activation models in the preceding section is that here the input stimulus is compared serially with each lexical entry in turn, whereas in the activation models all entries are compared with the stimulus *simultaneously*. Thus, lexical search theory is a serial-comparison theory, whereas an activation theory is a parallel-comparison theory.

The first model to explicitly consider the nature of the search process was developed by Rubenstein (Rubenstein, Garfield, and Millikan 1970). In this model it was suggested that the search process was literally a random search of a limited subset of the total lexicon (this subset being defined by a preliminary examination of the letters in the input word). The reason for proposing that the search was random was that Rubenstein wanted to explain why he had found that ambiguous words such as *chest* (which has two lexical entries) produced faster lexical decision times than unambiguous words. With two entries, an ambiguous word would have twice the chance of being sampled by a random search. Subsequent work, however, has not supported this result, so random search is no longer entertained as a possibility. The more common assumption now is that the search is *frequency-ordered*. That is, the entries for high-frequency words are compared to the stimulus before the entries for low-frequency words. This has the effect of minimizing the average search time.

It is also assumed that the lexicon can be accessed in several different ways. When we read, we have a visual display to recognize, but when we listen, we have a sequence of speech sounds. On the other hand, when we talk or write, we have some kind of meaning in mind, and we need to find a word that will express that meaning. Obviously, the same organization of entries is unlikely to serve the requirements of all three modes of access. Rather than have three totally different lexicons, Forster (1976) proposed three different access files: an orthographic access file, a phonological access file, and a semantic access file. Each such file consisted of a set of pointers to the actual lexical entries, plus an *access code*. For the orthographic access file, the access code would be some aspect of the spelling of the word—say, the first three letters. For the phonological access file, the access code would specify some aspect of the phonological specification of each word. Similarly, an access code in the semantic access file might specify the general semantic category to which a word belongs. Access now consists of first selecting the right access file (depending on what input mode we are in) and then comparing the properties of the input stimulus with the access codes in a strict frequency-ordered manner.

Once a match is found (for instance, in the orthographic case, the access code matches the first three letters of the input word), then the pointer to the location of the real lexical entry can be extracted from the access file, which enables the real entry to be selected without any further search (since its location is now known). The full orthographic specification of the word can now be retrieved and compared with the original letter input. This is referred to as a *postaccess check*. If this check reveals a match, then the correct entry has been found. If not, then the search of the access file must continue. In the now familiar terms of personal-computer data base systems, the set of lexical entries is the data base, and the access files are *index* files, where indexing has been carried out on something less than the total spelling of the word.

A relevant question to ask at this point is, "Why have a serial search procedure?" The implication of search is that the location of some desired piece of information is unknown. To set up an information retrieval system where the precise location of every conceivable piece of information is known in advance is extremely expensive. In practical terms, then, it is usually easier to have the general location known, but not the precise location. Consider a conventional printed dictionary as an example. Since words are listed in alphabetical order, we can predict the relative locations of pairs of words very precisely. However, from the spelling alone, we cannot predict which line a given word should appear on, or even which page. Hence, we still need to use search procedures even with alphabetized entries. Note that it is not *impossible* to design a system that would permit accurate prediction of location. In theory, we could print the dictionary according to a rule that assigned a line number to each word. But such a dictionary would at least have to reserve a separate line for every distinct combination of letters, whether a word is formed or not. Even if we ignore words over 10 letters in length, we will still have 26^{10} lines in the dictionary, with the overwhelming majority of those lines having no word listed. Allowing a generous 100 lines per page, this produces a mammoth book with more than one trillion mostly empty pages. Obviously, such a dictionary would be quite impractical, so much so that one wonders whether even the brain with its billions and billions of cells could afford such an extravagance.

What kinds of phenomena does the notion of search enable us to explain? First, it accounts for the frequency effect and explains why the function relating frequency to access time is logarithmic. Frequency works by establishing a rank order across all lexical entries, so that the search process compares the entries for high-frequency words with the input first. If we postulate that the entire lexicon is first subdivided into a number of "bins" according to their orthographic properties (as in Forster's (1976) model), then it can be seen that there is a reduced opportunity for frequency to exert an effect at the upper levels. That is, words with a rank of 1 in their bin will all be equivalent in access time, no matter what their frequency. All that is required is that they be of higher frequency than any other word in their bin. Thus, we may have a word that occurs at a rate of, say, 100 per million at the top of one bin, whereas the word at the top of the next might occur at a rate of 300 per million, but there will be no difference in access time between them. Hence, it is not surprising that the effect of frequency on lexical decision time tapers off at the high end.

Further, if we plot frequency as a function of rank, we discover that frequencies change very rapidly at the high end of the rank order but very slowly at the bottom end. In other words, the function relating frequency to rank is roughly logarithmic. Now, lexical search theory predicts that *rank* is the important variable and that the function relating rank to access time is linear. From this it follows that the function relating access time to frequency must be roughly logarithmic.

This theory also accounts nicely for the consequences of an *exhaustive search*. Consider what happens when a nonword is presented. Before we can say that it is a nonword, we must wait until all entries have been scanned. This predicts a longer decision time for nonwords than words, which is the case. Note that activation theories achieve the same result through the deadline mechanism. To avoid misclassifying any word as a nonword, we must wait for a time that is longer than the longest time required for any word detector to become activated.

Semantic priming effects are explained in Becker's verification model (a variant of lexical search theory; see Becker 1979 for details) by the postulation of a semantically defined search set, in addition to an orthographically defined search set. The latter includes words with a similar spelling to the input stimulus, whereas the former includes words that are semantically related to the context word. Thus, the prior context of the word *doctor* may preselect a set of words having to do with doctors, or perhaps more generally with medicine. If the target item is in fact on this list, and if this list is searched first, then the entry will be located more rapidly. Or, if we assume that both sets are searched in parallel, we will still get facilitation if the target entry has a higher rank in the semantic set than it does in the orthographic set.

5.4   Selected Issues in Current Research

In this very brief survey we can only get the flavor of the arguments and issues that are characteristic of the field. The key issue is, and always has been, whether we can adequately account for the phenomena of word recognition with simple detector circuits like those used in the logogen theory or in connectionist models. However, a direct assault on this issue has not proved to be rewarding, since as new phenomena were uncovered that were supposed to favor one particular approach, the other models have been easily extended to encompass the new findings. For this reason, we will focus more on fairly general issues that are independent of any particular theory.

5.4.1   Autonomy of Lexical Processing

Of very general concern is the claim that the lexical processor acts as an autonomous module in Fodor's sense (Fodor 1983; see section 5.4.6). A module acts in a highly automatic, reflex fashion and is driven totally by stimulus events of a very narrow sort. In the current context this amounts to the claim that conscious cognitive states such as expectations, beliefs, and desires can have no impact at all on the activity of the lexical access system. For example, being told that the next item in a lexical decision task is going to be a noun, or that it is going to begin with the letters FRE, should have no effect at all on access, although it might have an effect on some postaccess process.

Obviously, the existence of the sentence context effect raises serious problems for this view, since it appears to be top-down influence on access. Knowledge of what words are likely to occur in certain contexts cannot possibly be described as lexical knowledge, or even linguistic knowledge, since it must include a component that is based on real-world knowledge, and that is something totally outside the province of a modular lexical access system. Thus, realizing that WHEEL is a plausible continuation of the fragment *To stop the car from rolling, he put a brick under the* _____ , whereas SEAT is not, involves extensive knowledge about mechanics, relative sizes of bricks and car wheels, and inferences about the likely situation presupposed by the sentence (putting a brick under the wheel is no good if the car is rolling laterally).

If the facilitation observed in sentence context experiments is a genuine access effect, then the autonomy position must be given up. However, there are grounds for being suspicious of the premise of this argument. For one thing, much of the difference between WHEEL and SEAT in the above example is actually due to a slower-than-normal response to SEAT rather than a faster-than-normal response to WHEEL. For another, facilitation is usually restricted to just the most likely completion and does not extend to other appropriate words, such as TIRE in the example above (for discussion, see Fischler and Bloom 1979 and Forster 1981; for a different view altogether, see Stanovich and West 1983). What might be happening here is that the system responsible for making lexical decisions is unable to selectively attend just to the output of the lexical processor, as this experiment clearly requires. Instead, it cannot avoid attending to higher levels of processing, where the implausibility of SEAT might be strongly flagged as an indicator either that the sentence has not been processed correctly or that the situation involved must be quite different from what the reader presupposed. This error signal may in fact prompt a reanalysis of the sentence before a decision is made, or it may simply interfere with the making of a "Yes" decision.

It will be difficult to settle this question directly. But evidence from a totally different experimental paradigm has tipped the balance very much in favor of the autonomy position. This evidence concerns the priming effects of an ambiguous word. In the absence of any context, we might expect the ambiguous word PORT to prime responses to both the words WINE and SHIP. The interesting question is, What happens if PORT occurs in a sentence that clearly biases the interpretation? To answer this question, it was necessary to develop "on-line" measures of what happens during the processing of a sentence. The cross-modal priming technique (Swinney 1979; Seidenberg et al. 1982) was developed specifically to answer this question. In this task the subject hears a spoken sentence containing the ambiguous word, in this case *port*. Immediately after this ambiguous word the subject is given a visually presented probe for lexical decision that is related either to one meaning of the ambiguous word or to the other. The finding has been that *both* meanings of the ambiguous word are activated momentarily, regardless of the context. Thus, if the spoken sentence is *The waiter poured the port into the glasses*, then both WINE and SHIP show facilitation. However, if the probe is delayed for just a syllable or two, then only the contextually relevant meaning of *port* appears to be activated; that is, WINE shows facilitation, but SHIP does not. The implication, of course, is that the lexical access system initially provided *both* readings of the ambiguous word and that some higher-level system eventually discarded the irrelevant reading. Most striking is the fact that this result has also been obtained in cases where the biasing context places *syntactic* constraints on the interpretation of the ambiguous word (Seidenberg et al. 1982).

5.4.2   Interpretation of the Frequency Effect

As noted earlier, one way to tell whether a variable influences the access process itself, or some postaccess process, is to see whether it affcts performance in both the lexical decision task and the naming task. The idea is that these two tasks involve such radically different types of postaccess processing that any effect common to both tasks is likely to be an access effect. This was the argument originally used to identify the frequency effect as an access effect (Forster and Chambers 1973). However, it has long been noted that the size of the frequency effect is much smaller in the naming task than the lexical decision task. Thus, if we compare a set of high-frequency words with a matched set of low-frequency words in the naming task, we might find that the high-frequency words are named about 20 milliseconds faster than the low-frequency words, but in the lexical decision task the same set of high-frequency words might be classified 65 milliseconds faster than the low-frequency words. How could this be the case if the frequency effect reflects variations in access time? Since there is no reason to assume that the access process differs in the two tasks, we would expect the same-sized frequency effect in both tasks. Hence, we might be tempted to say that the frequency effect in the naming task reflects the true influence of frequency on access time, and the larger effect in lexical decision reflects an additional decision component (such as might be obtained if we were less certain of the correct spelling of lower-frequency words, for example).

In other words, the lexical decision task may overestimate the true size of the frequency effect. This might not seem to be very important, since the exact size of the frequency effect is not at issue in current theories. However, consider the following problem. Suppose we discover a set of experimental conditions that reduces the size of the frequency effect in the lexical decision task. Does this finding demonstrate that the effect of frequency on access time can be modulated? Not necessarily. If frequency also influences postaccess processes, then it could be these processes that are influenced by the experimental conditions, not the access processes. Clearly, it is of some importance to know what the "true" effect of frequency on access time might be, especially for theories such as lexical search theory that rely so strongly on this effect.

It seems, then, that we should abandon the lexical decision task and substitute the naming task. Unfortunately, this overlooks the possibility that it might be the naming task that is at fault—it might be underestimating the true frequency effect. This could occur in the following way. Suppose that the normal method of pronouncing a word involves accessing the lexical entry for that word, where information about the correct pronunciation is stored. But since pronunciations can be assigned quite readily to letter strings that we have never seen or heard pronounced before (such as *flink*), there must be some type of rule system that can also perform this task. Thus, there are two ways of responding in a naming task: the lexical method requires access of the relevant lexical entry, whereas the rule method does not. The lexical method is strongly influenced by word frequency, whereas the rule method is not influenced at all, being much more strongly influenced by variables such as the frequency of particular *letter* combinations, which have very little to do with word frequency (for instance, the fact that *have* is so much more frequent than *rave* has nothing to do with the likelihood of an initial *ha-* or *ra-*, as shown by the fact that *rate* occurs far more frequently than *hate*).

Forster and Chambers (1973) assumed that *both* procedures were typically used in the naming task and that the response was controlled by whichever process finished first (this type of assumption is generally referred to as a *race* model). Usually the lexical method finishes first, but if a very low-frequency word is being named, the rule method might generate usable output before the lexical method, since the rule method will not be adversely affected by the low frequency of the word. This means that the naming system does not always wait for access to occur, which must mean that the size of the frequency effect is reduced.

A fairly direct way to test this proposal would be to check whether subjects make errors in the naming task. The rule method is a fairly risky way to pronounce a real word, since in English the same letter sequence can be assigned several different pronunciations. For so-called regular words, where the pronunciation is predictable from the spelling, the rule method will work perfectly well, but for irregular words, it must produce errors, such as pronouncing *pint* to rhyme with *mint*. Certainly, such errors do occur, but they generally occur at a rate no greater than 1 or 2 percent, which seems too low if low-frequency words are named by rule. One possible explanation for this is that the rule system really only controls the initial segments of the vocalization response. By the time these have been initiated, lexical access has occurred, and the pronunciation is then guided by lexical information. Thus, in pronouncing the low-frequency irregular word *wool*, we might initially intend to pronounce it to rhyme with other *-ool* words, such as *pool* and *tool*, since we do not yet know that it is a word. The commands to the speech articulators for this response may be issued, but as lexically specified information about the pronunciation becomes available, corrections are made "on the fly," and the pronunciation of the vowel is adapted slightly, so that the correct form is produced. The result would be that at least as far as naming times are concerned (remember that this is the time taken to initiate vocalization only), the system behaves as though it were working by rule for low-frequency words but at the same time manages to avoid making the errors that a rule system would produce.

The preceding discussion presupposes that frequency does have at least some effect on access. A much more extreme position has been taken by Balota and Chumbley (1984, 1985). They noted that the frequency effect is very weak in a semantic categorization task, where subjects must classify words according to whether they refer to objects that belong to a certain category (say, *animal*). Since this task clearly requires access to be completed, it ought to show a strong frequency effect; yet it does not. This finding invites the inference that frequency has nothing to do with access at all. Balota and Chumbley suggest that it is really familiarity rather than frequency that is important. Since highly familiar letter sequences will usually be words, the decision-making system reaches a "Yes" decision in a lexical decision task faster for familiar words than for relatively unfamiliar words, thereby producing what looks like a frequency effect. But in the semantic categorization task, where familiarity is completely irrelevant to the decision, there is no such bias in the decision-making system, and therefore no frequency effect is observed. However, familiarity also plays no obvious role in the naming task, and hence an explanation is needed for the existence of a frequency effect with this task. Balota and Chumbley argue that this can be attributed to a response production effect. That is, because of their higher frequency of usage, the motor programs for the pronunciation of high-frequency words are executed more rapidly than are those for low-frequency words. As evidence for this interpretation, they demonstrate that a frequency effect is still obtained in a delayed naming task. In this type of task the subject views the target word for, say, 1000 milliseconds and then names the word when a cue is presented. Since access would have been completed during the preview time, any frequency effect that is detected could not be an access effect (assuming that subjects do not simply reaccess the target word when the cue is presented).

The generality of this effect is not yet known. Certainly, there may be many low-frequency words that are relatively difficult to pronounce, and such words would always produce a frequency effect in a delayed naming task; but whether this is true of the samples of low-frequency words used by other investigators is another matter.

Perhaps the clearest indication of the correct interpretation of the naming data has been provided by Paap et al. (1987). They argued that if the race model analysis of the naming task was correct, then the naming task should show exactly the same size frequency effect as lexical decision if one could somehow prevent the rule system from being used for low-frequency words. The method they chose involved creating nonwords out of words by adding letters at the beginning or at the end—for instance, *taklime, lifeber*. Subjects were instructed to find the word and pronounce it, ignoring the added letters. Under these conditions, a nonlexically based strategy will generate errors on 50 % of the trials, since on only half of the trials will it be appropriate to base a response on the initial letters in the string. As predicted, naming times produced a very strong frequency effect (107 milliseconds) under these conditions, comparable in size to the effect produced with lexical decision (99 milliseconds), and much larger than a normal naming task without the added letters (31 milliseconds). Obviously, one can no longer attribute the frequency effect to response production factors, since precisely the same set of articulatory responses produces a 107-millisecond frequency effect with the added letters, and only a 31-millisecond effect without them.

Perhaps the most compelling evidence in favor of the lexical decision estimates is the fact that in normal reading low-frequency words are fixated for about 80 milliseconds longer than high-frequency words (Rayner and Duffy 1986). This effect compares quite well with the typical value obtained in many lexical decision experiments. Thus, unless one argues that fixation times are influenced by exactly the same type of decision processes (a highly dubious proposal), it would seem clear that at least 80 milliseconds of the frequency effect must be a genuine access effect.

5.4.3   The Nature of the Access Code

Under the assumptions of a search model, an item of information is stored under a particular description, which is called the *access code*. Thus, if the word *destruction* is stored under the description "DES," then this implies that there is an entry in an access file under the header "DES," which contains a pointer to the full entry for the word *destruction* in the lexicon proper. When access occurs, it is the file of abbreviated access codes that is searched, not the listings of words in the lexicon proper. The advantage of this procedure might be that it speeds up the search considerably, since the time taken to make comparisons between the entries in the access file and the original stimulus may well depend on how many letters enter into the comparison. The disadvantage might be the increase in ambiguity, since there will now be many entries for "DES," each pointing to a different word (*destiny, desultory, desert, despicable*, and so on). The same notion can be expressed in activation terms, although perhaps with less force. The idea would be that sending activation out from a letter detector consumes a certain amount of energy, so anything that economizes on the number of letters that are necessary to activate the appropriate word detector leads to an overall increase in efficiency.

The available evidence suggests that something like this might actually occur. For example, Taft and Forster (1976) compared lexical decision times for "compound" nonwords that contained embedded words. The idea behind the experiment was that the time taken to *reject* these items as words would increase whenever the embedded word was detected, provided this detection took place before the lexical decision was made. The results showed that nonwords having a word as first syllable (for instance, FOOTMILGE) did in fact take longer to reject than nonwords with no embedded words (THRIMNADE), but that nonwords with two embedded words (TOASTPULL) showed no greater interference. Further, having a word as second syllable (TROWBREAK) seemed to produce no interference at all. These results can be readily interpreted if we assume that the access code consists of just the first syllable and that interference occurs only when a perfect match is encountered in the access file. Thus, FOOT-MILGE produces interference because its access code finds a perfect match with the entry "FOOT." However, when the stimulus TROWBREAK is converted to the access code "TROW," no match is found and hence no interference occurs. Obviously, the subjects would have noticed that TROWBREAK contained a word, but this evidently occurs too late to cause any interference with the decision.

Why should the first syllable be so important? One possibility is that subjects process the input from left to right, taking progressively larger segments of the word as the search target. For example, in the case of FOOTMILGE the successive targets might be FO, FOO, and FOOT. This guarantees that eventually the right access code will be generated. But problems arise when a large number of words begin with the same sequence of letters, as in *prefixed* words. For example, about 1500 words in English begin with RE: *reconsider, revel, remember, remark, return,* and so on. Programmers designing efficient dictionary lookup routines solve this problem by stripping off the prefix, so that a word like *remember* could be stored under "MEM" instead of the less informative "REM." Taft and Forster (1975) propose that an analogous process is performed by the human computer. They argue that if prefixed words were stored without their prefixes, then a search for a nonword such as VIVE should access the entry for the word *revive* and hence cause interference in the decision process. Since there is substantial letter overlap between these items, we need to compare VIVE with a control item that has the same overlap with a word but does not involve a prefix, such as LISH (coming from the nonprefixed word *relish*). The results indicated a very strong effect, with nonwords such as VIVE and JUVENATE taking longer to reject (and producing more errors) than control items such as LISH and PERTOIRE.

Fortunately, it is not necessary to postulate any special process for prefix stripping. If the prefixes are all listed in the access file, then the left-to-right scanning of the input will inevitably retrieve them. All we need to postulate is that if contact is made with a prefix, then the left-to-right scan recommences at the first letter after the prefix. This raises an interesting problem for "pseudoprefixed" words such as RELISH. The left-to-right scan should access RE, and then begin again at LISH, since there is no way to tell that this word is not prefixed until after it has been recognized. This would seem to make it impossible to recognize such words, and hence it is necessary to postulate an additional backup search procedure that searches for the whole word. As might be expected, such words take longer to classify than other words that are not mistakenly treated as pre-fixed words. So although VIVE takes more time to classify than LISH, the word REVIVE takes less time to classify than the word RELISH.

There is general agreement that these results indicate some sort of morphological decomposition of words during access, although the pre-cise details of the entire process are not absolutely clear. Subsequent work in this area has focused on the much more difficult problem of specifying how many letters are included in the access code. Taft (1979) has pro-posed that the access code includes all letters up to and including the consonants following the first vowel, providing that no orthographically illegal sequence is included. This unit is called the BOSS—the *Basic Orthographic Syllabic Structure*. For example, the BOSS of *lantern* is LANT, but the BOSS for *boycott* is BOY (since the sequence YC is not a legal sequence, except across a syllable boundary). A typical test of this proposal involves comparing BOSSes with non-BOSSes. Taft reports that lexical decision times for nonwords such as TRAUM (the BOSS of *trauma*) are reliably longer than for nonwords such as BLEN (not-the-BOSS of *blend*).

5.4.4   Phonological Processes in Reading

All of the above discussion assumes without question that the access code for a visually presented word is an orthographic array of some sort. How-ever, a great deal of work has concentrated on a radically different notion, namely, that the access code is expressed in a *phonological* code (see Colt-heart 1978 for a review of this material). That is, in order to access a word, we must first recode the orthographic stimulus in terms of a code that represents the speech segments involved in the pronunciation of the word. To some extent, this seems paradoxical, since we would not nor-mally expect to know the pronunciation of a word until *after* its lexical entry had been accessed.

The motivations for this proposal are mixed. There is the fact that every beginning reader already knows how to access the lexicon on the basis of speech sounds—hence, there would be an obvious economy if the beginning reader merely learned how to convert print into sound. Indeed, many children are ostensibly taught to read in just such a way. Then there is the clear but unmistakable "voice in the head" that many of us can hear while we are reading. What could be the purpose of this inner speech if not to aid recognition of the words?

Rubenstein, Lewis, and Rubenstein (1971) have produced perhaps the clearest experimental evidence for phonological recoding. They demonstrated that nonwords such as BRANE, which would sound the same as a word if pronounced, took longer to reject than nonwords such as BRONE, which do not sound the same as a word. Since the only difference between these nonwords is their closeness in sound to an English word, it follows that subjects must have determined the pronunciation before making their decision. However, this is not the same as phonological recoding. This theory asserts that the pronunciation must be determined before access can be attempted, whereas the experiment demonstrates only that pronunciation is determined before the final decision has been reached. Therefore, these findings are suggestive only.

Obviously, the procedure for generating a phonological representation must involve some nonlexical process, such as a set of grapheme-to-phoneme conversion rules. However, as we have already seen, many English words will receive the wrong phonological representation (for instance, both *rough* and *cough* cannot receive the correct assignment), so the recoding process can only be used for highly regular words. This indicates that there must at least be a purely visual route to meaning, since otherwise the irregular words could not be accessed. This suggests that the phonological route must play a fairly limited role in reading, especially since it is usually assumed that the phonological route is much slower than the visual route.

The limited utility of this system is further revealed when we consider that it can play no role at all in any language that uses ideographic rather than alphabetic representations. For example, in Chinese the character for a word represents the meaning of the morphemes making up the word— in some cases with highly stylized "pictograms" of the object designated by the word. In such a writing system, an unknown word could not be pronounced, and hence there is no way to determine the phonological code prior to lexical access.

At best, then, phonological recoding is a strategy used only in some languages, and then only for some words. Yet we hear the voice in the head for each and every word. How could this be so? Probably the best answer available is to suggest that as far as word recognition is concerned, phonological recoding is a backup strategy that is used when the visual access system fails. That is why we see children "sounding out" unfamiliar words, and also why the evidence for recoding is strongest with unfamiliar nonwords as stimuli. For example, when visual access for BRANE fails (as it must), a backup procedure is brought to bear on the problem, and that is to guess how the stimulus might sound, and then to attempt to access that representation instead of the visual representation. Thus, the inner speech we might observe when we are doing a lexical decision experiment is probably just a checking procedure. As far as reading text is concerned, it could be that recoding plays a more significant role, not in the process of word recognition, but in the process of sentence comprehension. By taking the products of a visually based analysis of the sentence and running them through a subvocalizing system, we may literally get a second exposure of the material, without having to retrace our steps.

5.4.5   Repetition Priming Effects

A phenomenon that presents considerable difficulties for lexical search theory is the *repetition* effect discussed earlier. Repetition priming occurs when a word is presented more than once in a lexical decision experiment. To explain the faster response on the second presentation, lexical search theory must propose that the entries are constantly changing their relative position as a function of recency, not frequency. This is no problem at all for activation theories. In the logogen model, we can postulate a sudden drop in threshold immediately after discharge of the logogen, with a gradual return to the original level. If the word occurs again before the return is complete, then the threshold will drop still further. Since only words with a relatively high rate of occurrence will achieve this, we could explain both the frequency effect and the repetition effect at once. The explanation in connectionist terms is quite similar. Instead of a postdischarge drop in threshold, we postulate a postdischarge increase in the letter-word connection weights, together with a gradual return to the predischarge weights.

The current controversy in this area is whether the repetition effect has anything to do with lexical access. Several investigators have raised the possibility that the faster response to repeated items is due to some kind of memory for the first presentation (Feustal, Shiffrin, and Salasoo 1983; Forster and Davis 1984). Somehow, recognizing that the test item has been presented in the experiment before is thought to give the subject some kind of an advantage, not in speed of access but in speed of decision making. Such an argument is difficult to spell out in detail, since subjects show repetition effects when they plainly cannot discriminate which items were repeated and which were not.

However, if this effect is really a lexical effect (that is, it reflects the increased accessibility of a lexical entry that has been accessed recently), then the circumstances under which the initial access took place should be quite irrelevant. However, Forster and Davis (1984) found that the repetition effect was severely weakened when the first presentation of a word was merely part of the context for another target item, despite the fact that they were able to show that the context words must have been processed. More striking is the evidence offered by Oliphant (1983), who showed no repetition effect at all when the initial presentation was part of the instructions for the experiment, which subjects were required to read aloud. These results make no sense if the sole requirement for the repetition effect is repeated access of the same lexical entry. However, they do make sense if the effect is due to the influence of the episodic memory trace of the first presentation on the lexical decision for the second presentation. The strength of such a trace would depend on factors like the amount of attention paid to the stimulus and the similarity of the circumstances surrounding the two presentations.

5.4.6   The Modular Lexicon

One of the issues that arises when we investigate the structure of cognitive systems is the extent to which they are modular (Fodor 1983). An information-processing system could be said to be modular if it is composed of self-contained systems that function independently of each other, operate in a limited domain, and have highly restricted access to information (or, in Fodor's terms, they are "informationally encapsulated"). The question of the autonomy of lexical processing discussed earlier is a specific issue that bears on modularity. A new issue that is currently emerging concerns the modularity of lexical *memory*. If the lexical processor is just one of the modules making up the language processor, then we might expect it to be informationally encapsulated—in other words, the lexical processor has access to a very limited type of memory, namely, memory for linguistic objects.

The stimulus for this research originated in Tulving's attempt to distinguish between semantic memory and episodic memory (Tulving 1972). Semantic memory probably should be broken down into at least two subsystems: memory for the properties of linguistic objects, and memory for generic facts or principles that have been abstracted away from individual, personal experience. Episodic memory, on the other hand, is a record of personal experiences. Thus, in principle, there ought to be a difference between "remembering" that *year* is a noun and remembering what one had for dinner yesterday.

The problem is to specify what sort of difference there might be and how to detect it. One approach is to try to show that different access mechanisms are involved. The aim is to show that variables that exert a strong influence on retrieval of information from lexical memory have no effect, or a quite different kind of effect, on retrieval from episodic memory. For example, semantic priming of the *doctor-nurse* variety is thought to be mediated by linkages between lexical entries. McKoon and Ratcliff (1979, 1986) asked whether similar effects could be obtained for episodically established linkages. They were able to demonstrate strong priming effects in a lexical decision task for word pairs that had been previously learned in a paired-associates learning task. That is, subjects first learned a list of word pairs such as *city-grass* and then were given *grass* in a lexical decision experiment, preceded either by the prime *city* or by some other word that was not originally paired with *grass*. Performance was faster in the former condition. The argument offered by McKoon and Ratcliff was that if semantic memory and episodic memory are really different systems, then an episodically established association should have no effect on a task that deals with retrieval of linguistic properties. Since it did, some doubt is cast on the validity of the distinction.

There are two ways to interpret this result and yet keep the distinction between lexical and episodic memory. One is to assume that the system of interlexical linkages has been changed by learning the list of word pairs. This is not a particularly attractive option. The other is to assume that the lexical decision task has rather broad *scope*. That is, the range of information taken into account when arriving at a decision is very broad and is by no means restricted just to the output of the lexical processor. Thus, the existence of a linkage between words in episodic memory (a nonlinguistic property) can influence decision making in much the same way as linkages within the lexicon (a linguistic property).

At first glance it seems that this must violate the modular principle that the lexical processor is informationally encapsulated. How could the lexical processor otherwise gain access to the episodic record of past experience? The answer is simple. It is the decision-making system, not the lexical processor, that needs to gain such access. In Fodor's system, the decision maker is not a low-level module at all; instead, it is part of the higher-level central processing system, and this has very broad scope indeed. As we surmised earlier, decision making might be influenced by a variety of nonlinguistic properties of the input data, and we can now add another property to that list.

However, it still remains to explain why this particular nonlinguistic property is relevant. Actually, it should come as no surprise that nonlinguistic relations might influence priming, since it has long been known that strong priming effects in lexical decision are produced by word pairs that are strongly associated, but not closely related linguistically (such as *mermaid-water*). One way to explain these kinds of effects is to propose a postaccess checking procedure that seeks to establish some meaningful relationship between the just-accessed word and the context. If no such relationship is found, then a very careful check of the spelling is carried out to make sure that the correct entry has been accessed. But if some kind of "fit" is obtained between the prior context and the accessed entry, then only the most superficial check is required. Thus, if we had accessed the entry for the word *chair*, and the context was the word *furniture*, the context check would reveal a connection, thereby permitting higher-level systems to proceed immediately, without waiting for any further confirmation. But if no connection can be found, then these higher-level systems must wait until the orthographic properties have been carefully checked. If the context-checking mechanism was strictly modular, then only semantic linkages would count. But if it is nonmodular, then a very wide range of relationships might be considered, including the connection between words like *mermaid* and *water*, and perhaps even the fact that the word in question was paired with the context word in a recently learned list. (For further discussion of context-checking mechanisms, see Norris 1986.)

It should be noted that we cannot appeal to the same decision-making system that we appealed to before, claiming that it is just the process of making a lexical decision that is facilitated, not the access process. This is because the priming effects that we are discussing are also found with the naming task, where no decision about the lexical status of the input is required. However, the naming task does involve at least one decision, and that is the decision that the correct entry has been accessed.

Put another way, we can say that the episodic priming effect represents a challenge to the modular conception of memory only if we believe that lexical decisions are based solely on linguistic properties. If there is any reason to doubt this assumption, then the strength of the challenge is diminished. As noted earlier, there are independent reasons for doubting this assumption in another area altogether—namely, *repetition* priming, where faster lexical decision times are observed for items presented more than once (see section 5.3.3). An episodic interpretation of these effects implies that the lexical decision maker has very wide scope and takes into account any piece of evidence that may be relevant. Evidently, discovering that the current test item has occurred before in the experiment is regarded as evidence in favor of the hypothesis that the stimulus is a word (there are several reasons why this might be so—the simplest is that nonwords are less likely to be remembered). However, when the initial presentation is stored under a different description from the second, recognition may not occur quickly enough to be relevant to the lexical decision task.

If this reasoning is correct, then McKoon and Ratcliff's result may demonstrate what many have suspected, namely, that the semantic priming effect does not reflect properties of the lexical processor but does reflect properties of the decision system. That is, *any* kind of relationship between the prime and target may be used as evidence, whether it be semantic, associative, formal, or even episodic.

Suggestions for Further Reading

Throughout this chapter we have considered only the case of a printed stimulus and have ignored the question of how a spoken word is recognized. In part this is the result of space limitations, but it also reflects the belief that the basic processes of word recognition are the same, regardless of modality (this not necessarily a widely held belief). However, there are some key features of speech that are completely absent in print, the most obvious being prosodic cues (pitch and stress), plus the fact that the speech signal is stretched out in time, whereas print is stretched out in space. The *cohort theory* of Marslen-Wilson is the best example of a theory of word recognition specifically designed for speech stimuli. The best up-to-date reference for a discussion of these matters is the special issue of *Cognition* on spoken word recognition, edited by Frauenfelder and Tyler (1987, vol. 25).

In section 5.4.4 we dismissed the possibility of a phonological access code for printed words. However, it has been shown that irregular words take longer to name than regular words. This implies that a rule system of some sort must be involved. These effects appear to be restricted to the naming task, however, since lexical decision times show no such effect (Coltheart et al. 1979). It has been suggested (Glushko 1979) that it is not regularity that is important, but rather consistency. Thus, both *mint* and *pint* should be slower to name because they have similar spelling but different pronunciations.

Stroke victims are often left with word-finding problems that can tell us a great deal about the normal, intact lexical access system. See Coltheart, Patterson, and Marshall 1980 for an excellent discussion of these issues.

Questions

5.1   Logogen theory accounts for frequency effects (and many others) in terms of a change in the threshold of a word detector. On the other hand, a connectionist account might be more likely to explain this effect in terms of stronger connection weights between letter and word units. Are these accounts perfectly equivalent?

5.2   It is claimed that a search model predicts that frequency should have absolutely constant effects under a wide range of conditions—that is, that there should be no interaction effects between frequency and other variables, such as the visual clarity of the input stimulus or the presence of a related context. Why should this be so? Are any special assumptions needed before this prediction can be made? What would activation models predict? See Mitchell 1982 for a discussion of these issues.

5.3   It is sometimes said that a search model is obviously out of the question, since the required search speeds are far too great, given the average lexical decision time. Is it possible to avoid this criticism by allowing for more than one search to be carried out at the same time? Would this alter the search model in any way?

5.4   How could you estimate how long it takes to carry out an exhaustive search under the assumptions of a search model?

References

Antos, S. J. (1979). Processing facilitation in a lexical decision task. *Journal of Experimental Psychology: Human Perception and Performance* 5, 527–545.

Balota, D. A., and J. I. Chumbley (1984). Are lexical decisions a good measure of lexical access? The role of word frequency in the neglected decision stage. *Journal of Experimental Psychology: Human Perception and Performance* 10, 340–357.

Balota, D. A., and J. I. Chumbley (1985). The locus of word-frequency effects in the pronunciation task: Lexical access and/or production? *Journal of Memory and Language* 24, 89–106.

Becker, C. A. (1979). Semantic context and word frequency effects in visual word recognition. *Journal of Experimental Psychology: Human Perception and Performance* 5, 252–259.

Carroll, J. B., P. Davies, and B. Richman (1971). *The American Heritage word frequency book.* Boston: Houghton Mifflin.

Carroll, J. B., and M. N. White (1973). Word frequency and age of acquisition as determiners of picture naming latencies. *Quarterly Journal of Experimental Psychology* 24, 85–95.

Coltheart, M. (1978). Lexical access in simple reading tasks. In G. Underwood, ed., *Strategies of information processing.* London: Academic Press.

Coltheart, M., D. Besner, J. T. Jonasson, and E. Davelaar (1979). Phonological encoding in the lexical decision task. *Quarterly Journal of Experimental Psychology* 31, 489–507.

Coltheart, M., K. Patterson, and J. C. Marshall (1980). *Deep dyslexia.* London: Routledge and Kegan Paul.

Feustal, T. C., R. M. Shiffrin, and A. Salasoo (1983). Episodic and lexical contributions to the repetition effect in word identification. *Journal of Experimental Psychology: General* 112, 309–346.

Fischler, I., and P. A. Bloom (1979). Automatic and attentional processes in the effects of sentence contexts on word recognition. *Journal of Verbal Learning and Verbal Behavior* 18, 1–20.

Fodor, J. A. (1983). *The modularity of mind.* Cambridge, MA: MIT Press.

Forster, K. I. (1976). Accessing the mental lexicon. In R. J. Wales and E. Walker, eds., *New approaches to language mechanisms.* Amsterdam: North-Holland.

Forster, K. I. (1981). Priming and the effects of sentence and lexical contexts on naming time: Evidence for autonomous lexical processing. *Quarterly Journal of Experimental Psychology* 33, 465–495.

Forster, K. I., and S. M. Chambers. (1973). Lexical access and naming time. *Journal of Verbal Learning and Verbal Behavior* 12, 627–635.

Forster, K. I., and C. Davis (1984). Repetition priming and frequency attenuation in lexical access. *Journal of Experimental Psychology: Learning, Memory, and Cognition* 10, 680–698.

Frederiksen, J. R., and J. F. Kroll (1976). Spelling and sound: Approaches to the internal lexicon. *Journal of Experimental Psychology: Human Perception and Performance* 2, 361–379.

Glushko, R. J. (1979). The organization and activation of orthographic knowledge in reading aloud. *Journal of Experimental Psychology: Human Perception and Performance* 5, 674–691.

Kucera, J., and W. N. Francis (1967). *Computational analysis of present day American English.* Providence, RI: Brown University Press.

McClelland, J. L., D. E. Rumelhart, and the PDP Research Group (1986). *Parallel distributed processing: Explorations in the microstructure of cognition.* Vol. 2, *Psychological and biological models.* Cambridge, MA: MIT Press.

McKoon, G., and R. Ratcliff (1979). Priming in episodic memory. *Journal of Verbal Learning and Verbal Behavior* 18, 463–480.

McKoon, G., and R. Ratcliff (1986). Automatic activation of episodic information in a semantic memory task. *Journal of Experimental Psychology: Learning, Memory, and Cognition* 12, 108–115.

Meyer, D. M., and R. W. Schvaneveldt (1971). Facilitation in recognizing pairs of words: Evidence of a dependence between retrieval operations. *Journal of Experimental Psychology* 90, 227–234.

Mitchell, D. C. (1982). *The process of reading.* New York: Wiley.

Morton, J. (1970). A functional model of human memory. In D. A. Norman, ed., *Models of human memory.* New York: Academic Press.

Norris, D. (1986). Word recognition: Context effects without priming. *Cognition* 22, 93–136.

O'Connor, R. E., and K. I. Forster (1981). Criterion bias and search sequence bias in word recognition. *Memory and Cognition* 9, 78–92.

Oliphant, G. W. (1983). Repetition and recency effects in word recognition. *Australian Journal of Psychology* 35, 393–403.

Paap, K. R., J. E. McDonald, R. W. Schvaneveldt, and R. W. Noel (1987). Frequency and pronounceability in visually presented naming and lexical decision tasks. In M. Coltheart, ed., *Attention and performance 12: The psychology of reading.* Hillsdale, NJ: L. Erlbaum Associates.

Rayner, K., and S. A. Duffy (1986). Lexical complexity and fixation times in reading: Effects of word frequency, verb complexity, and lexical ambiguity. *Memory and Cognition* 14, 191–201.

Rayner, K., and A. Pollatsek (1987). Eye movements in reading: A tutorial review. In M. Coltheart, ed., *Attention and performance 12: The psychology of reading.* Hillsdale, NJ: L. Erlbaum Associates.

Rubenstein, H., L. Garfield, and J. A. Millikan (1970). Homographic entries in the internal lexicon. *Journal of Verbal Learning and Verbal Behavior* 9, 487–494.

Rubenstein, H., S. S. Lewis, and M. A. Rubenstein (1971). Homographic entries in the internal lexicon: Effects of systematicity and relative frequency of meanings. *Journal of Verbal Learning and Verbal Behavior* 10, 57–62.

Scarborough, D. L., C. Cortese, and H. Scarborough (1977). Frequency and repetition effects in lexical memory. *Journal of Experimental Psychology: Human Perception and Performance* 7, 3–12.

Seidenberg, M. S., M. K. Tanenhaus, J. M. Leiman, and M. Bienkowski (1982). Automatic access of the meanings of ambiguous words in context: Some limitations of knowledge-based processing. *Cognitive Psychology* 14, 489–537.

Seidenberg, M. S., G. S. Waters, M. Sanders, and P. Langer (1984). Pre- and post-lexical loci of contextual effects on word recognition. *Memory and Cognition* 12, 315–328.

Shulman, H. G., and T. C. B. Davison (1977). Control properties of semantic coding in a lexical decision task. *Journal of Verbal Learning and Verbal Behavior* 16, 91–98.

Stanovich, K.E., and R. F. West (1983). On priming by a sentence context. *Journal of experimental Psychology: General* 112, 1–36.

Swinney, D. A. (1979). Lexical access during sentence comprehension: (Re)consideration of context effects. *Journal of Verbal Learning and Verbal Behavior* 18, 645–659.

Taft, M. (1979). Lexical access via an orthographic code: The Basic Orthographic Syllabic Structure (BOSS). *Journal of Verbal Learning and Verbal Behavior* 18, 21–39.

Taft, M., and K. I. Forster (1975). Lexical storage and retrieval of prefixed words. *Journal of Verbal Learning and Verbal Behavior* 14, 638–647.

Taft, M., and K. I. Forster (1976). Lexical storage and retrieval of polymorphemic and polysyllabic words. *Journal of Verbal Learning and Verbal Behavior* 15, 607–620.

Tanenhaus, M. K., and M. M. Lucas (1987). Context effects in lexical processing. *Cognition* 25, 213–234.

Thorndike, E. L., and I. Lorge (1944). *The teacher's wordbook of 30,000 words.* New York: Teacher's College, Columbia University.

Tulving, E. (1972). Episodic and semantic memory. In E. Tulving and W. Donaldson, eds., *Organization of memory.* New York: Academic Press.

Whaley, C. P. (1978). Word-nonword classification time. *Journal of Verbal Learning and Verbal Behavior* 17, 143–154.

6

Sentence Processing

Merrill F. Garrett

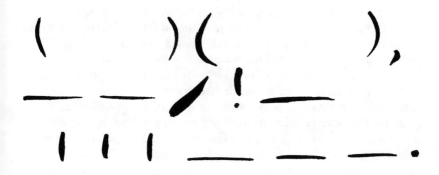

It is commonplace and perfectly correct to speak of language as the "glue" that holds human society together, that links past and future in a social, intellectual, and legal tradition. No other behavioral capacity is more central to our individual comfort and success in society. That capacity depends upon an incredibly complex set of cognitive systems, served by a set of motor and perceptual skills that are elaborately developed and delicately timed. Every day a normal human being utters thousands of words in the form of sentences and conversational fragments and listens to twice that number more. Every such word must be identified from an ensemble of 50,000 or more forms in less than a third of a second and assembled into a structure that correctly represents the meaning intended by the speaker. Moreover, the processes that eventuate in this association of meaning and utterance form are accomplished in major part without the conscious attention or intention of the speaker or listener.

These are the global facts of language use. The linguistic sciences comprise the technical fields that inquire into this process and are responsible for the study of the informational structures, the memory and processing systems, and the neurological and physiological functions that support language capacity. Broadly defined, these are the fields of formal linguistics (chapters 1, 2, 3), psycholinguistics (chapters 4, 5, 6), and neurolinguistics (chapter 7). Each of these areas may be more finely divided in ways that connect to study in the fields of logic, mathematics, computer science, cognitive psychology, neuroanatomy, and neurophysiology. Any specific inquiry into human use of language, deeply pursued, will inevitably breach the boundaries of any one discipline and be forced to call upon the richness of these multiple sources of information and theory.

In this chapter we will focus on the experimental study of the mental processes that assign sentence structure. We will give primary attention to language comprehension, though we will consider some observations about language production at the end of the chapter. The experimental study of real-time language processes revolves around several problem areas: speech processing, lexical recognition and retrieval, syntactic analysis (often referred to as "parsing"), and sentence interpretation (that is, the assignment of semantic and pragmatic consequence to sentences). The objectives of study are (1) to provide psychologically motivated, computational accounts of the informational structures and control processes that account for normal performance in each of these areas, and (2) to assay the character of brain structure and mechanism that support such behavioral systems. We will consider the first of these objectives; chapter 7 addresses some of the issues that relate to the second.

6.1   Some Real-Time Processing Constraints

6.1.1   Rate of Processing Decisions

Sentence processing is very fast and quite automatic. Even without appeal to sophisticated measurement or argument, we know that sentence-processing activities must approximate the rate of the input signals that represent language. We must process as we hear or as we read, rather than waiting for the end of a sentence to undertake some analysis. Memory would otherwise be quickly overloaded and early words in the sentence lost before their structural relation to later words could be established. Long pauses do not follow each word in speech or the ends of phrases and sentences during which our processing system can carry out its work; the next input is being presented before the echoes of the last have begun to fade.

Even so general a claim as this is valuable because it begins to establish boundary conditions on the class of processing machines that could be advanced as models of human performance: to a first approximation, their processing for interpretation must keep up with the normal rate of a spoken discourse or the normal rate for reading. To evaluate this condition more precisely, we must know just how closely tied are input presentation steps, measured in syllables or morphemes, and the various types of processing decisions that must be made. The fully detailed facts are not yet determined, and it will require many and very precise measurements of phonetic, morphological, syntactic, and semantic performance variables during sentence processing to establish them. But we do have a number of experimental findings that permit some rather specific claims. We can say, for example, that the decision about a word's identity, its syntactic class, perhaps its initial phrasal category, and some aspects of its semantic integration into the sentence of which it is a part are available within a syllable or two after its input.

How can we tell this? We will consider just three of many relevant findings. These come from studies of *speech shadowing*, *lexical ambiguity*, and *lexical decision* in sentences.

In speech shadowing, listeners are required to repeat aloud what they are hearing and to do so as accurately and with as little delay as possible. A few exceptional performers can sustain accurate shadowing at around an average syllable duration (300 milliseconds) but for the most part listeners do this task at delays of around 800 to 1000 milliseconds (Marslen-Wilson 1975). The salient fact for our purposes is that this performance has been shown to be responsive to lexical structure and to predictability of the text (Marslen-Wilson and Welsh 1978). For example, if a distortion were introduced into the latter portion of a word (as in pronouncing *cigaresh* for *cigarette*), shadowers would frequently restore it to its proper pronunication. This indicates that before they reach the point of the distortion, they have already identified the lexical target. The evidence that more than lexical structure (that is, the mere existence of a lexical entry for *cigarette*) is at work comes from the fact that such restorations are more likely to occur as the target word's predictability (from its preceding context) increases. It is also worth noting that most of these contextually constrained restorations are made fluently, without obvious indications that subjects consciously notice the deviance.

In the relevant lexical ambiguity studies, words are presented in contexts that bias their interpretation, and measurements of the meanings associated with an ambiguous term are taken at successive intervals following it. For example, subjects might listen to the sentence in (1):

(1) The gypsy read the young man's palm ∧ for only ∧ a dollar since he was nearly broke.

Measurements of what meanings for *palm* were available would be taken at the indicated points. One technique for making such measurements is called the *cross-modal priming* procedure (Swinney 1979): while listening to a sentence, subjects must simultaneously perform a lexical decision task for a visually presented target. From the perspective of a subject, targets can occur at any point in the sentence, but the crucial experimental observations are, of course, those taken at points following the ambiguous word. In separate experimental conditions, lexical decision targets related to each sense of the ambiguous word (in this case TREE and HAND) are tested and their response times compared with those for unrelated control words. The measurement method relies on effects of semantic priming of the sort described in chapter 5: priming of lexical decision targets should occur for the related words (that is, their reaction times should be lower than for their control words). However, when the sentence context has selected a sense of the ambiguous word, *only* that meaning (HAND, for (1)) should prime the lexical decision performance; the other (TREE) should behave like an unrelated word. It is therefore of great interest that two effects occur, and at different test positions. *Both* meanings of the ambiguous word prime their related lexical decision targets (HAND and TREE) when the targets are presented immediately after the ambiguous item, but only the contextually appropriate sense (HAND) is primed for tests made a syllable or two later (Swinney 1979; Seidenberg et al. 1982). This tells us something important about lexical retrieval in sentence contexts (it is not initially guided by semantic values derived from the sentence, and it yields multiple analyses where they exist; see section 5.4.1) and about sentence-processing rates (enough processing to resolve an ambiguity can occur in half a second or less). More precisely, the relation that the competing descriptions for the ambiguous word bear to the sentence and discourse structures that precede it can be evaluated in that interval.

Finally, we can consider experiments in which visually presented sentences occur on a computer display one word at a time, at rates of 4 to 8 words per second. At some point in the sequence the experimental item of interest occurs (signaled usually by a shift from lower to upper case) and the subject must make a lexical decision for that item—or, in some other experiments, must pronounce it (the naming task). When the target word is a syntactically well formed continuation of the sentence, response times are faster than when it is not (Wright and Garrett 1984; West and Stanovich 1986). This indicates that the subject has identified the phrasal role of the target word at delays of a few hundred milliseconds, even though in some cases considerable phrasal structure has to be evaluated for this to be done.

These observations tell us that sentence processing is very rapid and closely linked in time to the input. They also commit us to a view of processing that includes a kind of parallelism, or at least a very convincing pseudoparallelism at this level of observation. We are committed to the simultaneous action of (channel one) the perceptual processors that assemble the onrushing physical data into sensory representations and of (channel two, ...?) the systems responsible for building lexical, syntactic, and semantic descriptions. Certain sorts of parallelism—that is, the simultaneous action of different processing channels—are readily observed in human performance. What is problematic about the present case is to say what constitutes a "channel." The clear cases involve distinct motor and sensory systems. Here we are considering informational types as a basis for channel distinctions within a single modality. That notion of parallel processing is quite another matter—to which we will return.

6.1.2   Processing Errors: Garden Paths

We have been considering the rapid, multivalued, incremental processing that takes place as a language signal is taken in. A complementary point is also valid: it is sometimes necessary to take account of *late*-occurring sentence elements in order to achieve the correct analysis of initial sentence elements. Thus, incremental processing is a virtue in that it uses the time taken up by the sensory input process to do structural analysis, but it is sometimes a liability in that we pursue the wrong path of analysis. For example, read sentences (2)–(4):

(2)   Fatty weighted three hundred and fifty pounds of grapes.

(3)   The cotton shirts are made from comes from Arizona.

(4)   The horse raced past the barn fell.

For almost all readers (or listeners), the unexpected twist of interpretation at the end of these sentences produces a feeling of surprise. Such cases are often called *garden path sentences*, and their existence provides a powerful prima facie case for the incremental nature of sentence processing. Moreover, their careful experimental evaluation can provide significant insight into the time course of processing activity. If we could tell, for example, for any ambiguous stretch of sentence input, just how much of the "rightward" context (the words *following* the ambiguity) could influence its interpretation (that is, could forestall a garden path), we could get an estimate of just how closely the analysis processes and the input sequence are time-locked. Put another way, we could see whether—and how much—the system "looks ahead" before committing itself to an analysis consistent with the "leftward" information.

There is another important point to be made here. In the garden path cases, analysis goes astray. Normally, it does not. Moreover, and quite strikingly, we are normally altogether unaware of the analysis alternatives that present themselves. The garden path cases are the exception to this experience. For the most part, only a single interpretation of a sentence is made available to our awareness as we process it, and it is the situationally correct one. This is true even though, upon careful examination, many other analyses may be viable for substrings of the input. The range of (momentarily possible) analyses can be quite astounding. Examples (5)–(7) illustrate some of the kinds of phonetic, lexical, and syntactic ambiguity that may be encountered:

(5)   Remember,   a spoken   sentence   often contains   many words
       [ream ember   us poke can   cent tense   off in   men knee
       not   intended   to be   heard.
       knot   in ten did   tube bee   herd]

(6)   The old silver and jewels were very expensive.
       The old silver and the old jewels were very expensive.
       The old silver and the new jewels were very expensive.

(7)   Have the missionaries eaten.
       The bishop said, "Have the missionaries eaten their breakfast?"
       The cannibal said, "Have the missionaries eaten for breakfast."

By the time one has reached the end of a sentence or clause, a single interpretation, associated with a single lexical and syntactic analysis, has been selected from among the many possibilities that may be momentarily viable during the pass through a sentence. That interpretation is the one we become aware of, and it is almost invariably the one appropriate to our current communicative situation. The alternatives are "filtered" by the processing system in some way that permits the "selection" of the contextually appropriate analysis. Hence, cognitive processing of great power and flexibility occurs at levels prior to our conscious decision-making systems. How does this happen?

One way to shed light on this question is to ask why there are quotation marks on "filtering" and "selection." It is because the use of those terms might be taken to prejudge what is an empirical issue, namely, whether the mechanisms that account for our very high rate of correct (situationally apposite) analyses is to be accounted for by a mechanism that postulates the many lexical and syntactic analyses compatible with the sensory input and selects among them on the basis of criteria established by prior interpretation and compatibility with our general knowledge of the world, or whether analysis of the sensory data is guided from the very outset by "biases" derived from general world knowledge and from the semantic and pragmatic interpretation of the current communicative state of affairs. This contrast in possibilities is a version of the contrast between modular and nonmodular theories of language processing, and it is a crux in language processing and cognitive theory in general. We will discuss it more extensively in section 6.2.

6.1.3   Summary

The properties of sentence comprehension just reviewed characterize it as a left-to-right, single pass process, normally with a single readout. The goal of the process is to assign logical structure that will support an interpretation that is coherent in the prevailing communicative situation.

The objectives that processing must accomplish are (1) to associate with the sensory input a representation as a sequence of elements that can be organized into phrases (word identification), (2) to assemble those elements into phrasal groups that may be organized into sentences, and (3) to assemble sentence structures into a discourse structure that is systematically related to what the speaker knows about the real world.

6.2   The Organization of Language-processing Systems

6.2.1   Competence and Performance

The problems of speech perception raised in chapter 4, and those of word recognition and retrieval raised in chapter 5, represent two examples of a general kind of problem, namely, the problem of applying a *knowledge base* to a specific *performance task*. Language users clearly "know" the sounds, the words, and the sentences of their language because they use their language correctly—English speakers don't produce whistles and Bronx cheers, or sounds like buses or birds, or the phonetic classes of Hindi or Swahili, when they choose to speak their native tongue for purposes of communication. Neither do they utter just any sequence of English sounds. By intent, they use only those sequences that make up real English words in orders that make up real English sentences that make sense in the circumstances of their utterance. Whoever can behave in such fashion clearly "knows" English. But what is the sense of "know" that we appeal to when we make such an observation? Chapters 1, 2, and 3 offered detailed accounts of the structure of language, represented by rule systems called *grammars*, for the areas of syntax, semantics, and phonology. These, called theories of *competence*, are contrasted with theories of *performance*, in which the objective is to account for the exercise of language skills. Grammatical rule systems were characterized as representations of our knowledge of language. And so they indisputably are, insofar as they correctly represent the range of such structural distinctions as speakers make for the sentences of their language. But is representation by those rules of grammar the way in which such distinctions are coded in the minds of human beings in order to support the use of language as people speak and listen? To pose that question is to ask what relation holds between formal theories of grammatical structure and theories of the real-time computational processes that underlie human language use. In the domain of syntax, processors that assign structural descriptions to sentences are called syntactic *parsers*, and the question then becomes one of the relation that holds between grammar and parser.

The point to bear in mind is that the formal characterizations of grammatical knowledge have abstracted language structure from its context of use, and it is an empirical question whether the architecture of the mental processes responsible for real-time language use incorporates that abstract structure in a way that preserves the integrity of the representational types in grammars. The answer to this question lies at the heart of much of the development of theory and experiment in the language-processing area that has taken place since the 1960s.

That question has been variously answered, ranging from the claim that the mental operations that assign syntactic forms to sentences include representations precisely corresponding to those of a formal linguistic grammar (in other words, the grammar's rules are a real data base that must be accessed by procedures that determine their applicability to a given input), to the claim that grammatical rules represent the emergent properties of a system of processing elements for which no direct correspondence to grammatical categories or rules holds. To answer this question is evidently an empirical task, with the proviso that any proposed parser must assign a representation to sentences that is functionally equivalent to that assigned by an adequate grammar—that is, the range of structural distinctions that governs the form and meaning of sentences must be expressed in the representations assigned by the parser.

6.2.2   Modularity

The answers to questions about the relation between competence theories and performance theories are closely related to another issue, often referred to as the *modularity* of mental processes (Fodor 1983). At the most general level, for the case of language, this is the question of how language processes relate to our general inferential capacities and our general fund of information about the world. Is our knowledge of language, or the procedures for applying it (that is, the knowledge and procedures that account for the kinds of real-time performance features reviewed in section 6.1), encapsulated, set off from other kinds of cognitive structure?

To be more specific: We have noted that the ways processing systems use the several types of information represented in a grammar may not reflect the grammar's decomposition into separate rule systems. What are the implications of this? What if the procedures that effect the recovery of interpretations for sentences are not transparently related to the steps specified by application of the rules expressed in the formal systems? In particular, what if the procedures that effect a mapping from acoustic or orthographic representations to sentence meanings not only mix the grammar's informational types but also include representations of general nonlinguistic knowledge? Such a circumstance would amount to the denial of a separate language-specific processing faculty. It would not foreclose the possibility of an autonomous language faculty as an account of linguistic universals and of language learning, but it would certainly make the account of those facts quite different and perhaps more complicated than would otherwise be the case. We will turn momentarily to some experimental studies that address this issue. First, we need to put that work in perspective.

6.2.3   A Little History

The systematic experimental study of language processes began in earnest around 1960 and coincided with a shift in orientation from a predominantly behaviorist view in psychology (the tradition of John B. Watson, B. F. Skinner, and Clark L. Hull) to a cognitive perspective that emphasized the centrality of knowledge structures and mental processes in the determination of behavior. The views that fueled the transition made extensive appeal to the general background knowledge required to exploit contextual constraints in language use. Context-contingent processes were thus a central feature of the cognitive and perceptual/motor theories of the time.

Intelligent accommodation to the contextual circumstance of specific behaviors remains a central feature of cognitive theory today, of course. However, our view of the way in which contextual factors are to be incorporated into accounts of mental life has sharply changed from the 1960s to the present, and an examination of that change reveals much of the basis for the current excitement about the potential interactions among the several fields of linguistic and cognitive science.

A thumbnail sketch of language-processing theory circa 1965 could fairly go as follows: General wisdom had it that the study of language recognition and comprehension processes demonstrated pervasive interactions between language and general cognition. *Word recognition* was context driven in the strongest sense: primary perceptual activity was presumed potentially responsive to whatever the organism knew about the world. No principled distinction was drawn between the effects of specifically linguistic information and more general encyclopaedic knowledge in accounting for the processes of word recognition. The early logogen model Morton (1970), for example, discussed in chapter 5, is a case in point, and the many tachistoscopic studies of the time that showed powerful consequences of background knowledge on word recognition performance reflect the theoretical and experimental ambiance of the time.

Syntactic parsing was deemed heuristic and necessarily interactive with general semantic and pragmatic knowledge if anything like the efficiency (speed and accuracy) of human performance was to be achieved by computational models. Such constraints on the syntactic processing of sentences were deemed to derive from the level of *sentence interpretation*, in which general inferential mechanisms exploited knowledge of the world to restrict analysis to those structures with a plausible construal in the prevailing communicative context. Again, with respect to the real-time processing activities postulated, no principled distinction was drawn between linguistic and nonlinguistic informational types.

A similar, only marginally controversial sketch of theory today reflects a changed view of the essential architecture of language-processing systems. In particular, a principled distinction is drawn between processes that depend on the exploitation of general knowledge of the world and those that depend on language-specific structures. One cannot, of course, claim unanimity on this matter. But it is clear that the consensus has changed. That is not now for unbridled interaction, but rather for some degree of modularity, or autonomy of language processes. In succeeding sections we will identify some of the salient findings that provoked a change in theoretical attitude and we will see how the strong intuitions and evidence that fueled the interactive position may be preserved and reconstructed from a modular perspective.

6.2.4   An Experimental Example: The Processing of Active and Passive Sentences

We can illustrate the experimental evolution we have been discussing by looking at some investigations of active and passive sentences. Many early studies focused on this structural contrast because it seemed to provide a good testing ground for the evaluation of syntactic contributions to sentence-processing efficiency while controlling for variations in meaning. Actives and passives are, to a good first approximation, synonymous: *The boy was eaten by the shark* expresses the same essential content as *The shark ate the boy*. Thus, early experimental findings (see Fodor, Bever, and Garrett 1974, chap. 5) that passive sentences were more difficult to process than their corresponding active versions were taken as indications of syntactic effects on comprehension efficiency and as support for the existence of a purely syntactic mental processing system.

An early experimental challenge to that view arose from studies by Slobin (1966; see also Herriot 1969). These seemed to show that the processing cost for passives could be avoided *if* semantic or pragmatic constraints on the logical subject and object roles in passives were available, and thus to show an interaction between syntactic and semantic processes.

To take the example above, it is quite plausible that sharks should eat boys, but much less reasonable to assert the reverse, that boys eat sharks. Hence, the "reversibility" of the nouns in the example sentence is low. Similarly, and more so, for sentences like *The flowers were watered by the girl* or *The ice cream was eaten by the policeman*. These are nonreversible sentences because there is only one plausible assignment of their lexical content to the two argument positions in the sentence. Contrast these cases with ones like *The boy was kissed by the girl* or *The lion was chased by the tiger*. Either assignment of the nouns to argument positions is acceptable on grounds of plausibility; the only way to correctly interpret the sentence is to recover its syntactic analysis and relate the lexical items to it. For nonreversible sentences, however, this is not the case. Given an unstructured word string—say, *throw, football, boy*—one can infer the assignment of lexical items to argument positions from the semantic or pragmatic information associated with them. Hence, for such cases, syntax could be bypassed. The question for parsing theory was whether human sentence-processing systems could exploit that possibility, or whether syntactic processing was mandatory, unavoidable even when an alternative basis for analysis existed.

Slobin constructed stimuli that systematically crossed syntactic form and reversibility: active reversible and nonreversible, passive reversible and nonreversible. He tested the efficiency of processing by a timed picture verification task: subjects had to decide whether a test sentence was a correct description for a picture (presented immediately after the sentence). Performance was strongly affected by both variables, and they interacted—actives were easier to process than passives, but *only* for reversible sentences—nonreversible actives and passives had equal decision times. Thus, semantic constraint seemed to obviate a syntactic analysis problem.

The moral of this experimental outcome was taken to be quite general for language processes. It supported what seems antecedently reasonable and intuitively compelling: when we listen or read, our analysis of sentences is strongly influenced by what we know. It would, so the argument dictates, be absurd to hear a sentence like *I saw the Grand Canyon flying to New York* and analyze it as ambiguous (as some machine parsers of the time did) because of the existence of an analysis [I saw it: [The Grand Canyon flying to New York]] on the model of *I saw the eagle flying to its nest*. On this view, pure syntax is inefficient and fails to reflect the performance characteristics of human language users, so an autonomous language processor should not be postulated. Rather, general-purpose inferential mechanisms, with access to syntactic information to supplement the semantic and pragmatic information associated with the lexical items, was presumed to directly support sentence comprehension.

However, an alternative description of the effects observed by Slobin limits the generality of the interactive interpretation. Though the experimental effects are themselves robust, it is likely that they arise *after* sentence processing per se is complete—that is, at the point of picture analysis and comparison with sentence interpretation (Gough 1966). If so, the picture verification procedure does not reflect the processes at theoretical issue.

A particularly telling set of experiments in this regard was carried out by Forster and Olbrei (1973). They used two tasks: speeded judgments of well-formedness and the "RSVP" procedure (Rapid Serial Visual Presentation; Forster 1970). In RSVP the words of a sentence are rapidly projected one at a time onto a screen, each to the same point in the visual field. Each word thus masks the preceding one, forcing processing to proceed at the rate of input. When rates are relatively high (10 or more words per second), performance suffers, and accuracy of report can be used as a measure of processing efficiency. Forster and Olbrei used these procedures to test active and passive sentences with and without the semantic support provided by reversibility; both these procedures are linked to immediate processing of sentences and require no picture interpretation. Their experiments showed a strong and uniform difference between active and passive sentences in *both* reversible and nonreversible conditions. Moreover, they detected no effect of the reversibility variable at all, and this reinforces the view that reversibility effects arise quite late in the processing sequence, perhaps through interaction with picture interpretation processes.

The implication is that syntactic assignment processes are not directly affected by semantic constraint—not at least in the circumstances of these experiments, or, alternatively, not for the way logical and pragmatic factors are represented in reversible and nonreversible passives and actives. The performance interaction in the picture verification task is real enough, but it doesn't mean what it was initially taken to mean.

The measurement issue highlighted here is very significant. To properly assess the interaction and autonomy hypotheses, it is crucial to tap the processing of sentence structure as it unfolds. And the reason for that—as both the example just recounted and the earlier discussion of lexical and phrasal ambiguity attest—is that the interpretation we become aware of is the "final product" of processing, and that may reflect the contribution of several mental systems, linguistic and nonlinguistic. To assess claims about syntactic processes, one must evaluate the possibility that operations based on semantic and pragmatic plausibility apply to (potentially) independent products of a syntactic processor, yielding the appearance of interaction. This is a recurrent issue in contemporary psycholinguistic investigation, and the proper interpretation of experimental results requires its consideration.

6.3   Two Examples of Syntactic Processing

In the time since the studies just reviewed, considerable research has been invested in the question of how semantic and pragmatic factors relate to parsing. A substantial number of studies now indicate a significant degree of independence of syntactic processes from those inferential processes that are based on our general knowledge of the world. These experiments represent a variety of structures and methodologies, and the methods used are those in which real-time assessments of structural assignment are the target of investigation. We will consider several. We begin with a study that illustrates a basic parsing strategy, called minimal attachment.

6.3.1   A Parsing Strategy

The *minimal attachment* strategy requires the parser to take the first available structural option for assimilating each successive input into the parse tree and to change that only when forced to by subsequent input. This translates into an injunction not to build new phrasal nodes in order to attach a newly built simple phrase but instead to adjoin the new phrase to an already existing node (see figure 6.1). The principle minimizes processing locally by avoiding the proliferation of new phrasal nodes, but it does so at the potential cost of a garden path, with the necessary recomputation of structure that entails. (See Frazier 1979 for a review of evidence indicating the operation of such a principle of parsing.)

A number of experiments have studied the effect of interpretive constraints on parsing decisions to which minimal attachment may apply. We will consider one example from several that use eye-movement measures. In this technique, while subjects read test materials, the locations at which they fixate their gaze and the durations of those fixations are measured by an eye-tracking device. This provides an on-line measure of processing performance that has been found to be sensitive to lexical and syntactic properties of sentences.

Rayner, Carlson, and Frazier (1983) used this method to determine whether semantic and pragmatic constraints would modify the tendency of the parser to make a minimal attachment for prepositional phrases (as shown in figure 6.1). They compared eye-movement patterns for sentence pairs like those in figure 6.1 and those in (8a) and (8b):

(8)a.   The kids played all the albums on the stereo before they went to bed.

(a)

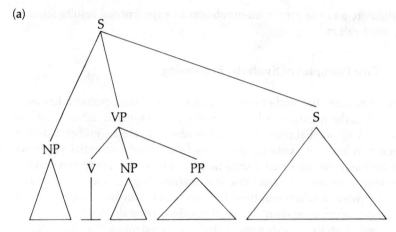

The spy saw the cop with binoculars but the cop didn't see him.

(b)

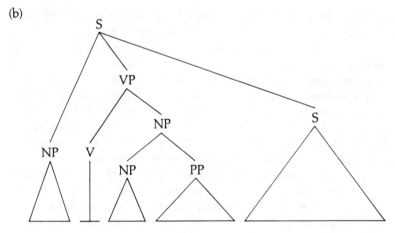

The spy saw the cop with a revolver but the cop didn't see him.

Figure 6.1
Minimal (a) and nonminimal (b) attachments for PP. Minimal attachment is accomplished by simple sister adjunction (in this case PP becomes a sister to V and NP under VP), and nonminimal attachment by first building a new phrasal node to which two phrases can attach (in this case NP and PP are both attached under the new node NP). Reprinted with permission from K. Rayner, M. Carlson, and L. Frazier (1983). The interaction of syntax and semantics during sentence processing: Eye movements in the analysis of semantically biased sentences. *Journal of Verbal Learning and Verbal Behavior* 22, 358–374.

b.   The kids played all the albums on the shelf before they went to
bed.

On grounds of plausible interpretation, the two versions of the prepositional phrase should attach to the VP in different ways: minimally for
(8a) and nonminimally (by first building a new NP to which both [the
album] and [on the shelf] could attach) for (8b). If plausibility determined
initial parsing decisions, then (8b) should not receive a minimal attachment
analysis at any point. But, in fact, the observed eye-movement patterns indicated initial commitment to a minimal attachment analysis in spite of
plausibility constraints: (8b) showed longer reading times than (8a) in the
biasing region (revolver/binoculars; shelf/stereo).

Rayner, Carlson, and Frazier took care to demonstrate that the plausibility variations in their sentences did influence the interpretation subjects
placed on them. Immediately after reading some test sentences, subjects
were asked for a paraphrase. This measure of the *final* product of the comprehension process showed strong effects of the semantic biases. Again,
we see that our conscious understanding of a sentence is the product of
multiple informational constraints, and again we see why the temporal factors in measurements of language performance are central to an understanding of the way in which the processing takes place.

A number of other studies have used eye-movement patterns to test for
the effect of interpretive constraints on parsing operations. These include
variations in the location of semantically constraining information and
tests of several other kinds of structures, with the same general outcome:
minimal attachment applies even for cases in which semantic constraint
militates against it. See Frazier 1987a and Clifton and Ferreira 1987 for
useful reviews that discuss the relations among such studies and their connection to other parsing research.

6.3.2   Noun Phrase Movement

Chapter 1 pointed out that certain structural properties of sentences can
be naturally described in terms of the movement of an NP from an initial,
underlying structure location to a different position that it occupies in surface structure. Such structures pose a problem for parsing. In order that a
sentence with a moved element be correctly interpreted, that element
must be linked to its original underlying structure site. In terms of the
trace theory discussed in chapter 1, this can be put as a question about
how traces are located and linked to the appropriate NP.

A number of important studies have focused on this problem area (see
Fodor 1979; Frazier, Clifton, and Randall 1983). We will consider one
study that uses an interesting methodology to measure the effects of
assigning an interpretation to a trace. The method differs from most pre-

viously applied to sentence processing. It uses scalp recordings of the electrical activity of the brain (*event-related brain potentials* or *ERPs*) to reveal changes in processing during reading. Several earlier studies have shown a particular wave pattern to be associated with semantic anomaly (Kutas and Hillyard 1980; Neville et al. 1986); for example, sentences like (9a) and (9b) elicit very different ERP patterns following their respective last words. (See chapter 7 for a related discussion.)

(9)a.   They spread the warm bread with butter.

  b.   They spread the warm bread with socks.

Garnsey, Tanenhaus, and Chapman (1988) used the ERP method to test cases like (10) and (11). The sentences were presented one word at a time, and ERP measures were taken after each word. The sentences in (11), which represent the question forms for those in (10), have a moved element in their structure (the noun introduced by *which*) that must be linked to its original site (the trace *t* in the examples) in order that the sentence be interpreted.

(10)a.   The children read the books in class.

  b.   *The children read the food in class.

  c.   The children read about the books in class.

  d.   The children read about the food in class.

(11)a.   Which books did the children read (*t*) in class?

  b.   *Which food did the children read (*t*) in class?

  c.   Which books did the children read about (*t*) in class?

  d.   Which food did the children read about (*t*) in class?

Garnsey, Tanenhaus, and Chapman found that the anomaly response was triggered by the NP following the main verb in sentences like (10b), but not for the other versions of (10). This is just what the earlier work on anomaly would indicate. The interesting result is that they also observed such a response for both (11b) and (11d) at the point immediately following the main verb. This indicates two things. First, it is evidence that the implicit elements (traces) that mark the sites of moved NPs and that permit the structural roles assigned by verbs and prepositions to be associated with the moved phrases are recovered during real-time language processing. Second, the fact that the anomalous (11b) and the nonanomalous (11d) showed the same ERP patterns immediately following the verb is evidence that the sentence-initial NP was inserted at the first location permitted by the syntax, in spite of the fact that the semantics of that verb and the NP in the introductory *which*-phrase are incompatible. If the parser were truly driven by interpretive possibilities in its initial syntactic assignments, such an anomaly response should be avoided—for instance, by waiting for definite indications that a preposition is not present to carry the NP as an argument. The anomaly response suggests that the initial assignments of the potential object NP role by the parser are blind to the semantic force of the association.

6.4   Mechanisms of Interaction

We turn now to a set of experiments that are interrelated in an informative way. These suggest some boundary conditions on ways in which interpretive constraints are brought to bear in parsing, and in so doing raise again the issue of parallel processing. We will begin with an experiment that makes an initially strong case for interaction of semantic and syntactic processes.

6.4.1   The "Landing Planes" Study

A significant and productive challenge to the view that discourse-level interpretation does not directly influence parsing operations was provided in an experiment by Tyler and Marslen-Wilson (1977). Their experiment sought to test whether the semantic interpretation of the first clause of a sentence could influence the syntactic analysis of its second clause. The syntactic feature they focused on was number agreement between NP and verb.

Sentence fragments, constructed in pairs like (12) and (13), were auditorily presented. At the point of the ellipsis, a visual target was presented, which subjects were required to pronounce aloud as quickly as possible. The target words were IS and ARE, both of which are grammatically acceptable continuations for both pair members; however, one (ARE) is intuitively preferred as the continuation for (a) and the other (IS) is preferred for (b).

(12)a.   If you walk too near the runway, landing planes . . . (ARE/IS)

   b.   If you are trained as a pilot, landing planes . . . (IS/ARE)

(13)a.   As they soar gracefully over the city, flying kites . . . (ARE/IS)

   b.   If the winds are too powerful, flying kites . . . (IS/ARE)

Task performance was affected by the preference pattern: ARE was pronounced faster after (a) versions of the sentence than after (b) versions.

Response times were in the 500-millisecond range, indicating that the bias provided by the initial clause had immediately determined which of two analyses of the NP was assigned: analysis as (14) or as (15):

(14)   [[Adj: landing][Head Noun: planes] NP_{plural}]

(15)   [[Gerund: landing][Noun: planes] $NP_{singular}$]

The application of number agreement then dictated verb form. When the target was congruent with that form, performance was faster than when it was incongruent. If this interpretation of the outcome were the only viable account, it would provide clear evidence for the penetration of general interpretive constraints (for example, effects of the plausible view that if you are walking around on the ground, it is unlikely that you are at the same time landing a plane) into analyses of the (putatively syntactic) parser.

This would pose a serious puzzle, given other evidence that such inferential constraints have their influence after the generation of syntactic representations for sentences. Moreover, it is difficult to see what interpretive features of the biasing clauses should be linked, in the general case, to the postulation of either an AdjN or a GerundN analysis. This, and the desire to have an account that covers all the reliable experimental results, suggests that we seek an alternative interpretation. Two possibilities present themselves.

6.4.2   Parallel Processing

The first possibility to consider is parallelism within the parsing system: both syntactic analyses are constructed, with subsequent filtering by syntactic and/or interpretive constraints. This is a strong version of the claim raised at the end of section 6.1.1, and it is one that preserves the autonomy of the parser. There is no a priori reason to exclude parallelism in the parsing system, although the general view in the past has been that parallelism is not a general feature of cognitive processing. That view has been changing, and proposals for parallelism have been made for several cognitive areas, including language (see Berwick and Weinberg 1984), for which it was formerly not a well-explored option.

Frazier and Rayner (1982) report evidence from eye-movement studies that is helpful here. They suggest that grammatical category ambiguities (words whose environment is compatible with more than a single assignment to a class: N, V, Adj) are not resolved immediately, as, for example, the lexical ambiguities referred to in section 6.1.2 seem to be. Rather, they argue, the resolution of categorial ambiguities is delayed until disambiguating material is encountered. Their tests involved the structures used by Tyler and Marslen-Wilson, as well as other structures. They found a pattern of fixation times that they interpreted as indicating a delayed assignment of category. Shorter fixation times (relative to unambiguous controls) were observed for ambiguous items (such as *landing* in *landing planes*) and longer fixation times at the disambiguating area (*is* or *are*). The latter fixation was longer for both terms of the ambiguity—an effect for only one term would indicate an initial selection process. Though Frazier and Rayner argue for delay rather than parallelism, their findings do reinforce the idea that the locus of effect in the "landing planes" experiment is after the ambiguous structure has been marked. That is, the parser is not antecedently biased to one analysis but rather is biased to a particular selection between alternatives, both of which must be considered, even if both are not fully computed.

6.4.3   The Pronoun Bias Effect

A second account of the effects in Tyler and Marslen-Wilson's experiment involves an alternative characterization of the bias source. It is likely that an important factor in these bias effects is a stimulus feature that was correlated with the experimental condition designed to produce a plural bias. That factor, however, does not depend on the actual interpretation of the biasing clause. Almost all the items in the plural bias condition contained the plural pronoun *they* (as in (13)). Whatever NP is coindexed with *they* will inherit its number feature, thus requiring the selection of *are*. The first candidate NP that could be so indexed was, in fact, the ambiguous AdjN/GerundN sequence that preceded the naming targets. If there were a processing strategy to take the first encountered NP for coindexation with the unbound pronoun, it would yield the observed bias—but not necessarily because general interpretive processes guide parsing decisions. Such a strategy might be language-specific or not, depending upon the kinds of influences that could trigger or block it.

Cowart and Cairns (1987) noted these possibilities and carried out a series of experiments to evaluate them. They first established the existence of a "pronoun bias" by contrasting naming latencies for *is* and *are* following plural lexical NPs with those following the plural pronoun *they*, as in (16):

(16) $\begin{cases} \text{As \textit{the birds} soar gracefully above the field,} \\ \text{As \textit{they} soar gracefully above the field,} \end{cases}$ flying kites ...

Reaction times for the two types of target were the same for the lexical NPs but showed a strong bias in the pronoun condition: times for the *is* targets were slowed down, indicating an interference effect with a normally proceeding process rather than facilitation of an incomplete one.

Cowart and Cairns then investigated constraints on the application of the coreference assignment strategy. If it is part of general interpretive processes, interpretive factors should modify it; if it is a restricted structural process, such factors should not be effective. They therefore tested syntactic (as in (17)) and semantic/pragmatic (as in (18)) blocking of the pronoun bias:

(17) $\begin{cases} \text{If they want to save money,} \\ \text{If they want to believe that} \end{cases}$ visiting uncles ...

(18) $\begin{cases} \text{Even though they use very little oil} \\ \text{Even though they eat very little oil} \end{cases}$ frying eggs ...

In (17) the phrasal configuration should block coreference if syntax is effective; in (18) the implausibility of making *eggs* the subject of *eat* should block coreference if semantic and pragmatic factors are effective. In fact, the pronoun bias was eliminated in the syntactic blocking cases like (17) but continued to operate for the semantic blocking cases like (18). This pattern clearly favors assignment of the mechanism to the language module.

The insensitivity of the pronoun bias effect to semantic influence indirectly increases the attractiveness of the parallel account. That account permits us to rationalize the rapid influence of contextual constraint on performance in the naming task and at the same time to preserve the capacity of the system to pursue syntactic analyses that have no immediate interpretive support. We have striking evidence from experiments like those of section 6.2.2 and from the pronoun bias experiment that even semantically aberrant analyses are, at least momentarily, entertained. The use of semantic and pragmatic constraint to resolve ambiguity must be done in a way that preserves the system's flexibility at lower levels of analysis. The limited parallelism proposal is one way to do this. In the following section we will examine that proposal in a different context.

6.5   Verb Structure and Parsing Operations

One of the richest areas of investigation of sentence processing—richest in controversy, richest in insight and pleasing potential solutions to complex issues—has to do with verbs. This is not surprising given the central role that verb structure plays in sentence organization. Recall the discussion in chapter 1 of verb subcategorization and thematic role assignments controlled by specific verbs—which verbs a sentence has, and in what positions, provides the structural matrix within which other phrasal elements are set. Accordingly, many studies of sentence processing have addressed the question of when and in what ways the information associated with specific verbs or verb classes is brought to bear on parsing decisions.

6.5.1   Transitive Verbs and Sentence Complements

Several such studies concern differences between simple transitive verbs like *solve* that take an NP—but not a sentence—in object position and verbs like *know* that may take either an NP or a sentence as complement. These studies raise interesting problems in evaluating the hypothesis of parallelism or delay for syntactic processing decisions, as compared with a hypothesis of immediate commitment, like that of minimal attachment.

Some early experimental findings indicated processing differences between these verb types. For example, using the RSVP procedure, Holmes and Forster (1972) found significant differences in accuracy of report for sentences differing only in verb type: those with simple transitive verbs were better reported than those with sentence complement verbs. A similar result was reported by Chodorow (1979). He used speech presented at much higher than normal rates (using techniques that sample the speech signal, then resynthesize it in intelligible but temporally abbreviated form) to increase auditory processing difficulty—in somewhat the way that RSVP affects visual presentation. In sentence pairs like (19a) and (19b), more errors were made following the sentence complement verbs than following the simple complement verbs (see also Chodorow, Slutsky, and Loring 1988).

(19)a.   The helicopter located the wreckage in the ravine.

   b.   The helicopter discovered the wreckage in the ravine.

Notice that the sentences in (19) contrast cases with very similar interpretations—and their syntactic structures are the same. They differ in the *potential* structures for the verbs. Several experimental measures have indicated an increased processing load in simple sentences at points following the sentence complement taking verbs. What causes that increase?

Two possibilities suggest themselves. One is that when two structural options are associated with a verb, sentence analysis processes either pursue both or delay structural commitment until the postverb context determines a path (a "look ahead" procedure; see Marcus 1980); the extra processing occasioned by multiple paths or delay accounts for poorer performance. A second possibility assumes that the *preferred* analysis path for the sentence complement verbs is the sentence complement analysis; that option is chosen and then must be revised when a simple NP structure is encountered (a "garden path" account). Some additional evidence suggests a choice between these options. Two types of findings are relevant.

6.5.2   Minimal Attachment

Frazier has argued for the application of the minimal attachment principle to the choice of a structural path following verbs like *discover*. Minimal attachment favors the simple NP object analysis. As evidence, Frazier and Rayner (1982) report reprocessing effects for eye-movement measures at the final VP in sentences like (20):

(20)   Sally found out the answer to the difficult physics problem was in book.

This result fits the minimal attachment principle, which calls for immediate assignment of a single phrasal analysis, with recomputation to cope with any errors. In this experiment the analysis that yields reprocessing is the sentence complement analysis, and that is the nonminimal one.

But this result paints us into a theoretical corner. It dictates the opposite garden path to the one considered in section 6.5.1, and that does not suit the experimental contrast between (19a) and (19b). To generate a garden path that will explain that contrast requires a bias to take the sentence complement path, and that directly contradicts the minimal attachment principle. Minimal attachment cannot help us with an explanation of the differences between (19a) and (19b). If it applies, both sentences receive the same, correct analysis.

This pair of findings shows that a simple preference account—whether preference for the sentence complement reading or preference for the simple NP—cannot be correct. If the sentence complement bias were correct, Frazier and Rayner's sentences, which do have sentence complement readings, should not have shown a recomputation effect. But a reverse simple preference account, which assumes a simple NP analysis, also cannot be correct. If it were, there would be no account of Chodorow's findings. Neither simple preference account will work for both results.

6.5.3   The Parallel Processing Option

How can we reconcile the results of these two sets of experiments? If we assume that the syntactic computation is parallel, we can assimilate both findings. The more complex verb yields more errors and more reading time because more computational paths must be represented and evaluated, hence the difference between (19a) and (19b). To account for the reprocessing effects in sentences like (20), we must assume that the parallelism is limited, sustained only briefly beyond the NP in object position, with a default to the minimal attachment analysis.

There is some evidence compatible with such bounds on the hypothesized parallelism. Frazier and Rayner (1982) varied the length of the stretch intervening between the main verb and the disambiguating region (compare *Sally knew the answer was in the book* with example (20)); the evidence for reprocessing effects was attributable to the longer condition, not the shorter one. On these grounds, it seems likely that if positive evidence of the presence of an embedded sentence is not encountered by a word or two past the head noun of the NP whose attachment is unfixed, the sentence complement path is abandoned.

There are other reasons to take this hypothesis seriously, coming from additional experimental evidence. Gorrell (1988) argues for a parallel account of processing for these structures (see also Kurtzman 1985). Gorrell tested at the point immediately following the NP whose attachment is ambiguous (for example, after *the wreckage* in (19b) or *the answer* in (20)). He added another verb type to the comparison as well: those that require the sentence complement analysis (for example, *realize*). He compared all three verbs: simple (*locate*), ambiguous (*discover*), and complement (*realize*) in terms of relative acceptability of a verb as a sentence continuation at that point. He found that the ambiguous verbs patterned with the unambiguous complement verbs rather than with the unambiguous simple verbs. The minimal attachment preference does not square with such an outcome. Gorrell argues that both paths are available at the point of evaluation.

Still another virtue of the parallel account is that it readily accommodates variations in the structural preferences that may be associated with particular verbs. So far we have been talking about the contrast in verb types in absolute terms—those that permit both sentence complement and simple transitive readings versus those that do not permit the sentence complement structure at all. But there are proposals (Ford, Bresnan, and Kaplan 1982; Holmes 1987) for associating priorities of processing paths with each verb's entry in the lexicon; those priorities reflect the frequency of exercise of the (sometimes several) structural options possible for a given verb. Such preferences might be applied at each choice point, with garden path consequences distributed accordingly, rather than by absolute structural possibility and minimal attachment. But preference biases might equally well be associated with the ordering of default choices when no decisive evidence appears within the window of the sustainable parallelism.

These discussions of processing performances associated with verb structures are meant to suggest the nature of argument and some of the possible hypotheses that must be addressed in the study of human parsing systems. The experiments reviewed sample from a larger range of relevant study, and the descriptions that can be given here do not represent many complex details of experimental design that must be evaluated in deciding how to fit any given finding into the mosaic of available results in the most parsimonious and productive way. Moreover, we have ignored other processing issues that might be appealed to in a full account of the way in which information associated with verbs must be incorporated in the procedures that permit the comprehension system to associate the correct phrasal analysis with a sentence and to do so with the fluency and accuracy that is characteristic of normal human performance. To explore these areas further, see the Suggestions for Further Reading.

6.6   Overview for Comprehension Studies

As orienting overview, let us consider the strong version of the modular thesis for language-processing systems proposed by Forster (1979), which is shown in figure 6.2. On this model, processing components interact only via their outputs. Their internal states are not directly affected either by other language modules or, in particular, by general world knowledge.

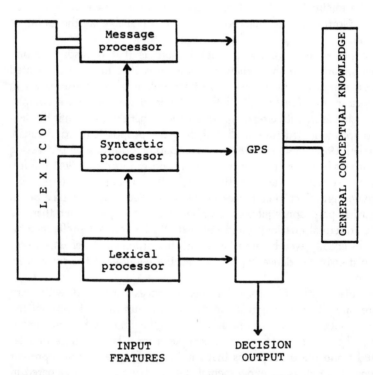

Figure 6.2
A modular language-processing system for language comprehension. From Forster 1979.

Thus, two aspects of modular process are represented: that between language and nonlanguage processes, and that internal to the language system.

The evidence we have reviewed indicates that the processes responsible for the assignment of simple phrasal structure are not directly influenced by semantic/pragmatic factors. However, it must be stressed that the evidence reviewed in sections 6.1 and 6.4 requires mechanisms that project constraints at several levels of analysis simultaneously. It is difficult to see how the very rapid resolution of lexical and structural ambiguities could otherwise be achieved. In order to permit the necessary application of interpretive constraints, some parallelism between syntactic and semantic processes seems essential.

Consider, for example, Forster's (1979) suggestion that semantically relevant properties of the lexical content of a sentence may be processed in parallel with their syntactic properties to provide a check on syntactic analysis, or Rayner, Carlson, and Frazier's (1983) suggestion that thematic relations associated with the heads of phrases may be evaluated for their plausible construals and used to filter the output of the parser. One way to achieve such effects might be to permit the GPS (General Problem Solver) system in figure 6.2 to provide input to Message-level processing. Given the lexical input, general knowledge of plausible possibility could be applied via thematic structures to construct a message in much the way that normal language production mechanisms might do, with the evolving representation serving as a test for the evaluation of the syntactically driven parser's products.

The principal question of modularity that we have examined concerns the degree to which parsing procedures are insulated from general inferential mechanisms. But figure 6.2 also contains a more detailed claim: modular boundaries within the language processor are indicated. Some reasons to separate lexical and sentence processes were given in chapter 5. Evidence reviewed there suggested that sentence context influences word recognition at a postaccess stage. Other relevant findings may be cited.

First is the evidence that syntactic constraint does not block the access of lexical entries (Prather and Swinney 1977; Seidenberg et al. 1982). Thus, where the terms of an ambiguity come from distinct grammatical categories (*he rose* versus *the rose; she tires* versus *the tires*), and the syntactic environment selects one, both senses are nonetheless accessed, as indexed by cross-modal priming measures.

Second, in chapter 4, evidence for a *nonmodular* relation between phonetic analysis and lexical status was cited. Recall that the phoneme restoration effect is influenced by lexical structure: phoneme restoration is more likely for sound deletions from real words than from nonwords. Work by Samuel (1981) indicates that this is a perceptual effect and not a bias effect. However, in the same experimental series Samuel also tested for effects of *sentence*-level bias on phoneme restoration. There was indeed an influence on performance, but it was identified as a postperceptual bias effect. (See also Conine 1987.)

Thus, several lines of evidence lead to something like the outline of relations among processors in figure 6.2. It represents a working hypothesis about processors, most of whose internal structure remains to be determined. Some indication of the kind of detail we need was given in section 6.5. As more becomes known about these mechanisms, the questions that can be put about their possible interdependencies will be far more sharply drawn. Identifying the sorts of constraints on interaction that we have been discussing is a helpful first step in the formulation of proposals for the much more sophisticated characterizations of mechanism that will be required for an adequate theory of human language performance.

6.7   Language Production Processes

Questions about lexical retrieval and the integration of syntactic form are central to the study of real-time language production processes, just as they are for the study of comprehension processes. We will consider some representative findings in the production area to increase the generality of our theoretical analysis and test the robustness of conclusions based on the study of language comprehension. The finding of modular processing structure in comprehension systems suggests the outcome for language production study—it would be remarkable if the two major performance systems diverged in so fundamental a respect. And this, in fact, is the general tenor of the results: similar architectural constraints are found in both cases.

By way of preliminary assumption, we will talk of a speaker's particular communicative intention as the input to the production system; we will refer to that input as a *message* and the processes associated with it as the *Message level*. Our focus is on the operations that map from messages to instructions that will correctly guide the articulatory system.

6.7.1   The Kinds of Data

Compared to work on comprehension, the study of language production has been less experimentally and more observationally oriented for most of its history. This is partly because the input conditions (message structure) cannot be controlled with the directness possible in comprehension study, and partly because of a compensating virtue—one can directly observe the output of the system, as one cannot for comprehension. The work therefore has emphasized analysis of speech errors, hesitations, and correction patterns in speech. There has been more experimental activity in recent years, however, and many of the hypotheses derived from the observational work have been put to that sort of test. We will concentrate on observations and arguments from the speech error literature; a guide to related experimental findings is given in the Suggestions for Further Reading.

The speech errors we will consider are those from the spontaneous speech of normal speakers. "Normal speech" is, of course, not pristinely grammatical and fluent. Nonfluencies, misarticulations, and various infelicities of expression are fairly common in normal conversational interchanges. These arise in a number of ways—changes of mind, interruptions, haste—and all are in some general sense "errors." But references to "speech errors" in the study of language production have a more restricted sense than this. Analysis focuses on those errors in which the specific target of utterance is quite clear, but the speaker misorders the elements or substitutes some other element for an intended one. Examples (21)–(23) give some representative cases:

(21) Substitutions

    a. "Sue keeps food in her *vesk*." (d)

    b. "Why d'you eat that with white *wed* anyway?" (bread)

    c. "I think my *foot* just ran over it." (tire)

    d. "She must be a very *morbid* lady." (married)

(22) Shifts

    a. "Keep you cotton-pickin' hands off my weet *speas*." (sweet peas)

    b. "He's hit the fastball*ing* hard into ... right field." (he's hitting the fastball hard)

    c. "... with our hand on our head*s*, we'll ..." (hands on our head)

    d. "Who did you meet *else* there?" (who else)

(23) Exchanges

    a. "... got a lot of po*ns* and pa*ts* to wash." (pots and pans)

    b. "Jeez, he's *Wittle Wed Liding-hood*." (Little Red Ridinghood)

    c. "We'll sit around the *song* and sing *fires*." (fire and sing songs)

    d. "That *kid's toy* makes a great *mouse*." (mouse makes a great kid's toy)

Though not frequent with respect to the base rate of correct performance, these and similar types of error are nonetheless common enough events: if you begin to listen for them carefully, you will observe a few every day.

The background assumption is that constraints on the distribution of such errors reflect the structure of the real-time processing system for language production. We will concentrate on two general classes of error: word substitution errors, because they indicate lexical selection processes, and movement errors, such as sound and word exchanges, because they are particularly relevant to inferences about phrasal-level processes.

6.7.2   Lexical Retrieval in Production

The production problem addressed here is analogous to the comprehension problem treated in chapter 5: What mechanisms support the retrieval of specific words from a speaker's lexicon during normal, continuous speaking? In this case the governing representation is an aspect of meaning derived from the communicative intention of a speaker rather than the sensory representation for an acoustic or visual language stimulus. We want to know how the production retrieval system is organized and how its processes relate to phrasal construction.

Word substitution errors have a prima facie relevance to this process, and their regularities provide a starting point for theory development. To study word retrieval processes, however, we must focus on those cases in which we are reasonably confident that a lexical representation is the effective one. Therefore, we must take care to exclude ambiguous cases from our analyses (like the one in (21b), in which it is very likely that a sound error rather than an error in word selection processes has occurred). If we make this and some similarly motivated exclusions (see Garrett 1988), we find that the clear cases of word substitution fall into two broad classes: errors like (21c) and (24) that seem to have some sort of meaning relation between target and intrusion, and errors like (21d) and (25) that seem to have a form relation.

(24)   *finger* for *toe*; *sword* for *arrow*; *walk* for *run*

(25)   *guest* for *goat*; *mushroom* for *mustache*; *envelope* for *elephant*

The influences on these errors show a striking complementarity: Those with a clear meaning relation show few similarities of form, and those with a strong form relation show few similarities of meaning. Errors that display both meaning and form similarity do occur (see (26)), but they are not a dominant error type.

(26)   *read* for *write*; *hair* for *head*; *lobster* for *oyster*

This outcome is both surprising and significant. Error processes should be opportunistic—they should highlight properties of the system conducive to inappropriate interactions among the elements of the planning process. If the system in which lexical retrieval processes take place were one in which representations of form and meaning function simultaneously, then cases in which both kinds of similarity are present should produce the most error. On the other hand, if representations of form and meaning are effective at different points in the process of sentence construction, the dissociation observed in these errors would be understandable.

The separation of meaning- and form-based processes has been called the *two-step lexical retrieval* hypothesis for language production. (Other interpretations of the apparent separation of meaning and form have been argued for—see the Suggestions for Further Reading.) On the two-step hypothesis, the calculation of a meaning description leads to the recovery of a lexically specific record that does not itself contain information about word form. An error made at this point in the process produces a meaning-related lexical substitution. Word form information must be retrieved in a separate step, using an address stored with the meaning representation—a "linking address" from word meaning to word form. An error made at this point results in a form-related word substitution. This will be an item nearby in the similarity space defined by the form parameters that organize the space and govern retrieval from it.

The similarities between target and intrusion words for form-based errors provide hypotheses about retrieval parameters at this processing stage. Fay and Cutler (1977) note that segmental similarity is greatest at word onset and declines with each succeeding segment; stress position and length in syllables are significantly similar as well. Later work (Hurford 1981; Cutler and Fay 1982) indicates that although form similarity is greatest at the beginnings of target/intrusion pairs, overall segmental similarity is also a factor.

This pattern for word substitutions is reinforced by observations of a related phenomenon, tip-of-the-tongue states. These are occasions, familiar to everyone, when we know a word (often a name) perfectly well but cannot recover it in the normal way. Investigations of this problem (see, for example, Brown and McNeill 1966) show that the lost word and abortive targets (words we recover in an attempt to find the errant word but know immediately are wrong) are often related in the same way as target/intrusion pairs in form-based word substitutions. Moreover, if people in such a state are asked to guess what they can about the target word, they recover information about initial segments, stress, and length better than other aspects of word form.

A dissociation of meaning and form and the particular features of word form that are prominent appear to be generally characteristic of lexical processing. The retrieval process for word forms in language production is quite similar to that for the comprehension system, a fact that led Fay and Cutler to propose that the same word form inventory was, in fact, used for both processes. Moreover, these properties of normal word retrieval are strongly reflected in the patterns of certain aphasic language disturbances (see the Suggestions for Further Reading).

6.7.3   Phrasal Construction

What can we say of the constructive processes that intervene between message (M) construction and articulatory programming? Various evidence indicates at least three levels of processing: one that provides detailed phonetic information, one that provides surface syntactic and prosodic information as well as more abstract word form information, and one that provides a phonologically uninterpreted syntactic representation. Two features of speech errors support this claim: (1) accommodation of error elements to error-induced environments, and (2) the existence of distinct classes of movement errors, defined by an association of error element types (word, morpheme, sound) with specific phrasal and categorial constraints on error.

The phenomenon of *accommodation* in speech errors (Fromkin 1971; Bierwisch 1971) gives one clear indication that multiple levels of processing intervene between M and articulatory control. Errors like those in (27) show that regular morphological and phonological processes must apply *after* the processing stage that gives rise to errors that mislocate sound elements.

(27)a.   "an angwage lacquisition device" (a language acquisition device); *a/an* alternation

   b.   "... even the best team losts." (even the best teams lost); [z] changes to [s]

This dictates *two* processing levels at which aspects of the sound structure of sentences are represented: one providing abstract segmental and lexical structure (hereafter called *Positional* or *P*) and one that fixes detailed phonetic properties (hereafter called *Phonetic*).

Knowing that one must distinguish levels is a first step. A second is to associate more detailed representational and computational claims with each such level. Several properties of sound exchange errors (like those in (23a,b)) suggest important features of the representations being constructed at *P*. First, there are strong phonological similarities between the interacting sound elements themselves and between the immediate segmental and syllabic environments of the exchanged elements (Fromkin 1971; MacKay 1969; Meringer 1908). This reinforces the claim that abstract phonological information is present (recall that the accommodation evidence forces the conclusion that *phonetic* detail comes after the error locus). Second, the majority of such errors occur within phrases, the source syllables are metrically similar, and the word with primary phrasal stress is more often involved than chance would predict (Boomer and Laver 1968; Nooteboom 1969; Garrett 1975). This tells us that the level at which these processing errors occur is constrained by phrasal boundaries, and that at least the surface constituent structure needed to represent major phrasal stress is present.

We now turn to the case for a third processing level (prior to *P*), based on differences between sound exchange and word exchange errors. Word exchanges (like (23c,d)) take place predominantly *between* phrases rather than within phrases, occur almost exclusively for words of corresponding grammatical category, and frequently span several intervening words (Fromkin 1971; Bierwisch 1971; Garrett 1975). Sound exchanges are primarily phrase-internal, do not show a category constraint, and usually span only a word or two. Though some of these constraints covary, there is evidence that they are independently defensible (Garrett 1980). An additional and important point is the marked difference in the degree of phonological involvement for the two error classes: the word exchanges show, at best, rather weak evidence of such influence (see Dell and Reich 1981).

These differences, and some others to be discussed momentarily, suggest a level of processing distinct from *P* at which the syntactic relations among words, but not their phonological representations, are calculated; we will refer to this as the *Functional* or *F* level. It is a multiphrasal level (as compared with the single-phrase processes implicated in sound errors), probably with a two-clause limit; word exchanges rarely involve elements of nonadjacent clauses.

Another salient feature of the *F* level concerns the role of meaning relations: word exchanges are not constrained by the kind of similarities expressed in meaning-related word substitutions. If the meaning of the expressions constructed at this point were being used to directly support processing operations, meaning similarity might well be expected to influence the incidence of error. That it does not suggests that constructive algorithms at the *F* level do not depend on the interpretive value of the elements being manipulated.

These patterns and a number of related findings may be summarized as a proposal for the successive assignment of lexical content to planning frames for phrasal structures as outlined in figure 6.3. There is a good fit between the *independently motivated* two-step lexical retrieval hypothesis we considered in section 6.7.2 and the distinction between syntactic and phonological levels of phrasal integration (*F* and *P* in figure 6.3). The meaning-based word substitutions may be associated with the selection of lexical content for *F*-level structures, and the form-based substitutions with the selection of lexical forms needed for the development of *P*-level structures. Thus, there is a natural articulation of the findings that derive from

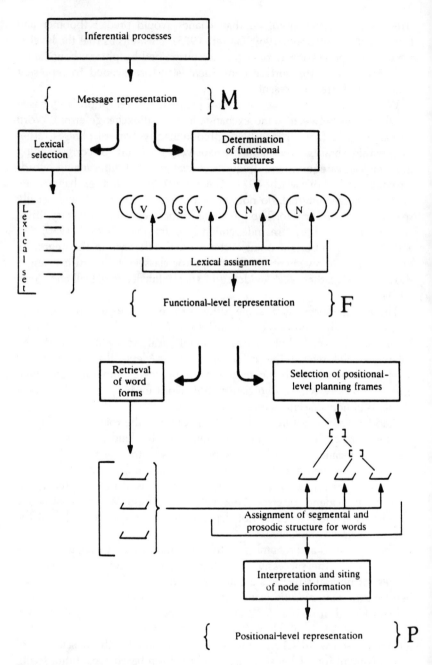

Figure 6.3
Successive assignment of lexical content to phrasal structures. From Garrett 1984.

word substitution errors on the one hand, and word and sound movement errors on the other.

6.7.4   Open and Closed Class Vocabularies

Figure 6.3 may be used to express another interesting claim, namely, that different processes underlie the recovery and phonological interpretation of *open* and *closed* class words. This contrast is roughly coextensive with that between major and minor grammatical categories, often also called "content" and "function" words. The distinction has a long history in psychology, with links to developmental processes (Brown 1973; Gleitman and Wanner 1982) and language disorders (see chapter 7), as well as a suggestive relation to parsing processes (Thorne, Bratley, and Dewar 1968; Marcus 1982). There have been various efforts to sharpen this distinction in terms of its computational role in language production and language comprehension. The production processes outlined here provide an illustration.

In section 6.7.3 discussion of error processes was restricted to open class elements—nouns, verbs, adjectives. This is not by chance. With a few noteworthy exceptions, these are the classes that participate in word or sound exchanges and word substitutions. Closed class elements, both bound and free, rarely participate in sound exchange errors, though they do appear in other types of error. That constraint is represented in figure 6.3 by identifying the elements that contribute to sound movement and word movement exchange errors with the lexical lists that are mapped into F and P frameworks. Closed class elements are not on the lexical list and are instead assumed to be features of the frames. If exchange arises as a function of misassignment of list members, or segmental features of list members, to planning frames of F or P, elements of the planning frames should not exchange—and this is the empirical observation. An error type that *is* compatible with closed class involvement on this view is shifts (22b–d). These may be described as single element mislocations that arise in the process of mapping features of the frames into sites in the terminal string. And, indeed, closed class elements are prominent factors in such errors.

On this hypothesis, the closed and open class elements have a different retrieval history. Open class elements are retrieved and phonologically specified as outlined section in 6.7.2. But closed class elements would be retrieved by association with a role in F or P representations and their form specified there or at the *Phonetic* level. The different processes thus suggested are compatible with a number of quite independent observations from normal and disordered language performance. Some of these are discussed in chapter 7.

6.7.5   Parallelism in Production

In many respects, the investigation of production and comprehension systems has had similar outcomes with respect to claims for modular processing. Brief further comment is in order concerning this point.

First is the issue of parallelism, raised earlier in discussion of comprehension systems. It is clear that similar plausibility attaches to the role of parallel processes in production. Five levels of processing activity were identified (*M, F, P, Phonetic, Motor*). These are simultaneously active and have different structural scope (hence potentially different time factors) associated with their activity. *M*-level processes encompass structure that is only roughly correlated with the temporal ordering of output elements, for example, and the *F* level represents multiclausal structures, only some portion of which is in the focus of the detailed planning activity for *P*-level structures. A more acute issue of parallelism, of course, is whether more than a single set of structures is computed as a possible realization of a given *M*-level representation. There is good reason to believe this happens, both because of the existence of another class of speech errors (blends; for discussion, see Butterworth 1982) and because of our need to monitor and adjust our production during the course of sentence planning. We routinely shape our utterance form not only to be responsive to pure semantic intent, so to speak, but also to vary the style and force of our remarks in order to produce particular effects on our listeners. The ability to do that with the speed and flexibility we normally exhibit suggests the availability of alternative utterance forms from which we "filter" the ones most apposite to our current intent. Whether this represents a true parallelism or a pseudoparallelism is a matter that we cannot settle on current evidence. Suffice it to say that there is good reason to pursue the matter.

Finally, we should recall the suggestion made in section 6.6, that we might accommodate the effects of interpretive constraint on comprehension processes by incorporating something like the message processor as the way to generate a representation for comparison with the products of the parsing system. The complementary point is that the production system uses the comprehension system to monitor its own products. We do listen to what we say ourselves, and we do this not only to adjust the form of our utterance more closely to our communicative objectives but also to monitor for error in the operation of the systems that generate spoken form. In the relations thus suggested between comprehension and production, each system provides an error-checking mechanism for the other. Viewed in this way, the two are closely linked in their functions, and the fact of their similar design seems more inevitable than surprising.

6.8   Sentence Processing: The State of the Art

We have considered representative findings from studies of language comprehension and language production. These suggest the general structure of the two systems and some ways in which that structure connects to a modular theory of mind. The results reviewed invite more detailed inquiry along several lines.

Studies of real-time syntactic processing reflect a concern for the precise temporal locus and structural conditions on the assignment of specific features of sentence form. We now understand a number of the conditions that govern the real-time resolution of lexical and phrasal ambiguities, recovery of coreferential NP expressions in relative clauses, assignment of verb subcategorization constraints, and interpretation of pronouns and related anaphoric elements. More generally, there has been and continues to be a productive controversy over the role of interpretive constraints in real-time parsing decisions. The aim is to discover the point at which the meaning of a word, phrase, or sentence can have an influence on the phrasal analysis of what we are hearing or reading. That controversy has given rise to a systematic effort to establish the range of and limits on the interaction between semantic/pragmatic structures in discourse and the procedures that effect the sorts of specific parsing assignments just mentioned. These questions are under active investigation, but it is quite clear that some truth attaches to both sides—there are unquestionably some syntactic processes that are indifferent to the presence of semantic constraint, and indubitably some processes susceptible of a pristine syntactic description that nonetheless reflect semantic influences. Establishing the boundaries of these processing classes will contribute greatly to our understanding of the architecture of linguistic systems in particular and cognitive systems in general.

The theoretical structure that has begun to emerge in the domain of language production reflects the same general organizational features as that of comprehension theories. A major area of experimental elaboration in the immediate future will be the attempt to evaluate the parallels in these two major processing domains and to determine the extent to which the two performance systems rely upon common computational resources and, possibly, common underlying neural systems.

The research conclusions for the study of real-time language processes exemplify a general change in perspective on cognitive systems that has begun to emerge. Qualitatively, the change has been to establish the notion of modularity in mental processes as a presupposed general condition. The question at present is not whether significant modular structure exists for cognitive systems (namely, those that deal in informational structures more abstract than motor and sensory representations); rather, the question is where the boundaries are to be drawn. What is the inventory of modular systems and how do they interact? What are the conditions that foster the development of modular processing systems and what exceptions to that general condition exist?

For language, the broad-scale modular contrast is between language-specific function and general background knowledge. The evidence for some such division is rather clear. Of acute interest for the immediate future will be attempts (1) to draw the currently rough line between the two domains more finely and (2) to explore the thesis of modular structure within the domain of language itself (What relations hold among systems for processing phonological, morphological, syntactic, logical, and thematic structures?) and within the general cognitive domain (What is the "parliament of expert systems?").

Suggestions for Further Reading

An excellent starting point for broadening one's historical appreciation of psycholinguistic research beyond the account given in section 6.2.3 is Miller 1951, written within the behaviorist tradition of the 1940s and 1950s. Miller was also instrumental in the rebirth of psycholinguistics that followed the "Chomskyan revolution" in linguistics. Seminal papers that reflected the new interaction between psychological and linguistic theorizing include Miller and Chomsky 1963. This style of theorizing was also evident in Lenneberg 1967, an influential monograph devoted to the biological basis of language use and acquisition. Fodor, Bever, and Garrett 1974 provides an overview and discussion of much of that initial psycholinguistic research that was prompted by the quest for a linguistically inspired psychological theory of language use.

In section 6.1 and indeed throughout the chapter we argued that human language use approximates a real-time processor: by the time one reaches the end of a sentence (plus, perhaps, a small constant time factor), its structure has been determined, and if one checks at any point internal to a sentence, most of its structure has been worked out up to that point. Contemporary computational theory provides another way to use that kind of information. We can put boundary conditions on the kinds of processors that are candidates for human processing models by associating limits for processing times with properties of the grammars that generate sentences. You may wish to consult the discussion in chapters 1–3 of Berwick and Weinberg 1984 and references suggested there, for some insight into the way that structure and length affect the time required for parsing.

In section 6.4.3 we considered some aspects of the processes that determine coreference relations among the phrases of a sentence. That discussion implicated lexical, semantic, syntactic, and discourse factors in such assignments. Somehow the strategic and discourse factors must be coordinated with the syntactic constraints to produce the real-time solutions that people make. The examination of such processes is an active research area in language processing at present, and a number of interesting studies that bear on the role of interpretive and syntactic influences in this process are available. See Nash-Webber 1979 for a general treatment, and Dell, McKoon, and Ratcliff 1983, Bever and McElree 1988, and Cloitre and Bever, in press, for some recent experimental examples and references to other experimental work.

In section 6.5 we examined some issues concerning verb structure in parsing decisions. For further discussion of these issues, see Mitchell 1987 and Holmes 1987. In section 6.6 we considered the suggestion that thematic structure be used to apply interpretive constraints for the resolution of syntactic indeterminacy: thematic structure associated with the lexical content of the sentence would be used to construct test frames for the products of the parser. A number of versions of this basic notion are possible, and in addition to the references given in section 6.6, relevant discussion can be found in Frazier 1987, Stowe, in press, and Tanenhaus and Carlson, in press.

In section 6.7 we considered language production research from the perspective of speech error analysis. For some important experimental studies of the language production process, see Bock 1986, 1987, in press. In particular, Bock addresses the role of thematic structure in what we have called F-level processes, and she reports a number of experimental findings that evaluate semantic and phonological factors in the selection of phrasal planning frames.

The account of word retrieval and phrasal planning in language production presented in section 6.7 made a strong case for segregation of form and meaning processes. It is important to note that some investigators have expressed reservations about the absoluteness of that separation. Dell and Reich (1981) and Stemberger (1985) have reported evidence of "form contamination" of meaning-dependent errors—specifically, that the correspondence of target and intrusion in meaning-related substitutions at the first segment position exceeds estimates of chance convergence. This may indicate that that similarity plays some facilitatory role in the occurrence of the error. Similarly, Dell and Reich have argued for the same form effect on F-level word exchanges. They have suggested that such effects might be accounted for by the representation of lexical structures in a network that permits some interaction among different levels of lexical structure. Dell has written extensively on different aspects of such a network lexicon and its bearing on error processes. See Dell 1986.

For discussion of the relation between normal lexical processing and some features of aphasia, see Buckingham 1979, Garrett 1984, and Patterson, Marshall, and Coltheart 1985, as well as references in chapter 7.

For a comprehensive review and discussion of the entire range of language production study, see Levelt, in press. This work treats each of the relevant subareas and provides valuable background as well as up-to-date theoretical treatments.

Questions

6.1   One of the problems we considered was the need to deal with ambiguous input sequences. The possibility of different construals of the input sequence poses great problems for machine parsing systems but not, apparently, for people. It is instructive to make an approximation to one of the ambiguity problems faced by a speech analysis system using a written record.

Ask an unsuspecting friend to read three versions of the same short passage:

1. the passage itself,
2. the same passage, from which you have removed all the spaces between words,
3. the same passage, from which you have removed all the normal word spaces and into which you have randomly inserted new spaces between letters.

Time your friend's reading performance in all three conditions. See what effects practice has on performance time. You should make up your own materials, but the following examples illustrate some interesting possible variations:

(i)   Youreaseinreadingaseriesofwordsissomehowinfluencedina
seriouswaybyspacesmarkingoffeachoftheboundaries.

(ii)   Ifyoumakethelettertransitionsformostofthewordboundariesof
lowprobabilityorillegalthenpeoplehavelessdifficulty.

(iii)   I fyo uca nu seemp tysp ace ina nart ful lymis lead in gwa yit
seven wor se.

(iv)   Try decoding this sentence in one pass:
Man yt he me son gsf rommo vies oft he thir ties we rem ore
pop ul araft ert hey appe are dont el evi sion.

What might these examples suggest about the way in which listeners solve the speech segmentation problem?

6.2   As an exercise in lexical ambiguity, consider this sentence: *Light lights lightly light light lights* (Osgood 1971). It is indeed a sentence, with a quite acceptable sense (try to find some semantically equivalent forms to substitute at each slot; answer below). How do we find the distinct meanings associated with a given form? What are the options?

Pick a paragraph of a dozen or so sentences from a magazine or a newspaper story and count the number of ambiguous words you can find without major delay. You may tire of this game after a brief period, but you might last long enough to note that any machine solution will need access to more than the lexicon and the parser. Does this imply any conclusion about the notion of modularity discussed in section 6.2? (Note: There are at least 18 ambiguous words in preceding lines of this paragraph.)

Osgood's paraphrase:
"Pale flames gently illuminate airy lanterns."

6.3   Consider the following sentences:
(i)   The women discussed the dogs on the beach.
The women left the dogs on the beach.
The women kept the dogs on the beach.

(ii)   Mary put the dresses on the rack.
Mary bought the dresses on the rack.
Mary bought the dresses at the fleamarket.

Determine in each case how you should most naturally understand the relations between the PP and the NP that precedes it and state how the minimal attachment principle fits or does not fit your interpretations. Try writing some sentences with these sorts of structure that seem to vary in the strength of preference for the two analysis options. What implications do your observations have, if any, for parsing theory? We noted that suggestions have been made for associating a preference ordering with verbs as a basis for parsing decisions. For discussion of this issue, see Mitchell 1987, Holmes 1987, Frazier 1987b, and Gorrell 1988.

6.4   You can assemble a small corpus of speech errors by systematic observation of your own errors and those of your friends and acquaintances. Here are some things to think about if you should try such an exercise: What factors could influence the character of the data you collect? How feasible would it be just to carry around a tape recorder to record the errors? What practical and ethical problems exist? If you record errors in written form, when should you record them? Why? For some guidance in thinking about these problems, see Cutler 1982.

References

Berwick, R., and A. Weinberg (1984). *The grammatical basis of linguistic performance.* Cambridge, MA: MIT Press.

Bever, T., and B. McElree (1988). Empty categories access their antecedents during comprehension. *Linguistic Inquiry* 19, 34–43.

Bierwisch, M. (1971). Linguistics and language error. Reprinted in Cutler 1982.

Bock, J. K. (1986). Syntactic persistence in language production. *Cognitive Psychology* 18, 355–387.

Bock, J. K. (1987). Coordinating words and syntax in speech plans. In A. Ellis, ed., *Progress in the psychology of language*, vol. 3. London: L. Erlbaum Associates.

Bock, J. K. (in press). Closed class immanence in sentence production. *Cognition.*

Boomer, D., and J. Laver (1968). Slips of the tongue. *British Journal of Disorders of Communication* 3, 2–12.

Brown, R. (1973). *A first language: The early stages.* Cambridge, MA: Harvard University Press.

Brown, R., and D. McNeill (1966). The tip of the tongue phenomenon. *Journal of Verbal Learning and Verbal Behavior* 5, 325–337.

Buckingham, H. (1979). Linguistic aspects of lexical retrieval disturbances in the fluent aphasias. In H. Whitaker and H. A. Whitaker, eds., *Studies in neurolinguistics*, vol. 4. New York: Academic Press.

Butterworth, B. (1982). Old data in search of new theories. In Cutler 1982.

Chodorow, M. (1979). Time compressed speech and the study of lexical and syntactic processing. In W. Cooper and E. Walker, eds., *Sentence processing.* Hillsdale, NJ: L. Erlbaum Associates.

Chodorow, M., H. Slutsky, and A. Loring (1988). Parsing non-deterministic verb phrases. Paper presented at the 1st CUNY Conference on Human Sentence Processing, CUNY Graduate Center, New York, March 1988.

Clifton, C., and F. Ferreira (1987). Modularity in sentence comprehension. In J. Garfield, ed., *Modularity in knowledge representation and natural-language understanding.* Cambridge, MA: MIT Press.

Cloitre, M., and T. G. Bever (in press). Pronouns and noun anaphors access distinct levels of representation during discourse processing. *Language and Cognitive Processes.*

Conine, C. (1987). Constraints on interactive processes in auditory word recognition: The role of sentence context. *Journal of Memory and Language* 26, 527–538.

Cowart, W., and H. Cairns (1987). Evidence for an anaphoric mechanism within syntactic processing: Some reference relations defy semantic and pragmatic constraints. *Memory and Cognition* 15, 318–331.

Cutler, A., ed. (1982). *Slips of the tongue.* Amsterdam: Mouton.

Cutler, A., and D. Fay (1982). One mental lexicon, phonologically arranged: Comments on Hurford's comments. *Linguistic Inquiry* 13, 107–113.

Dell, G. (1986). A spreading activation theory of retrieval in sentence production. *Psychological Review* 93, 283–321.

Dell, G., G. McKoon, and R. Ratcliff (1983). The activation of antecedent information during the processing of anaphoric reference in reading. *Journal of Verbal Learning and Verbal Behavior* 22, 121–132.

Dell, G., and P. Reich (1981). Stages in sentence production. *Journal of Verbal Learning and Verbal Behavior* 20, 611–629.

Fay, D., and A. Cutler (1977). Malapropisms and the structure of the mental lexicon. *Linguistic Inquiry* 8, 505–520.

Fodor, J. A. (1983). *The modularity of mind.* Cambridge, MA: MIT Press.

Fodor, J. A., T. G. Bever, and M. F. Garrett (1974). *The psychology of language.* New York: McGraw-Hill.

Fodor, J. D. (1979). Superstrategy. In W. Cooper and E. Walker, eds., *Sentence processing.* Hillsdale, NJ: L. Erlbaum Associates.

Ford, M., J. Bresnan, and R. Kaplan (1982). A competence-based theory of syntactic closure. In J. Bresnan, ed., *The mental representation of grammatical relations.* Cambridge, MA: MIT Press.

Forster, K. I. (1970). Visual perception of rapidly presented word sequences of varying complexity. *Perception and Psychophysics 8,* 215–221.

Forster, K. I. (1979). Levels of processing and the structure of the language processor. In W. Cooper and E. Walker, eds., *Sentence processing.* Hillsdale, NJ: L. Erlbaum Associates.

Forster, K. I., and I. Olbrei (1973). Semantic heuristics and syntactic analysis. *Cognition 2,* 319–347.

Frazier, L. (1979). *On comprehending sentences: Syntactic parsing strategies.* Bloomington, IN: Indiana University Linguistics Club.

Frazier, L. (1987a). Theories of sentence processing. In J. Garfield, ed., *Modularity in knowledge representation and natural-language understanding.* Cambridge, MA: MIT Press.

Frazier, L. (1987b). Sentence processing: A tutorial review. In M. Coltheart, ed., *Attention and performance 12: The psychology of reading.* Hillsdale, NJ: L. Erlbaum Associates.

Frazier, L., C. Clifton, and J. Randall (1983). Filling gaps: Decision principles and structure in sentence processing. *Cognition 13,* 187–222.

Frazier, L., and K. Rayner (1982). Making and correcting errors during sentence comprehension: Eye movements in the analysis of structurally ambiguous sentences. *Cognitive Psychology 14,* 178–210.

Fromkin, V. (1971). The non-anomalous nature of anomalous utterances. *Language 47,* 27–52.

Garnsey, S., M. Tanenhaus, and R. Chapman (1988). Monitoring sentence comprehension with evoked brain potentials. Paper presented at the 1st CUNY Conference on Human Sentence Processing, CUNY Graduate Center, New York, March 1988.

Garrett, M. F. (1975). The analysis of sentence production. In G. Bower, ed., *Psychology of learning and motivation,* vol. 9. New York: Academic Press.

Garrett, M. F. (1980). Levels of processing in sentence production. In B. Butterworth, ed., *Language production,* Vol.1, *Speech and talk.* London: Academic Press.

Garrett, M. F. (1984). The organization of processing structure for language production: Applications to aphasic speech. In D. Caplan, A. R. Lecours, and A. Smith, eds., *Biological perspectives on language.* Cambridge, MA: MIT Press.

Garrett, M. F. (1988). Processes in sentence production. In F. Newmeyer, ed., *The Cambridge linguistics survey.* Vol. 3, *Biological and social factors.* New York: Cambridge University Press.

Gleitman, L., and E. Wanner (1982). Language acquisition: The state of the art. In E. Wanner and L. Gleitman, eds., *Language acquisition: The state of the art.* Cambridge: Cambridge University Press.

Gorrell, P. (1988). Establishing the loci of serial and parallel effects in syntactic processing. Paper presented at the 1st CUNY Conference on Human Sentence Processing, CUNY Graduate Center, New York, March 1988.

Gough, P. (1966). The verification of sentences: Effects of delay of evidence and sentence length. *Journal of Verbal Learning and Verbal Behavior 5,* 492–496.

Herriot, P. (1969). The comprehension of active and passive sentences as a function of pragmatic expectation. *Journal of Verbal Learning and Verbal Behavior 8,* 166–169.

Holmes, V. M. (1987). Syntactic parsing: In search of the garden path. In M. Coltheart, ed., *Attention and performance 12: The psychology of reading*. Hillsdale, NJ: L. Erlbaum Associates.

Holmes, V. M., and K. I. Forster (1972). Perceptual complexity and underlying sentence structure. *Journal of Verbal Learning and Verbal Behavior* 11, 148−156.

Hurford, J. R. (1981). Malapropisms, left-to-right listing, and lexicalism. *Linguistic Inquiry* 12, 419−423.

Kurtzman, H. (1985). Studies in syntactic ambiguity resolution. Doctoral dissertation, MIT, Cambridge, MA.

Kutas, M., and S. Hillyard (1980). Reading senseless sentences: Brain potentials reflect semantic incongruity. *Science* 207, 203−205.

Lenneberg, E. H. (1967). *Biological foundations of language*. New York: Wiley.

Levelt, W. J. M. (in press). *Language production*. Cambridge, MA: MIT Press.

MacKay, D. (1969). Forward and backward masking in motor systems. *Kybernetik* 6, 57−64.

Marcus, M. (1980). *A theory of syntactic recognition for natural language*. Cambridge, MA: MIT Press.

Marcus, M. (1982). Chapter 6 in M. Arbib, D. Caplan, and J. Marshall, eds., *Neural models of language processes*. New York: Academic Press.

Marslen-Wilson, W. (1975). Sentence perception as an interactive, parallel process. *Science* 189, 226−228.

Marslen-Wilson, W., and A. Welsh (1978). Processing interactions and lexical access during word recognition in continuous speech. *Cognitive Psychology* 10, 29−63.

Meringer, R. (1908). *Aus dem Leben der Sprache*. Berlin: Behr.

Miller, G. A. (1951). *Language and communication*. New York: McGraw-Hill.

Miller, G. A., and N. Chomsky (1963). Finitary models of language users. In R. D. Luce, R. R. Bush, and E. Galanter, eds., *Handbook of mathematical psychology*. New York: Wiley.

Mitchell, D. (1987). Lexical guidance in human parsing: Locus and processing characteristics. In M. Coltheart, ed., *Attention and performance 12: The psychology of reading*. Hillsdale, NJ: L. Erlbaum Associates.

Morton, J. (1970). A functional model of human memory. In D. A. Norman, ed., *Models of human memory*. New York: Academic Press.

Nash-Webber, B. (1979). *A formal approach to discourse anaphora*. New York: Garland Press.

Neville, H., M. Kutas, G. Chesney, and A. Smith (1986). Event related brain potentials during initial encoding and recognition memory of congruous and incongruous words. *Journal of Memory and Language* 25, 75−92.

Nooteboom, S. (1969). The tongue slips into patterns. In A. Sciarone, A. van Essen, and A. Van Raad, eds., *Leyden studies in linguistics and phonetics*. The Hague: Mouton.

Osgood, C. E. (1971). Where do sentences come from? In D. Steinberg and L. Jakobovits, eds., *Semantics*. Cambridge: Cambridge University Press.

Patterson, K., J. Marshall, and M. Coltheart (1985). *Surface dyslexia*. Hillsdale, NJ: L. Erlbaum Associates.

Prather, P., and D. Swinney (1977). Some effects of syntactic context on lexical access. Paper presented at the American Psychological Association Meeting, San Francisco, August 26, 1977.

Rayner, K., M. Carlson, and L. Frazier (1983). The interaction of syntax and semantics during sentence processing: Eye movements in the analysis of semantically biased sentences. *Journal of Verbal Learning and Verbal Behavior* 22, 358−374.

Samuel, A. (1981). Phonemic restoration: Insights from a new methodology. *Journal of Experimental Psychology* 110, 474−494.

Seidenberg, M. S., M. K. Tanenhaus, J. M. Leiman, and M. Bienkowski (1982). Automatic access of the meanings of words in context: Some limitations of knowledge-based processing. *Cognitive Psychology* 14, 489–537.

Slobin, D. (1966). Grammatical transformations and sentence comprehension in childhood and adulthood. *Journal of Verbal Learning and Verbal Behavior* 5, 219–227.

Stemberger, J. (1985). An interactive action model of language production. In A. Ellis, ed., *Progress in the psychology of language*, vol. 1. Hillsdale, NJ: L. Erlbaum Associates.

Stowe, L. (in press). Thematic structures and sentence comprehension. In G. Carlson and M. Tanenhaus, eds., *Linguistic structure in language processing*. Dordrecht, Holland: Reidel.

Swinney, D. (1979). Lexical access during sentence comprehension: (Re)consideration of context effects. *Journal of Verbal Learning and Verbal Behavior* 18, 645–659.

Tanenhaus, M., and G. Carlson (in press). Lexical structure and language comprehension. In W. Marslen-Wilson, ed., *Lexical representation and process*. Cambridge, MA: MIT Press.

Thorne, J., P. Bratley, and H. Dewar (1968). The syntactic analysis of English by machine. In D. Michie, ed., *Machine intelligence*. New York: American Elsevier.

Tyler, L. K., and W. Marslen-Wilson (1977). The on-line effects of semantic context on syntactic processing. *Journal of Verbal Learning and Verbal Behavior* 16, 683–692.

West, R. F., and K. E. Stanovich (1986). A robust effect of syntax on visual word recognition. *Memory and Cognition* 14, 104–112.

Wright, B., and M. F. Garrett (1984). Lexical decision in sentences: Effects of syntactic structure. *Memory and Cognition* 12, 31–45.

7

Language and the Brain

Edgar B. Zurif

This chapter is about the kinds of relations that hold between the organization of the language faculty and the organization of the neural system that supports it. It's about a "neural theory of language."

What do we want from such a theory? Several possibilities have been imagined and are currently being explored. Acting on one possibility, some investigators seek a *dynamic* model of brain function underlying language processing—a model of how linguistic computations are translated into neural action. To this end, they study correlations between language processing and temporospatial patterns of activity in the brain. At present, however, a dynamic characterization of this sort is still far off; accordingly, we will consider it only briefly, at the end of the chapter.

For the most part, we will focus instead on another means of achieving a theory of language-brain relations: namely, on analyses of the aphasias, the various language disorders that arise as a consequence of focal brain damage. Remarkably, focal damage does not lead to an across-the-board reduction in language proficiency. Rather, lesions appear quite selective in

Preparation of this chapter was supported by NIH grants NS 11408, 21806, and 06209.

the manner in which they undermine language. And the question is whether or not this selectivity can be interpreted within particular theories of language. Do the components that are so seamlessly assembled for the purposes of normal speech and comprehension reveal themselves following brain damage? Does the unraveling of the language capacity in aphasia permit a scientific understanding of language?

These questions can be approached quite apart from any direct neural considerations. But a number of investigators remain optimistic that the manner in which language is selectively disrupted can be correlated with where in the brain the lesion, or damage, is. We will start with a review of what is known about what parts of the brain are crucial for which aspects of language processing.

7.1   Aphasia

7.1.1   Language Activities and Cerebral Localization

Charting change in language performance associated with damage to various regions of the brain has been a recognized part of neurology for well over 100 years. The neurologists who have been involved in this activity have been those with a philosophical bent and with an inclination to speculate about the mind. Two facts about the aphasias have encouraged such speculation. First, lesions that cause language disorders often cause disruptions to other cognitive activities, and this has fueled hypotheses about the relation of language to thought. Second, the language disruptions themselves appear to be selective; lesions in different locations seem to undermine language in different ways, and this has led to notions about the kinds of constituents that are assembled to form the normal faculty of language.

It is this last concern that is at the center of a model of brain-language relations established in the 1870s—a model dating from the earliest scientific explorations of aphasia (see, for example, Lichtheim 1885; Wernicke 1874/1977). This model focuses on two patterns of selective disruption and on the relation of these two patterns to two different sites of brain damage.

One of these, now called *Broca's aphasia* after the nineteenth-century neurologist Paul Broca, who first brought attention to the disorder, results from damage to the left frontal lobe of the brain, including an area now marked as Broca's area. This involves at least that portion of the cortex that lies just in front of the primary motor zone for the muscles of the lips, tongue, jaw, palate, vocal cords, and diaphragm—that is, in front of the cortical area for the muscles serving speech (see figure 7.1). The clinical signs of Broca's aphasia are these: Although the patients show relatively

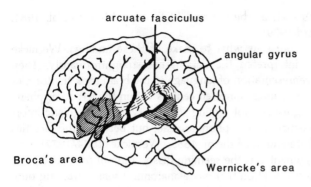

Figure 7.1
A side view of the left hemisphere of the brain. The arcuate fasciculus is the nerve tract hypothesized by Wernicke and his colleagues to be the carrier of information from Wernicke's area to Broca's area.

good comprehension, they produce little speech and do so slowly, with effort and with poor articulation. Further, their speech is "agrammatic": grammatical morphemes, bound and free—items, that is, of the closed class of minor lexical categories (determiners, auxiliaries, and other function words)—tend to be omitted, and there is a corresponding reliance on "open" class items—mostly on nouns, and to a lesser extent on verbs, the latter often appearing in nominalized form (Goodglass and Kaplan 1972; Lecours, Lhermitte, and Bryans 1983).

The second of the two patterns originally observed, now termed *Wernicke's aphasia* after the nineteenth-century German neurologist Carl Wernicke, who first described it, results from a lesion in the posterior region of the left hemisphere. This is now referred to as Wernicke's area; it is adjacent to the cortical region known to be involved in hearing (see figure 7.1). Patients with such lesions produce a form of speech strikingly different from that of patients with Broca's aphasia—one that is rapid and effortless. Also, there is no palpable omission of closed class or function word vocabulary items; phrasal construction seems grossly intact, although features of sentence form can sometimes be aberrantly produced, whether through errors of word choice or through the disruption of some sentence-level processes. Importantly, patients with Wernicke's aphasia show a marked comprehension deficit (Goodglass and Kaplan 1972; Lecours, Lhermitte, and Bryans 1983).

These descriptions, although provided well over 100 years ago, still serve a rough diagnostic purpose. That is, they still have lesion-localizing value, though, to be sure, lesion localization no longer depends, as it did in Wernicke's era, on postmortem examination. Now we have in vivo brain-imaging techniques such as the CT and PET scans (Metter et al. 1981; Naeser and Hayward 1979).

The problem, of course, is what to make of these findings. Wernicke and his colleagues interpreted the data rather straightforwardly. They theorized that the representation of language in the brain took the form of anatomically discernible interconnected centers within the left hemisphere. These centers distinguished, not among various types of linguistic information (syntactic, semantic, and phonological), but between the faculties of speaking and listening (Lichtheim 1885; Wernicke 1874/1977). The bulwark for this argument was the seeming dissociation of production and comprehension—a dissociation that made anatomical sense, granting only the assumption that speaking depended upon principles of motor system organization and that comprehension depended upon the organization of auditory perceptual mechanisms. After all, it is well known—was well known even then—that Broca's area implicates motor function and Wernicke's area, auditory sensory function. In effect, then, Wernicke's theory was that the distinction between comprehension and production mechanisms in the brain is built upon a motor-sensory distinction.

More particularly, word usage was hypothesized to depend upon sensory and motor images of words. Wernicke's area was claimed to contain the sensory images—that is, spoken word memories—whereas Broca's area was held to be crucial for the motor images—that is, for memories by which words were coded into articulatory form. Further, under the assumption that the auditory form of words was necessary for the proper guidance of word production, damage to Wernicke's area could be held accountable not only for the comprehension deficit in Wernicke's aphasia but also for the abnormal output seen in that syndrome (Geschwind 1970).

Two things about this theoretical effort are immediately apparent. It fails to connect with—failed even to anticipate—analyses of language knowledge and use that turn on distinctions among abstract information types that we refer to as syntactic information, semantic information, and the like. And it could not account for important aspects even of the language disruptions themselves. Nothing about function word omission or the tendency to nominalize verbs, for example, is captured by the production-comprehension distinction. These failures were noticed very early on, almost from the inception of the theory. And it is fair to say that a significant part of the subsequent history of aphasia research has been in reaction to Wernicke's theory.

7.1.2   From Language Activities to Symbolic Capacity

One reaction can be traced to the nineteenth-century neurologist John Hughlings Jackson's insistence that the essential unit of language was the proposition, not the word, and that aphasia reflected a breakdown in the capacity to propositionalize (Jackson 1884; see also selected writings, 1958). On Jackson's account, brain damage released the activity of lower centers from higher cortical control and thereby released more primitive behaviors.

This notion led, in turn, to a view wherein aphasia is not a linguistic disruption but rather the reflection in language of a more general conceptual limitation—witness such explanations of aphasia as "loss of abstract attitude" (Goldstein 1948), "asymbolia" (Finkelnburg (see Bay 1964)), and "disorder of conceptual thinking" (Bay 1964).

This general limitation is held to account for a wide variety of quite specific behavioral disruptions. But the details of such connections are never explicitly offered, and the fact remains that the relation of aphasia to other "symbolic" disruptions—primarily disruptions of pantomimic activity (gesturing what one does with objects) and concept formation—is, at the very least, inconsistent. Aphasia can occur alone; these other disruptions can occur alone; and when aphasia and these other disruptions do cooccur after left-brain damage, the aphasic feature implicated by the cooccurrence appears only to be what Goldstein (1948) has termed the "nominal" defect—that is, a defect in the ability to name objects, events, and so on. Conversely, the aphasia feature of no apparent relevance to the correlation is the type of grammatical deformation: pantomimic disruptions, impaired classification performances, and even word-finding difficulties appear in the context of very different (easily distinguishable) forms of grammatical disruption (Gainotti and Lemmo 1976; Goodglass and Kaplan 1963). Given this pattern, and granting the intuition that pantomime and naming are symbolically alike insofar as both index an ability to connect symbols to their referents, it seems reasonable to suggest a neurological distinction between, on the one hand, a system supporting reference (one that is likely embedded in, and structured by, our knowledge about objects in the world) and, on the other hand, a uniquely linguistic system for the representation of grammatical knowledge.

This broadly drawn generalization also holds up from a different perspective. This different perspective is provided, not by the focal damage underlying one or another type of aphasia, but by the effects of the kind of diffuse brain damage that leads to a general diminution of cognitive function, that is, to the condition known as dementia. Specifically, whereas disorders of symbolic gesturing, purposeful movement, and naming are commonly seen as some of the earlier signs of dementia, grammatical disruptions are not (Curtiss and Kempler 1982; Schwartz, Marin, and Saffran 1979). In fact, grammatical capacity has been observed to be spared even in the face of substantial cognitive deterioration (Curtiss and Kempler 1982).

Again, then, the left hemisphere of the brain does not house some undifferentiated symbolic capacity. Rather, it appears to sustain grammatical capacity as a distinct neurological entity.

7.1.3   From Language Activities to Abstract Information Types

The attempt to homogenize cognition in the left hemisphere of the brain was not, however, the only manner of reaction to Wernicke's theory. A second body of work, although also reacting to the limitations of Wernicke's word-based, activity-centered analysis, nonetheless continued to view the aphasias as linguistically specific phenomena. Here the change, simply, was a shift from the word to the *sentence* as the unit of analysis. The agrammatism of Broca's aphasia and the sentence-level errors in Wernicke's aphasia were no longer ignored.

This shift occurred fairly early on with the work of Pick and Salomon (reviewed in De Bleser 1987). But within the last few years there have been significant revisions in the kinds of analyses taking place at the sentence level. From a representational standpoint, analyses of aphasia are now being approached in terms of fairly far-reaching principles stated within the transformational grammar framework, and from a processing standpoint, analyses are being directed to the real-time operations that implement linguistic information for the purpose of production and comprehension.

These new approaches have their roots in the 1970s with a number of studies of comprehension in Broca's aphasia—studies that sought to determine the basis for what clinically appeared to be relatively intact comprehension (for example, Caramazza and Zurif 1976; Heilman and Scholes 1976; von Stockert and Bader 1976; Zurif, Caramazza, and Myerson 1972). Typically, these studies employed a sentence-picture matching paradigm in which aphasic patients were presented with a sentence and were asked to demonstrate their understanding of it by pointing to its correct depiction (embedded in a multiple-choice array of pictures). Distinguished by their systematic examination of semantic and grammatical cues, these studies documented the patients' abnormal reliance on semantic cues and their corresponding inability to carry out normal syntactic analyses. Thus, the Broca's patients could interpret sentences of the type *The apple that the boy is eating is red*, but they seemed to base their interpretation on semantic constraints: boys can eat apples, not vice versa. When such constraints were absent, they had trouble. They failed to interpret who did what to whom in sentences like *The girl whom the boy is pushing is tall*—sentences in which both entities are capable of performing the action (Caramazza and Zurif 1976).

Other experiments pointed to the Broca's patients' relative inability to correctly comprehend sentences in situations where interpretation crucially depended upon the processing of the article *the* (Goodenough, Zurif, and Weintraub 1977; Heilman and Scholes 1976). For example, Heilman and Scholes (1976) observed that the patients had difficulty distinguishing the meaning of *He showed her baby the pictures* from the meaning of *He showed her the baby pictures.*

Taken together, these various analyses indicated that the Broca's patients' relatively intact comprehension skills were somewhat illusory. They appeared unable to use features of sentence *form* to guide interpretation. In the sweeping terms used at the time, Broca's patients were said to be as agrammatic in listening as in speaking (see, for example, Caramazza and Zurif 1976). Left anterior brain damage was claimed to produce an overarching syntactic limitation, even as it spared the capacity to carry out semantic inference. Optimistically, then, it seemed at that time that Wernicke and his colleagues had correctly localized the language centers in the brain and that further research would serve simply to redefine their functions: Broca's area seemed to be a syntactic center; perhaps Wernicke's area would be discovered to sustain semantic inference.

7.1.4 Complications

The matter has turned out to be more complex. To start, we will examine this complexity from a representational perspective. That is, we will seek to "unpack" the notion of a syntactic limitation solely in *grammatical* terms, without also being concerned to account for *processing* disruptions that might yield the limitation. As we will see, however, even from only a representational perspective, complications arise.

The original claims notwithstanding, agrammatic Broca's aphasic patients do not seem totally reliant on semantic and pragmatic cues. They do not, that is, seem entirely without syntax. Rather, they show a partial disruption: even when plausibility and semantic cues are absent—even when the patients do not have such cues available so that they can bypass syntactic analysis—still they can interpret some kinds of sentences. In this respect, consider the following contrast. Even though these patients do not assign agency appropriately for an object-relative construction like *The girl whom the boy is pushing is tall* (that is, they aren't sure who is doing the pushing), when the relations between the boy and the girl are cast into a subject-relative construction, *The boy who is pushing the girl is tall*, they show a near normal ability to comprehend who is doing what to whom (Grodzinsky 1984; Wulfeck 1984).

Two other paired contrasts of this general sort have been reported. Specifically, although agrammatic Broca's patients show uncertain comprehension for passive-voice sentences (*The girl was pushed by the boy*), they have no problem with the corresponding actives (*The boy pushed the*

girl) (Caplan and Futter 1986). And again, even as they have difficulty
with object cleft sentences (*It is the girl who the boy is pushing*), they do well
with subject clefts (*It is the boy who is pushing the girl*) (Caplan and Futter
1986).

7.1.5   A Trace Theory Analysis of Agrammatic Broca's Aphasia

We can make sense of these findings within the framework of recent de-
velopments in transformational grammar (see chapter 1). In order to do so,
however, we need to review some general features of this theory. First, it
includes two levels of representation: deep and surface structure. These
two levels are related to each other by transformation rules that can move
constituents around. For example, in the case of the passive, a transformation moves a noun phrase (NP) from object position at deep structure; this
leaves a trace—an abstract, phonologically unrealized marker—in the
vacated position at surface structure; and the trace is linked to the moved
NP by a mutual index. This maneuver is shown in the following deep and
surface structure representations, where *e* stands for a position in the deep
structure that is unfilled and *t* is the empty (trace) position resulting from
the transformation:

(1)a.   [*e*] was pushed the boy   (deep structure)

b.   [the boy]$_i$ was pushed t_i (surface structure)

If we look only at surface structure—the level that most determines
what we hear—then clearly traces are crucial for semantic interpretation—for determining who does what to whom. How traces function in
this respect is intimately bound up with the notion of how thematic roles
are assigned in a sentence. Examples of this assignment are presented in
chapter 1. What needs to be specified here is that thematic roles like agent
(the "doer"), source (where the action originates), and goal (what the action is directed toward) are assigned to *hierarchically structured sentence positions regardless of the identity of the assignee*. If a thematic position is filled
with a lexical NP (say, the subject of an active sentence or the object of
an active sentence), then this NP receives its thematic role directly. (The
assigner is usually the verb (V) or verb phrase (VP).) However, if a
thematic position contains a trace, then the trace is assigned the thematic
role and the moved NP that left the trace receives its thematic role indirectly, via its trace (because the two are, by convention, coindexed).

The pattern of comprehension failures and successes in agrammatic
Broca's aphasia can now be captured by the following generalization. The
sentences that were randomly interpreted by the agrammatic patients involve a transformation of a particular type: they involve movement from
object position, and consequently their surface structure representations

contain a trace in that position. By contrast, the constructions that were interpreted relatively normally either do not have a trace in their surface structure representation (as in the active), or if there is a trace, it appears in the subject position. This situation is illustrated by the following approximate surface structure representations:

(2)a. Object-relative construction
       [$_{NP}$ the girl]$_i$ whom [$_{NP}$ the boy] is pushing [$_{NP}$ t]$_i$ is tall
       (Trace is in object position.)
       vs.
       Subject-relative construction
       [$_{NP}$ the boy]$_i$ who [$_{NP}$ t]$_i$ is pushing [$_{NP}$ the girl] is tall
       (Trace is in subject position.)

   b. Passive construction
       [$_{NP}$ the girl]$_i$ was pushed [$_{NP}$ t]$_i$ by [$_{NP}$ the boy]
       (Trace is in object position.)
       vs.
       Active construction
       [$_{NP}$ the boy] pushed [$_{NP}$ the girl]
       (There is no trace.)

   c. Object-cleft construction
       it is [$_{NP}$ the girl]$_i$ whom [$_{NP}$ the boy] is pushing [$_{NP}$ t]$_i$
       (Trace is in object position.)
       vs.
       Subject-cleft construction
       it is [$_{NP}$ the boy]$_i$ who [$_{NP}$ t]$_i$ is pushing [$_{NP}$ the girl]
       (Trace is in subject position.)

A very important detail is the kind of comprehension performance each pair member elicits from the Broca's patients. The first sentence of each pair (wherein a trace appears in object position) yields chance performance; the second sentence of each pair yields a level significantly above chance (Caplan and Futter 1986; Grodzinsky 1984; Wulfeck 1984). In no instance is performance significantly below chance. In effect, in none of the studies were the patients observed to consistently invert thematic roles—in none did they get, say, 10 sentence-picture matching trials wrong and 0 right. If the agrammatic Broca's patient found the construction difficult to interpret, the difficulty would emerge as, roughly, 5 right, 5 wrong.

These features of agrammatic aphasic performance—the pattern of success and failure as a function of trace location and the fact of random, as opposed to consistently inverted, thematic assignment—have been most clearly articulated by Grodzinsky (1986), who moreover has an explanation for them. His account makes two assumptions. The first has to do with agrammatic Broca's aphasia. It is that patients exhibiting this syndrome, although they appreciate hierarchical syntactic organization, have one syntactic problem: they cannot represent traces in surface structure. The second has to do with the application of a comprehension strategy: namely, that an NP that does not receive a thematic role syntactically (either directly or through a trace) is assigned a default thematic role, that of agent. Following Bever's (1970) early formulation, the default strategy assigns roles to *linear* position (as opposed to position in the hierarchical, tree structure). This default strategy is considered to be nonlinguistic. It does not obey grammatical principles but instead is based on general nonlinguistic knowledge—knowledge induced through experience that in English the clause-initial position is usually filled by an agent role.

Applying these assumptions, chance performance on passive, object-relative, and object-cleft constructions—on all of the first-listed members of each pair in (2)—is explained as the consequence of the agrammatic Broca's patients' assigning the agent role to two different NPs in the same sentence. Since *for agrammatic patients* the clause-initial NP does not have a trace with which to be coindexed and from which to inherit a thematic role, it is assigned a thematic role by the default strategy. The application of this strategy yields an agent role for the dangling NP. And this is inappropriate. With verbs of motion, as in the sentence *The girl was pushed by the boy*, the NP undergoing the motion—*The girl*—should be given the role of theme.

Since all other representational features are intact in agrammatism, the role of agent also is assigned (appropriately) to the second NP—that is, to the NP that receives its thematic role from the verb, or, in the case of passives, from the preposition *by*. In the above example this NP is *the boy*. Thus, there are two agents, one assigned by the normal grammatically based procedure in which assignment is given in terms of the sentence's overall hierarchical configuration, and the other, by a nonlinguistic default procedure sensitive only to linear (nonhierarchical) positions.

But there can only be one agent. As a consequence, the patient is forced into a guessing situation that leads to random performance. In the above example, having assigned the role of agent to both *the boy* and *the girl* and faced with two depictions, one showing a boy pushing a girl and the other, a girl pushing a boy, the patient is reduced to guessing which is the correct picture (Grodzinsky 1986).

No such conflict arises in the active, subject-cleft, and subject-relative constructions, however. In the active case there is no trace in the representation and thus no need for applying the default strategy. In the remaining two constructions, although the default strategy is invoked to assign the agent role to the first NP this happens to be the role it would receive had it been linked normally to its trace (Grodzinsky 1986).

This appealing theory is not problem free, however. It has been criticized for restricting the representational limitation in agrammatism only to a problem with traces. Discussion of this criticism, and Grodzinsky's counterarguments, would take us too far off our present introductory course, but they can be pursued by reading Caplan and Futter 1986, Caplan and Hildebrandt 1986, Caplan 1987, Grodzinsky, in press, and, for a more general view, Kean 1984.

7.1.6 Representational Theories and Brain Localization

What does warrant examination here, however, is a problem common to all representational theories. It turns on the fact that none of the efforts to characterize the agrammatic patient's failure in linguistic terms—neither Grodzinsky's nor anyone else's—has been shown to have any very certain lesion-localizing value. Thus, although Grodzinsky's analysis seems to capture the comprehension limitation in some, even many, patients with anterior lesions, other patients with these lesions and with agrammatic output do not show comprehension limitations admitting such an analysis (Goodglass and Menn 1985). Conversely, it is uncertain whether Grodzinsky's analysis applies just to Broca's patients or whether it also applies to some or many patients fitting within the classical Wernicke's aphasia category—that is, to patients with posterior lesions (Goodglass and Menn 1985). (The data are very scanty in this respect—indeed, very few linguistic analyses have been carried out on posterior, Wernicke's aphasics.)

In light of this, we can no longer securely maintain our early optimism that the brain centers isolated in Wernicke's theory could stay where placed but simply be functionally redefined. Efforts to redescribe the functions of these centers may end up blurring their edges. Whereas deficits stated over activities taken whole—for instance, impaired output, relatively intact comprehension—seem most often to implicate particular cortical areas, deficits stated in the abstract terms of current linguistic theory have not been shown to have this impressive lesion-localizing value.

7.1.7 Processing Analyses

There is a modern perspective that does allow us to be more forceful on the matter of brain localization, however. It has to do, not directly with the representation of language knowledge, but rather with the nature of the real-time processes that make use of such knowledge representations. In shifting from a representational to a processing perspective, we will shift our focus in yet another way. Whereas representational accounts of sentence knowledge in aphasia (for example, Grodzinsky 1986) deal with what remains of a full-blown hierarchical grammatical organization, processing accounts of aphasia have been directed to only a very small part of sentence processing—to that early stage in which an entry in the lexicon is contacted and its meaning and structural properties accessed for further (syntactic and semantic) analysis.

Yet even with this restricted focus, processing accounts appear difficult to achieve. Investigators who have sought such accounts cannot allow themselves merely to chart *endpoints* of the comprehension process—patterns of ultimate success or failure of comprehension. This provides no basis for thinking about a processing-representational separation. Without an independent theory of the processor or without seeking to provide evidence for processing modules in terms of real-time operating characteristics (see chapters 5 and 6), these comprehension patterns indistinguishably support claims about the processing unit *and* about the knowledge representation it operates on.

How, then, have investigators sought to achieve an account of aphasic limitations in relatively independent processing terms? Largely by studying the fixed and mandatory operating characteristics of the processing systems. And, as already noted, these analyses have primarily been restricted to those systems that access lexical information (but compare Marcus 1982). In turn, much of this effort has focused on the possibility that the comprehension deficit in agrammatic Broca's aphasics—and only in that group—can be captured in terms of a processing distinction between open class vocabulary elements (content words) and closed class vocabulary elements (function words such as articles and grammatical morphemes such as the English plural -s).

7.1.8   The Processing of Open and Closed Vocabulary Classes in Aphasia

No formal analysis is required to make the obvious point that the distinction between the open and closed vocabulary classes broadly implicates the contrast between sentence form and sentence meaning. Whatever their other functions, open class words generally bear reference, whereas closed class items support the construction of syntactic groupings, namely, phrases (see chapter 5). As we have already seen, even only the inability to use articles severely limits syntactic analysis.

The question we are asking here, however, is intended to probe deeper: Is the agrammatic patient's failure to use articles and other closed class items for syntactic purposes a failure of stored representations? Are the closed class items unalterably unavailable in their representations? Or is the failure the reflection of a processing problem—an inability, say, to make these elements available at the right time for subsequent comprehension operations?

On balance, the data side with the processing alternative. These data have been gained primarily from experimental situations that require the patients to simultaneously interpret sentences and monitor the presence of preselected targets such as particular words or letters (Friederici 1983, 1985; Rosenberg et al. 1985; Swinney, Zurif, and Cutler 1980).

In one of these experiments (Rosenberg et al. 1985) the dual task paradigm was used to examine a phenomenon known as the "invisibility" effect. When neurologically intact subjects were faced with the requirement to cross out target letters in a printed text, they were more apt to notice and cancel the letters when they appeared in open class words than when they appeared in closed class words. In some sense, properties of closed class items less readily intruded themselves into conscious attention—they tended toward "invisibility." One plausible assumption is that this pattern arises because of differences in the way that the products of an open and closed class processing distinction contribute to processes of sentence comprehension.

Indeed, this position is reinforced by the additional finding that the invisibility effect was significant only when the subjects were reading prose passages, not when they were reading scrambled word passages. That is, the effect appeared only when parsing and interpretation were at stake. Moreover, the closed class invisibility phenomenon was not altered by alerting subjects to potential error in that class. Thus, the failure to detect target letters in closed class items was not the consequence of some task-specific scanning strategy. Rather, the pattern proved to be intractable—the likely reflection of an unconscious and impenetrable processing mechanism employed in the service of phrasal analysis.

By contrast to these signs of normal processing, agrammatic Broca's aphasics were found to detect targets with an almost equal facility in the two vocabulary classes. In fact, they performed better than neurologically intact subjects in detecting target letters in the closed class items. Presumably, their failure to process closed class items normally made these items more accessible to conscious attention.

In the context of these findings, we can now pick up on the promissory note given earlier: that a processing perspective would show important differences between agrammatic, nonfluent Broca's and fluent Wernicke's patients. The promise holds. The various dual task paradigms routinely yield some difference between the two groups (Friederici 1983; Rosenberg et al. 1985). Thus, in contrast to the performance of the Broca's group on the letter detection task, the Wernicke's patients, like the neurologically intact subjects, were less able to detect target letters in closed class items than in open class items.

The Wernicke's patients did not perform entirely normally, however. They failed to show a pattern shift when presented with scrambled word sequences. Even in this condition they were less able to detect targets in closed class items than in open class items. If we are right in supposing that the invisibility effect is the consequence of the normal operation of a lexical access device in the service of parsing, then the question arises, How can such a device persist in its operation when faced with unparsable ("scrambled prose") passages?

The answer turns on the notion of processing modularity. One facet of a modular process, as described in chapter 6, is that it accesses lexical information but does not evaluate the context in which the lexical item appears. In this view, contextual constraints apply only *after* the information has been accessed. Accordingly, initial access based on word forms may be spared in Wernicke's aphasia, but since patients with this syndrome have an interpretation problem, they are unable to apply context —or more properly in the present instance, lack of context—to then block efforts to assign phrasal constituents on the basis of the distribution of the closed class vocabulary elements (Rosenberg et al. 1985).

To return to the central point, when aphasic performance is analyzed in mechanistic terms, in terms of the operating characteristics of a word access system, the distinction between Broca's and Wernicke's aphasia is upheld. And since, as we have seen, this distinction has lesion-localizing value, the processing analyses provided here inherit this value. Thus, damage to Broca's area in the brain appears to disrupt access of closed class items and attendant real-time phrasal construction; damage to Wernicke's area seems to limit later stages of sentence processing.

7.1.9   Priming Patterns in Aphasia

It is misleading, however, to describe the Broca-Wernicke processing distinction solely in terms of the closed class of vocabulary items. The Broca's patients' failure to make normal use of this vocabulary class is likely one instance only—the most sensitive reflection, perhaps—of a failure to access any restricted lexical domain normally.

The data supporting this claim come from studies of lexical priming. As described in chapter 5, priming refers to the finding that lexical decisions —deciding whether or not an item is a word—are faster for target words when these are immediately preceded by semantically related words than when preceded by unrelated words. This pattern indicates that the meaning of the related prime has been activated or somehow contacted.

Actually, there are a number of variations on—and a number of purposes served by—the priming paradigm. Two are relevant here: Milberg and Blumstein's studies of priming effects on isolated words to analyze the effects of focal brain damage on access to lexical semantic information (Milberg and Blumstein 1981; Blumstein, Milberg, and Shrier 1982; Milberg, Blumstein, and Dworetzky 1987), and the use by Swinney et al. (1985) and Swinney, Zurif, and Nicol (1989) of a cross-modal priming technique to study the effects of brain damage on lexical access in the service of sentence comprehension (Zurif, Swinney, and Garrett, in press).

The cross-modal priming technique, introduced in chapter 5, has been an important tool in the analysis of autonomous processing devices. Before we turn to its use in aphasia research, some of its particulars warrant brief review. Basically, the technique turns on the inclusion in sentences of words with two or more meanings—potentially ambiguous words. In this situation, priming is assessed for both meanings of the word in sentential contexts that are relevant to only one of its meanings. For example, in the sentence *The man saw several spiders, roaches, and other bugs in the corner of his room*, priming is assessed for both meanings of the word *bugs*— the contextually relevant 'insect' sense, and the contextually irrelevant 'espionage' sense. In the first instance the lexical decision time for the letter string ANT is charted; in the second instance the decision time for the string SPY is examined; and in each instance the reaction time is compared to the decision time for a letter string unrelated to either meaning of *bugs*.

Two phenomena are repeatedly observed with neurologically intact subjects. First, when the letter string is flashed on a screen at a point immediately after the subject has heard the word *bugs* in the aurally presented sentence, there is a priming effect for *both* of its meanings—in other words, for SPY as well as for ANT. Second, if the lexical decision probe is delayed—if the letter string does not appear until about one and a half seconds after the word *bugs* is heard—only the contextually relevant, insect meaning (ANT) shows a priming effect (Swinney 1983). These observations have been taken to indicate that lexical access during normal sentence comprehension is an autonomous process that cannot be penetrated by contextual information, that it involves the retrieval of all interpretations for a lexical item, and that contextual information has its effect upon lexical processing only after access (as was also suggested in our analysis of performance on the letter detection task).

With this background, we can turn to the aphasic data. These can be simply summarized: In both the isolated word situation and the cross-modal sentence situation Wernicke's patients showed the normal pattern. In the isolated word situation they responded more quickly to a target when it was preceded by a semantically related prime than when it was preceded by an unrelated or a nonword prime (Milberg and Blumstein 1981); in the cross-modal sentence situation they showed priming for both interpretations of an ambiguous word when the lexical decision probe immediately followed the word (Swinney et al. 1985; Swinney, Zurif, and Nicol 1989).

In marked contrast to these patterns, the Broca's patients generally showed no priming in the isolated word situation (Milberg and Blumstein 1981), and in the cross-modal sentence situation they showed priming only for the most frequent meanings of the "ambiguous" words, *regardless of context* (Swinney et al. 1985; Swinney, Zurif, and Nicol 1989). As a general point, then, even though the Broca's patients knew the meanings of individual words—a fact that is always established before undertaking priming studies—they were nonetheless unable to access them normally.

The details of this processing failure, at least so far as it emerges during sentence processing, remain to be filled in. The researcher's task is to reconcile the aberrant lexical access pattern with the fact that the patients routinely demonstrated understanding of the sentences containing the ambiguous primes. To have understood these sentences, the Broca's patients necessarily had to understand the words in them, including the ambiguous words. Nevertheless, they showed priming *only* for the most frequent meaning of these ambiguous words, even though on half of the trials this meaning was irrelevant to sentence interpretation.

One possible explanation requires the following scenario for *normal* processing: (1) that accessing the range of meaning candidates within the set defined by an ambiguous word takes the form of a serial search; (2) that the order of this search is controlled by frequency of meaning occurrence; and (3) that when the number of candidates in the set is very limited, the search is normally carried out at a rate too fast to measure with our existing techniques. On this view, the lexical search device in agrammatic aphasics operates with a slower-than-normal rise time, and only the most frequent meaning representation is engaged within the time frame imposed by the on-line experimental paradigm. Pursuing this line of speculation, the facilitation for all senses of an ambiguous word, for the Broca's aphasics, should appear at a point in the sentence that is noticeably later than usual.

The idea developed here is that agrammatic Broca's patients are slower processors all down the line. Indeed, it may be supposed that this processing inefficiency also underlies the problem that these patients show for closed class items. Perhaps these items constitute a more vulnerable class, simply by virtue of stricter time requirements for phrasal construction than for semantic inference to take place—the former, but not the latter, depending crucially on the distribution of closed class items. Whatever the reason, the general point of the account offered here is that the agrammatic Broca's patients' failure to contact lexical representations—whether of the closed class or open class vocabularies—cannot be seen as some failure of stored representations; rather, it must be viewed as a processing failure—*as a failure, presumably, to make these elements available at the right time in the processing sequence.* How such processing failures yield their full-blown representational consequences is at this time an unsolved problem. And indeed, we have yet to determine the fit between patients categorized in processing terms and those categorized in representational terms.

A final consideration: to the extent that agrammatic patients cohere as a group in terms of an underlying disruption to fast-acting processing devices, it is quite possible that this coherence is brought about by the dependence of such devices on elementary motor systems—in the sense that the motor systems serve as a resource for the processing devices. If this turns out to be the case, we will have returned, in part, to Wernicke's formulations in which linguistic processes in the brain were seen as an extension of sensorimotor operations that had obvious cerebral localizing value. However, our account cannot be construed as simply old wine in new bottles: for although the component processors that we have analyzed here are possibly rooted to sensorimotor activities with discrete cortical localizations as originally formulated, the fact remains that such processors must, in the first instance, be identified in terms of the information they access. More than that, they must be shown to be dedicated to one or another type of information in virtue of their encapsulation during processing. Therefore, we have positioned ourselves to evaluate processing devices in two ways: in terms of their localizable sensorimotor resources and in terms of their computational operations and goals.

7.2   Dynamic Analyses of Brain-Language Relations

The foregoing analyses of aphasia have incorporated static, neuroanatomical facts. By contrast, in what follows we will focus on some *dynamic* properties of brain activity. We will focus, that is, on analyses of the electrical activity arising from the millions of neurons participating in the processing of one or another piece of linguistic information. This sort of analysis seems, somehow, to bring us closer to neurophysiology, the machine code in which our language capacity is realized. It also seems more compatible with the aim of psycholinguistic analysis, which is to describe language capacity in terms of the real-time operation of information-processing systems.

The fact is, however, that the electrophysiological research paradigm has yet to supplant the centrality of aphasia research for neurolinguistic theorizing. This is the reflection neither of habit nor of any principle. As we will see, it simply has to do with the present level of development of electrophysiological analysis. Still the technique also shows some promise and hopefully this too will be apparent in what follows. (See also chapter 6 for some indication of its promise.)

7.2.1   Some Assumptions and Problems

Although nerve activity is a physiochemical process, most of our information about language-related neural conduction comes from recording its electrical consequences. The recordings that concern us here are *event-related potentials* (ERPs). These are the transient voltage fluctuations generated by millions of active neurons and picked up by electrodes placed on the scalp. They are referred to as event-related potentials because these are electrical signals that cooccur with specific cognitive acts, such as when subjects process linguistic input.

The use of ERPs to study the brain's involvement in language processes turns entirely on the assumption that some part of the neural activity yielding the scalp potentials has a functional role in some aspects of cognitive activity. Hence, correlations are sought between ERP parameters and cognitive processes.

By studying how the waveform changes with an experimental manipulation—with, say, the requirement to do a certain kind of syntactic analysis on certain input strings—researchers seek to explore whether such a process is discretely represented in the brain. If it can be isolated, they can also examine the timing of this process relative to others, when it kicks in during sentence interpretation, and whether it is influenced by other kinds of input information.

This would seem to be a relatively uncomplicated business—but it is not. First, if only one event at a time is analyzed, the ERP is too small to emerge from the welter of ongoing electrical activity. Hence, to distinguish the ERP from background noise, the signal must be averaged over many trials. The random "noise" tends to disperse—the random peaks and troughs cancel each other out—and the constant peaks and troughs of the ERPs thereby become more recognizable.

Even with this maneuver, however, many difficulties for ERP interpretation remain, of which the following three (from a list provided by Picton and Stuss (1984)) are representative. First, the fields recorded at the scalp can be generated by many artifactual sources: by the eyes, the scalp muscles, the skin, and the tongue. Second, scalp ERPs represent only those cerebral activities that generate electric fields at a distance, and to generate such fields, the neural events must be synchronous and spatially oriented. However, many cerebral activities occur in neurons that are not similarly oriented or synchronically activated; they do not contribute to the scalp recordings even though they may be essential to the cognitive process being assessed. Third, any ERP recorded at the scalp can be generated by several sources with temporally and spatially overlapping fields. Each peak recorded at the scalp does not necessarily reflect a separate cerebral process.

This last complication is to be expected, however. The claim that a linguistic process is discretely represented in the brain depends only upon the existence of some correspondence between the two levels. It is not necessarily a straightforward relation—one in which a single cluster of neurons alone is responding to a particular linguistic process.

7.2.2 Some Experimental Studies

The ERP is an imperfect instrument to measure a very complicated correlative relation. Still, some workers in the field remain sanguine about its possibilities. They argue that with proper care to minimize artifactual signs and with appropriate statistical techniques to parcel out the various subwaves and sources contributing to the waveform—both reasonably achievable—the ERP can provide an important physiological litmus test for claims about linguistic processing (see, for example, Kutas and Hillyard 1984).

They may be right. For the most part, however, this litmus has been applied to broad distinctions of very limited value to current linguistic theory. For example, it has been shown that there are consistent ERP differences, especially over the left anterior scalp region, as a function of whether aurally delivered target words in sentences are nouns or verbs (*Sit by the fire* versus *Ready, aim, fire*) (Brown, Marsh, and Smith 1973). Are these differences due to the meaning contrast between the two appearances of *fire*? Or do they reflect a lexical category difference, picked up by a syntactic processing device? Investigators do not yet know.

There are, however, some clues pointing to electrical patterns specifically correlated to sentence-processing requirements. Thus, sentences presented visually, one word at a time, and completed by semantically inappropriate words, were observed to yield a peak in the waveform around 400 milliseconds post offset. This peak was not present in sentences ending with semantically appropriate words. Moreover, this "surprise" component did not occur in response to all types of "sentence surprises." If the "surprise" was a visual one, as when the last word in the sentence was presented in a very different typeface, the waveform showed a late-appearing trough, not a peak. Also, these two distinct ERP effects—the peak and the trough—could be elicited concurrently by the same word when it was both semantically inappropriate and in a suddenly different type face (Kutas and Hillyard 1984).

Although this work can hardly be claimed to support the burden of current theoretical linguistic concerns, it at least shows how the brain distinguishes language from nonlanguage processing requirements.

Also, as alluded to earlier and as can be seen in chapter 6, there are more encouraging signs of progress. Indeed, one study focuses directly on a functional architectural distinction already much chewed upon in our discussion of aphasia: the distinction between open class and closed class words.

The finding is this: whether presented in sentences (Kutas and Hillyard 1984) or in isolation (Neville 1984, cited in Kutas and Hillyard 1984), the processing of open class words is associated with greater positive components than is the processing of closed class words. Thus, in line with the aphasia research data, the ERP findings also indicate some level of neural organization at which the brain treats the processing of these two vocabulary classes as distinct. And it indicates this neural organization in a very palpable fashion.

Suggestions for Further Reading

There are a number of surveys of current research in brain-language relations: Caplan 1980, Studdert-Kennedy 1983, and Caplan, Lecours, and Smith 1984. These edited volumes are notable for their mix of different research methodologies and strategies, including neural modeling, for their introduction of cross-language considerations, and for their inclusion of some lively exchanges between neuroscientists and cognitive scientists.

An account of aphasia featuring explicit ties to linguistic theory is provided in Kean 1985.

Question

7.1   One of the possibilities noted in this chapter is that agrammatic patients are limited in their ability to construct phrases because they fail to process closed class lexical items in the normal fashion. It has also been shown that these patients are unable to process traces in surface structure. Is there any generalization to be drawn in terms of processing efficiency that links these two limitations? And why should the capacity for semantic inference be relatively spared?

References

Bay, E. (1964). Principles of classification and their influence on our concepts of aphasia. In A. V. S. de Reuck and M. O'Connor, eds., *Ciba Foundation Symposium: Disorders of language*. London: J. and A. Churchill.

Bever, T. G. (1970). The cognitive basis of linguistic structures. In J. R. Hayes, ed., *Cognition and the development of language*. New York: Wiley.

Blumstein, S., W. Milberg, and R. Shrier (1982). Semantic processing in aphasia: Evidence from an auditory lexical decision task. *Brain and Language* 17, 301–315.

Brown, W. S., J. T. Marsh, and J. C. Smith (1973). Contextual meaning effects on speech-evoked potentials. *Behavioral Biology* 9, 755–761.

Caplan, D., ed. (1980). *Biological studies of mental processes*. Cambridge, MA: MIT Press.

Caplan, D. (1983). Syntactic competence in agrammatism: A lexical hypothesis. In M. Studdert-Kennedy, ed., *Psychobiology of language*. Cambridge, MA: MIT Press.

Caplan, D. (1987). Agrammatism and the coindexation of traces: Comments on Grodzinsky's reply. *Brain and Language* 30, 191–193.

Caplan, D., and C. Futter (1986). Assignment of thematic roles to nouns in sentence comprehension by an agrammatic patient. *Brain and Language* 27, 117–133.

Caplan, D., and N. Hildebrandt (1986). Language deficits and the theory of syntax: A reply to Grodzinsky. *Brain and Language* 27, 168–177.

Caplan, D., and N. Hildebrandt (in press). *Disorders of syntactic comprehension*. Cambridge, MA: MIT Press.

Caplan, D., A. R. Lecours, and A. Smith, eds. (1984). *Biological perspectives on language*. Cambridge, MA: MIT Press.

Caramazza, A., and E. B. Zurif (1976). Dissociation of algorithmic and heuristic processes in sentence comprehension: Evidence from aphasia. *Brain and Language* 3, 572–582.

Curtiss, S., and D. Kempler (1982). Language and cognition in dementia: A case study. In *UCLA Working Papers in Cognitive Linguistics* 3, UCLA, Los Angeles, CA.

De Bleser, R. (1987). From agrammatism to paragrammatism: German aphasiological traditions and grammatical disturbances. *Cognitive Neuropsychology* 4, 187–256.

Friederici, A. D. (1983). Aphasics' perception of words in sentential context: Some real-time processing evidence. *Neuropsychologia* 21, 351–358.

Friederici, A. D. (1985). Levels of processing and vocabulary types: Evidence from on-line comprehension in normals and agrammatics. *Cognition* 19, 133–166.

Gainotti, G., and F. Lemmo (1976). Comprehension of symbolic gesture in aphasia. *Brain and Language* 3, 451.

Geschwind, N. (1970). The organization of language and the brain. *Science* 170, 940–944.

Goldstein, K. (1948). *Language and language disturbances*. New York: Grune and Stratton.

Goodenough, C., E. B. Zurif, and S. Weintraub (1977). Aphasics' attention to grammatical morphemes. *Language and Speech* 20, 11–19.

Goodglass, H., and E. Kaplan (1963). Disturbances of gesture and pantomime in aphasia. *Brain* 86, 703–720.

Goodglass, H., and E. Kaplan (1972). *The assessment of aphasia and related disorders*. Philadelphia: Lea and Febiger.

Goodglass, H., and L. Menn (1985). Is agrammatism a unitary phenomenon? In Kean 1985.

Grodzinsky, Y. (1984). The syntactic characterization of agrammatism. *Cognition* 16, 99–120.

Grodzinsky, Y. (1986). Language deficits and the theory of syntax. *Brain and Language* 27, 135–159.

Grodzinsky, Y. (in press). *Theoretical perspectives on language deficits*. Cambridge, MA: MIT Press.

Heilman, K. M., and R. J. Scholes (1976). The nature of comprehension errors in Broca's, conduction, and Wernicke's aphasics. *Cortex* 12, 258–265.

Jackson, J. H. (1884). Evolution and dissolution of the nervous system. *Popular Science Monthly* 25, 171–180.

Jackson, J. H. (1958). *Selected writings of John Hughlings Jackson*. New York: Basic Books.

Kean, M.-L. (1984). Linguistic analysis of aphasic syndromes: The doing and undoing of aphasia research. In Caplan, Lecours, and Smith 1984.

Kean, M.-L., ed. (1985). *Agrammatism*. New York: Academic Press.

Kutas, M., and S. A. Hillyard (1984). Event-related potentials in cognitive science. In M. S. Gazzaniga, ed., *Handbook of cognitive neuroscience*. New York: Plenum.

Lecours, A.- R., F. Lhermitte, and B. Bryans (1983). *Aphasiology*. London: Bailliere Tindall.

Lichtheim, K. (1885). On aphasia. *Brain* 7, 433–484.

Marcus, M. P. (1982). Consequences of functional deficits in a parsing model: Implications for Broca's aphasia. In M. A. Arbib, D. Caplan, and J. C. Marshall, eds., *Neural models of language processes*. New York: Academic Press.

Metter, E. J., C. G. Wasterlain, D. E. Kuhl, W. R. Hanson, and M. E. Phelps (1981). FDG positron emission computed tomography in a study of aphasia. *Annals of Neurology* 10, 173–183.

Milberg, W., and S. E. Blumstein (1981). Lexical decision and aphasia: Evidence for semantic processing. *Brain and Language* 14, 371–385.

Milberg, W., S. E. Blumstein, and B. Dworetzky (1987). Processing of lexical ambiguities in aphasia. *Brain and Language* 31, 138–150.

Naeser, M. A., and R. W. Hayward (1979). The resolving stroke and aphasia: A case study with computerized tomography. *Archives of Neurology* 36, 233–235.

Picton, T. W., and D. T. Stuss (1984). Event-related potentials in the study of speech and language: A critical review. In Caplan, Lecours, and Smith 1984.

Rosenberg, B., E. Zurif, H. Brownell, M. Garrett, and D. Bradley (1985). Grammatical class effects in relation to normal and aphasic sentence processing. *Brain and Language* 26, 287–303.

Schwartz, M., O. Marin, and E. Saffran (1979). Dissociations of language function in dementia: A case study. *Brain and Language* 7, 277–306.

Studdert-Kennedy, M., ed. (1983). *Psychobiology of language*. Cambridge, MA: MIT Press.

Swinney, D. (1983). Theoretical and methodological issues in cognitive science: A psycholinguistic perspective. In W. Kintsch, J. Miller, and P. Polson, eds., *Methodology in cognitive science*. Hillsdale, NJ: L. Erlbaum Associates.

Swinney, D., E. B. Zurif, and A. Cutler (1980). Effects of sentential stress and word class upon comprehension in Broca's aphasia. *Brain and Language* 10, 132–144.

Swinney, D., E. B. Zurif, B. Rosenberg, and J. Nicol (1985). Modularity and information access in the lexicon: Evidence from aphasia. Paper presented at the Academy of Aphasia, Los Angeles.

Swinney, D., E. B. Zurif, and J. Nicol (1989). The effects of focal brain damage on sentence processing: An examination of the neurological organization of a mental module. *Journal of Cognitive Neuroscience* 1, 25–37.

Von Stockert, Th., and L. Bader (1976). Some relations of grammar and lexicon in aphasia. *Cortex* 12, 49–60.

Wernicke, C. (1874). The aphasia symptom complex: A psychological study on an anatomical basis. Reprinted in G. H. Eggert (1977). *Wernicke's works on aphasia*. The Hague: Mouton.

Wulfeck, B. (1984). Grammaticality judgment and sentence comprehension in agrammatic aphasia. Paper presented at BABBLE, Niagara Falls, Canada.

Zurif, E. B., A. Caramazza, and R. Myerson (1972). Grammatical judgments of agrammatic aphasics. *Neuropsychologia* 10, 405–417.

Zurif, E. B., D. Swinney, and M. Garrett (in press). Lexical processing and sentence comprehension in aphasia. In A. Caramazza, ed., *Advances in cognitive neuropsychology and neurolinguistics*. Hillsdale, NJ: L. Erlbaum Associates.

8

Language Acquisition

Steven Pinker

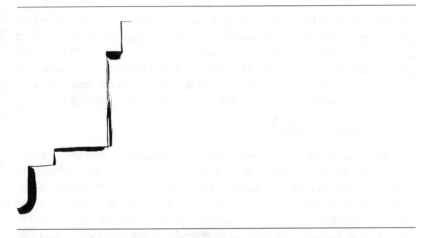

8.1 The Importance of Understanding Language Acquisition

Language acquisition is one of the most important topics in cognitive science. Every theory of cognition has tried to explain it; probably no other topic has aroused such controversy and so much strong feeling. It is not hard to see why. Possessing a language is the quintessentially human trait: all normal humans speak, no nonhuman animal does. Language is the main vehicle by which we know about other people's thought processes, and the two must be intimately related. Every time we speak we are revealing something about the nature of language, so the facts of language structure are easy to come by—facts that hint at a system of extraordinary complexity. Nonetheless, learning a first language is something every normal child does successfully, in a matter of a few years and without the need for formal lessons. With language so close to the core of what it means to be human, it is not surprising that children's acquisition of language has re-

Preparation of this chapter was supported by NIH grant HD 18381 and by a grant from the Alfred P. Sloan Foundation to the MIT Center for Cognitive Science.

ceived so much attention. Anyone with strong views about the human mind would like to show that children's first few steps are steps in the right direction.

Language acquisition is not only inherently interesting; studying it scientifically is one way to look for concrete answers to the important theoretical questions that permeate cognitive science, concerning modularity, human uniqueness, the relation between language and thought, and the interaction between heredity and environment.

8.1.1   Modularity

Do children learn language using a distinct "mental organ," whose principles of organization are not shared with other cognitive systems such as perception, motor control, or reasoning (Chomsky 1975, 1986; Fodor 1983)? Or is language acquisition just another problem to be solved by general intelligence, in this case the problem of how to communicate with other humans over an auditory channel (Anderson 1983; Minsky 1975)?

8.1.2   Human Uniqueness

A related question is whether language is unique to humans. At first glance the answer would appear to be yes; other organisms often have communication systems consisting of a fixed repertoire of behaviors, but none appears to have the generative rule system that characterizes human language. On the other hand, many other claims about human uniqueness, such as that humans were the only animals to use tools or to fabricate them, have turned out to be false. Some researchers have thought that apes have the capacity for language but never profited from a humanlike cultural milieu in which language was taught, and they have thus tried to teach apes languagelike systems. Whether they have succeeded, and whether human children are really "taught" language themselves, are questions we will soon turn to.

8.1.3   Language and Thought

Is language simply grafted on top of cognition as a way of sticking communicable labels onto thoughts (Fodor 1975; Piaget 1926)? Or does learning a language somehow mean learning to think in that language? A famous hypothesis, outlined by Whorf (1956), asserts that the categories and relations that we use to understand the world come from our particular language, so that speakers of different languages quite literally conceptualize the world in different ways. This is an intriguing hypothesis, but virtually all modern cognitive scientists believe it is false. (For a review of some of the evidence, see Fodor 1975; Shepard and Cooper 1982.) There are many reasons for this. One can show that adults think in terms of images and abstract logical propositions, not just words (see chapters 2 and 4). Individuals without language can demonstrate considerable intelligence (such as deaf people who have not acquired a sign language, infants before they learn to speak (see chapter 3), and nonhuman animals). Human languages are too ambiguous to use as a medium of internal computation (when people think about "spring," surely they are not confused about whether they are thinking about a season or something that goes "boing"). And if there really are fundamental differences in thought processes corresponding to the different languages people speak, no one has been able to document them; in fact, there are remarkable similarities in people's perception of color and shape despite widespread differences in how languages categorize them in words (Rosch 1973).

Language acquisition has several unique contributions to make to this issue. It is virtually impossible to show how children could learn a language unless it is assumed that they have a considerable amount of cognitive machinery in place before they start. On the other hand, learning different languages does require one at least to pay attention to different aspects of the world. For example, English speakers can say *The dog ran through the forest* but not *The dog ran through the table* (they have to say *The dog ran under the table*); speakers of certain other languages have to use the word *through* for both. It is as though English speakers had to conceptualize a table as essentially "being" its top, and its legs as minor appendages that "don't count" as part of it one could run through. Thus, learning a language does involve learning to categorize the world in particular ways, even if only for the purpose of using language itself; an English speaker must think of a table as being more like a board than a forest when referring to it in a sentence.

8.1.4   Learning and Innateness

Since all normal humans talk but no house pets or house plants do, no matter how pampered, heredity must be involved in language. But since a child growing up in Japan speaks Japanese whereas the same child brought up in California would speak English, the environment is also crucial. Thus, there is no question about whether heredity or environment is involved in language, or even whether one or the other is "more important." Instead, language acquisition might be our best hope of finding out *how* they interact. We know that adult language is extremely complex, and we know that children become adults. Therefore, whatever exists in children's minds that allows them to learn a language must be capable of attaining that degree of complexity. Any theory that posits too little innate structure, so that the hypothetical child ends up speaking something less than a real language, thus meets a brutal empirical end. The same is true for any theory that posits too much innate structure, so that the hypothetical child can acquire English but not, say, Bantu or Serbo-Croatian. And not only do we know about the *output* of language acquisition; we also know a fair amount about the *input* to it, namely, parents' speech to their children. Thus, even if language acquisition, like all cognitive processes, is essentially a "black box," we know enough about its input and output to be able to make precise guesses about its contents.

The scientific study of language acquisition began around the same time as the birth of cognitive science, in the late 1950s, and we can see now why that is not a coincidence. The historical catalyst was Noam Chomsky's review of B. F. Skinner's *Verbal Behavior* (Chomsky 1959). At that time Anglo-American natural science, social science, and philosophy had come to a virtual consensus about the answers to the questions listed above: the mind consisted of sensorimotor abilities plus a few simple laws of learning governing gradual changes in an organism's behavioral repertoire. Therefore, language must be learned, it cannot be a module, and thinking must be a form of verbal behavior, as verbal behavior is the prime manifestation of "thought" that can be observed externally. Chomsky argued that language acquisition falsified these beliefs in a single stroke: children learn languages that are governed by highly subtle and abstract principles, and they do so without explicit instruction or any other environmental clues to the nature of such principles. Hence, language acquisition depends on an innate, species-specific module that is distinct from general intelligence. Much of the debate in language acquisition has attempted to test this once-revolutionary collection of ideas. The implications extend to the rest of human cognition.

8.2   Learning about Language Acquisition

Understanding language acquisition is not just a matter of listening carefully to children's speech; it is a complex computational and biological problem that has to be broken down into parts. Different subdisciplines within cognitive science pay attention to different parts. It is useful to explain any cognitive faculty at three levels: What problem is the mind solving? What steps does the mind go through in solving it? And what kind of neural machinery allows these steps to be executed? (For a similar distinction, see the Introduction.)

8.2.1   What Is Learning, and How Can It Happen?

The most general question to ask about language acquisition is, What is it, in principle? A branch of theoretical computer science (also called "the mathematical theory of automata") called *learnability theory* attempts to answer this question (Gold 1967; Osherson, Stob, and Weinstein 1985; Pinker 1979). According to learnability theory, learning involves four things (the theory embraces all forms of learning, but language learning will be used as the example here):

1. A class of languages. One of them has been selected as the "target" language, to be attained by the learner, but the learner does not know which. In the case of children the class of languages would consist of the existing and possible human languages.

2. An environment. This is the information in the world that the learner has to use in trying to acquire the language. In the case of children it might include the sentences parents utter, the context in which they utter them, feedback to the child (verbal or nonverbal) in response to the child's own speech, and so on. Parental speech can be a random sample of the language, or it might have some special properties: it might be ordered in certain ways; sentences might be repeated or uttered only once; and so on.

3. A learning strategy. The learner, using information in the environment, tries out "hypotheses" about the target language. The learning strategy is the algorithm that creates the hypotheses. In the case of children it is the "grammar-forming" mechanism in their brains—their "language acquisition device."

4. A success criterion. If we want to say that "learning" occurs, presumably it is because the learner's hypotheses are not random but are related in some systematic way to the target language. The learner may arrive at a hypothesis identical to the target language after some fixed period of time, arrive at an approximation to it, or waver among a set of hypotheses, one of which is correct.

Theorems in formal learning theory show how assumptions about any of the three components impose logical constraints on the fourth. It is not hard to show why learning a language, on logical grounds alone, is so hard. In language acquisition, as in all "induction problems," there are an infinite number of hypotheses consistent with any finite sample of environmental information. Learnability theory shows which induction problems are solvable and which are not.

A key factor is the role of *negative evidence*, or information about which strings of words are not sentences in the language to be acquired. Children might get such information by being corrected every time they spoke ungrammatically. If this is not the case (and it probably is not; see section 8.3.2)—the acquisition problem is all the harder. Consider figure 8.1, where languages are depicted as circles corresponding to sets of strings of words, and all the logical possibilities for how the child's language could differ from the adult language are depicted. There are four

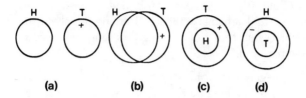

Figure 8.1
Four situations that a child could be in while learning a language. Each circle represents the set of sentences constituting a language; "H" stands for "hypothesized language"; "T" stands for "target language."

possibilities. (a) The child's hypothesis language, H, is disjoint from the language to be acquired (the "target language," T). That would correspond to the state of the child learning English who cannot say a single well-formed English sentence. For example, the child might only be able to say things like *We breaked it* and *We goed*, never *We broke it* or *We went*. (b) The child's hypothesis language and the target language intersect. Here the child would be able to utter some English sentences, like *He went*. However, the child would be unable to produce certain other English sentences, such as *We broke it*, and would also use strings of words that are not English, such as *We breaked it*. (c) The child's hypothesis language is a subset of the target language. Here the child would have mastered some (but not all) of English, but everything the child had mastered would be part of English. The child might not be able to say *We broke it* but would be able to say some grammatical sentences, such as *We went*; no errors such as *We breaked it* or *We goed* would occur. (d) The child's hypothesis language is a superset of the target language. That would occur, for example, if the child could say *We broke it*, *We went*, *We breaked it* and *We goed*.

In cases (a)–(c) the child can realize that her hypothesis is incorrect by hearing sentences from parental "positive evidence" (indicated by the " + " symbol) that are in the target language but not the hypothesized one: sentences such as *We broke it*. This is impossible in case (d); negative evidence (such as parental corrections of the child's ungrammatical sentences) would be needed. In other words, without negative evidence, if a child guesses too large a language, the world can never tell her she's wrong.

This has several consequences. For one thing, the most general learning algorithm one might conceive of—one that is capable of hypothesizing any grammar, or any computer program capable of generating a language —is in trouble without negative evidence. Without negative evidence (and even in many cases with it), there is no general-purpose, all-powerful learning machine; a machine must in some sense "know" something about the constraints in the domain in which it is learning. More concretely, if children do not receive negative evidence, it is ridiculously easy for them to make overly large hypotheses. For example, children actually do go through stages in which they use two or more past tense forms for a given verb, such as *broke* and *breaked*. They derive transitive verbs from intransitives much too freely: where an adult might say both *The ice melted* and *I melted the ice*, children also can say *The girl giggled* and *Don't giggle me!* In each case they are in situation (d) in figure 8.1, and unless their parents slip them some signal in every case that lets them know they are not speaking properly, it is puzzling that they eventually stop. Without negative evidence, we would need to explain how they grow into adults who are more restrictive in their speech—or, another way of putting is that it is puzzling that the English language does not allow *Don't giggle me* and *She ated*, given how children are likely to grow up talking. If the world is not telling children to stop, something in their brains is, and we have to find out who or what is causing the change. We will return to the question of negative evidence and children's errors later in the chapter.

8.2.2   What Is Learned

To understand how X is learned, we first have to understand what X is. Linguistic theory is thus an essential part of the study of language acquisition (see chapters 1 through 3). It tries do three things. First, it must characterize the facts of English, or any other language whose acquisition we are interested in explaining. Second, since children are not predisposed to learn English or any other particular language, linguistics must examine the structure of other languages. In particular, linguistics characterizes which aspects of grammar are universal, prevalent, rare, or nonexistent across languages. Contrary to early suspicions, languages do not vary arbitrarily and without limit; there is by now a large catalogue of *language universals*, properties shared exactly, or in a small number of variations, by all languages (see Comrie 1981; Greenberg 1978; Shopen 1985). This obviously bears on what children's language acquisition mechanisms find easy or hard to learn. Third, then, linguistics ideally must contribute a theory of *universal grammar* (Chomsky 1965, 1981). This specifies the allowable mental representations and operations that all languages are constrained to use, and of course it must be consistent with grammars for particular languages and with language universals. The theory of universal grammar is closely tied to the theory of the mental mechanisms children use in acquiring language; their hypotheses about language must be couched in structures consistent with universal grammar.

To see how linguistic theory tells us about how language acquisition must work, consider sentences (1)–(5). In each example a learner who heard the (a) and (b) sentences could quite sensibly extract a general rule that, when applied to the (c) sentence, would yield version (d). Yet in each case the result is actually not the kind of sentence any speaker of English would say or hear without a sense of oddness.

(1)a.   John saw Mary with her best friend's husband.

  b.   Who did John see Mary with?

  c.   John saw Mary and her best friend's husband.

  d.   *Who did John see Mary and?

(2)a.   Irv drove the car into the garage.

  b.   Irv drove the car.

  c.   Irv put the car into the garage.

  d.   *Irv put the car.

(3)a.   I expect the fur to fly.

  b.   I expect the fur will fly.

  c.   The fur is expected to fly.

  d.   *The fur is expected will fly.

(4)a.   The baby seems to be asleep.

  b.   The baby seems asleep.

  c.   The baby seems to be sleeping.

  d.   *The baby seems sleeping.

(5)a.   John liked the pictures of Bill that Mary took.

  b.   John liked Mary's pictures of Bill.

  c.   John liked the pictures of himself that Mary took.

  d.   *John liked Mary's pictures of himself.

The solution to the problem must be that children's learning mechanisms ultimately do not allow them to make the generalization. (For a discussion of some of these mechanisms, see chapter 1.) For example, in (1) the constraint that prevents extraction of a single phrase out of a coordinate structure would block what would otherwise be a natural extension of all the examples of extraction that the child would actually hear, such as (1a,b) and the dozens of other kinds of questions that parents might use. Each of the other sentences presents another puzzle that the theory of universal grammar, as part of a theory of language acquisition, must solve. It is because of the subtlety of these examples, and the abstractness of the principles of universal grammar that must be posited to explain them, that Chomsky has claimed that the overall structure of language must be innate, based on his examination of the facts of language alone.

8.2.3   How Language Acquisition Actually Proceeds

Ultimately, it is children, not computer programs or abstract algorithms, that actually do the language learning, and by examining their behavior and that of their parents, we can try to figure out how their learning strategies operate. Although many scholars in the last 100 years and more have kept diaries of their children's speech (Charles Darwin was one of the first), it was only after portable tape recorders became available in the late 1950s that children's spontaneous speech began to be analyzed systematically within developmental psychology (see Brown 1973; Maratsos 1983; Gleitman and Wanner 1982). These *naturalistic studies* of children's spontaneous speech have become even more accessible now that they can be put into computer files and disseminated and analyzed automatically (MacWhinney and Snow 1985). They are complemented by *experimental methods*; in *production* tasks children utter sentences to describe pictures or scenes, in response to questions, or to imitate target sentences; in *comprehension* tasks they listen to sentences and then point to pictures or act out events with toys; in *judgment* tasks they indicate whether or which sentences provided by an experimenter sound "silly" to them.

To make the discussion more concrete, let us consider three examples of studies from developmental psycholinguistics. They illustrate some of the common methodologies and some of the important theoretical questions that these methodologies provide answers to. Furthermore, they illustrate points about language acquisition that we will return to frequently in the rest of the chapter.

Productivity

One of the earliest and most famous experiments on language development was done by Berko (1958). A common naive conception of language acquisition is that it is a form of "imitation" of parental speech. Berko showed that, on the contrary, children have the ability to create completely new forms, by applying some internal mechanism that captures the effects of a rule of language. The technique was a very simple elicited production task. Children between the ages of 4 and 7 were shown a picture of a cartoon bird and told that it was a "wug." Then they were shown a second picture, with two cartoon birds. "Now there are two of them," the children were told; "There are two _____." Most children completed the sentence with the word *wugs*. Similarly, they were shown a picture of a man swinging an instrument and were told, "Here is a man who likes to rick. Yesterday he did the same thing. Yesterday he ____." (Children's response: "Ricked.") Clearly, children had never said or heard the words *wugs* or *ricked* before, because they are not part of English. Therefore, their performance cannot be explained by any straightforward notion of "imitation" (or of reinforcement, since the children had never uttered the words before and so could not have been rewarded for uttering them). Instead, they had clearly internalized the relevant regularities of English, which they could apply *productively*. Where and when children will apply a regularity productively is a crucial issue in language acquisition, since children must go beyond the finite sample of information in the input and generalize to the infinitely large language of their community.

The laboratory results were nicely confirmed by the naturalistic studies of Ervin (1964), who showed that children's spontaneous speech contained many examples of the overapplication of these regularities to irregular verbs and nouns that do not take the *-ed* or *-s* ending, resulting in errors such as *bringed, goed,* or *foots.* Again, since adults do not say such words, children could not have picked them up through imitation; they must be using something like a rule. Interestingly, before children make these errors, they use the irregulars correctly, saying *brought, went,* and *feet.* At some point they get worse, using the correct forms and errors side by side. Slowly, the errors begin to drop out during the late preschool and early school-age years.

The standard explanation for these results runs as follows (see, for example, Pinker 1984). Children first simply memorize present and past tense forms directly from the input. They correctly use irregular forms because the overregularized forms do not appear in the input, and all they are doing is reproducing what they have heard. Regular past tenses such as *walked* are acquired in the same way, without being analyzed yet into a stem plus an inflection. In the meantime the child has recorded the fact that, say, *walked* is used reliably to refer to past instances of walking, whereas *walk*, similar in phonological structure to *walked*, is used in non-past circumstances to refer to the same kind of action. The child juxtaposes *walk* and *walked*, notes that the second is created by adding *d* to the first, and creates the corresponding rule: "To form the past, add *d* to the stem." This rule can then be applied to other stems, including (mistakenly) irregulars such as *go*. At some point, though, the child has to realize that *goed* is not allowable. He might do so by applying an innate *Uniqueness Principle*, a constraint from universal grammar that has the effect of ensuring, roughly, that every verb has no more than one past tense form. When the child realizes that *went* is nothing but the past tense form of *go*, he can begin to get rid of *goed*.

Structure-dependence

Sentences are linearly ordered strings of words. No child could fail to notice word order in learning and understanding language. Most regularities of language, however, are couched in terms of hierarchically organized structures (see chapter 1). If the structures of linguistic theory correspond to the hypotheses that children formulate when they analyze parental speech and form rules, they should create rules and processes that are defined over hierarchical structures, not simple properties of linear order such as which word comes before which other word or how close two words are in a sentence.

Another classic experiment in developmental psycholinguistics comes from Carol Chomsky (1969). Languages often have embedded clauses missing a subject, such as *John told Mary to leave*, where the embedded "downstairs" clause *to leave* has no subject. The phenomenon of *control* governs how the missing subject is interpreted; in this sentence it is Mary who is understood as fulfilling the subject role, namely, the person doing the leaving. We say that the phrase *Mary* "controls" the missing subject position of the lower clause. For most verbs, there is a simple principle defining control. If the upstairs verb has no object, then the subject of the upstairs verb controls the missing subject of the downstairs verb. For example, in *John tried to leave, John* is interpreted as the subject of both *try* and *leave*. If the upstairs verb has a subject and an object, then it is the object that controls the missing subject of the downstairs verb, as in *John told Mary to leave*. Chomsky showed that children apply this principle quite extensively, even for the handful of verbs that are exceptions to it. In act-out comprehension experiments with children between the ages of 5 and 10, she showed that even relatively old children were prone to this kind of mistake. When told "Mickey promised Donald to jump; make him jump," the children would make Donald, the object of the first verb, do the jumping, in accord with the general principle. The "right answer" in this case would have been Mickey, because *promise* is an exception to the principle, calling for an unusual kind of control where the subject of the upstairs verb, not the object of the upstairs verb, should act as controller.

But what principle are the children overapplying? One possibility can be called the *Minimal Distance Principle*: the controller of the downstairs verb is the noun phrase nearest to it in the linear string of words in the sentence. If children analyze sentences in terms of linear order, this should be a natural generalization. However, it is not correct for the adult language. Consider the sentence *Mary was told by John to leave*. The phrase *John* is closest to the subject position for *leave*, but adult English speakers understand the sentence as meaning that Mary is the one leaving. The Minimal Distance Principle gives the wrong answer here. Instead, for the adult language we need a principle sensitive to grammatical structure, such as the "c-command" structural relation discussed in chapter 1. A simplified version of such a principle, which we may call the *Structural Control Principle*, might say that the controller of a missing subject is the grammatical object of the upstairs verb if it has one; otherwise, it is the grammatical subject of the upstairs verb (both of them c-command the missing subject). The object of a preposition in the upstairs clause, however, is never allowed to be a controller, basically because it is embedded "too deeply" in the sentence's tree structure to c-command the missing subject. That is why *Mary was told by John to leave* has *Mary* as the controller. (It is also why the sentence *Mary was promised by John to leave* is virtually uninterpretable—it would require a prepositional phrase to be the controller, which is ruled out by the Structural Control Principle.)

It would certainly be understandable if children were to follow the Minimal Distance Principle; it is easily stated in terms of surface properties that children can easily perceive, and sentences that would disconfirm it like *Mary was told by John to leave* are rare in parents' speech. Maratsos (1974) did the crucial experiment. He gave children such sentences and asked them who was leaving. Of course, on either account children would have to be able to understand passive sentences in general to interpret these sentences, and Maratsos gave them a separate test of comprehension of simple passive sentences to select only those children who could. And indeed, he found that such children interpreted passive sentences with missing embedded subjects just as adults would. In accord with the Structural Control Principle and in violation of the Minimal Distance Principle, they interpreted *Mary was told by John to leave* as having the subject (*Mary*) as the controller.

A demonstration making a similar point comes from Crain and Nakayama (1986), based on a case frequently used by Noam Chomsky to illustrate how he predicts language acquisition should work. The sentence *The man is in the room* can be turned into a question: *Is the man in the room?* Two versions of the rule relating these sentences are possible. A linear rule might say, "Find the first example of *is* and move it to the front." A structural rule would say, "Find the example of *is* that is in the highest clause in the tree and move it to the front." The two rules behave differently in sentences like *The man who is tall is in the room.* The linear rule yields an incorrect version: *Is the man who tall is in the room?* The structural rule yields the correct version: *Is the man who is tall in the room?* Crain and Nakayama had children play a game in which they had to convert an experimenter's sentences into questions. Even though the linear rule is in some sense "simpler," Crain and Nakayama showed that children performed in an adultlike fashion, never asking questions like *Is the man who tall is in the room?* Therefore, they must have formed their answers by using a structural rule, never a linear rule. Furthermore, the children's rules were not restricted to subjects with certain types of meanings: they had no trouble converting *It is raining* to *Is it raining?*, despite the meaninglessness of *it*. Young children look for abstract structural relations in sentences, as we would expect given the kinds of knowledge they must acquire.

Innate constraints

Arguments that the child must come to the language-learning task with inborn constraints about the possible form of linguistic rules are usually defended by comparing the facts of adult grammar with the facts of parental input to children and inferring what children must possess to go from the latter to the former. Sometimes it is possible to corroborate such theories with children's behavior in experimental settings.

An elegant illustration of how this might be done comes from Gordon (1985). According to a theory of word structure proposed by Kiparsky (1982), words are built in layers or "levels." To build a word, a speaker starts with a root (say, *Darwin*) and applies rules of a certain kind to it, called "level 1 rules," to yield a more complex word. For example, there is a rule adding the suffix *-ian*, turning the word *Darwin* into *Darwinian*. Level 1 rules, according to the theory, can affect the sound of the stem; in this case the stressed syllable in *Darwin* changes from *Dar* to *win*. Level 2 rules apply to a word after any level 1 rules have been applied. An example of a level 2 rule is the one that adds the suffix *-ism*, yielding, for example, *Darwinism*. Level 2 rules generally do not affect the pronunciation of the words they apply to; they just add material onto the word, leaving it intact. Finally, level 3 rules apply to a word after any level 2 rules have been applied. Many regular rules of "inflectional morphology" are examples of level 3 rules, such as the rule that adds an *-s* to the end of a noun to form its plural—for example, *Darwinians* or *Darwinisms*. Crucially, the rules cannot apply out of order, so the input to a level 1 rule must be a word root; the input to a level 2 rule must be either a root or the output of level 1 rules; and the input to a level 3 rule must be a root, the output of level 1 rules, or the output of level 2 rules. That constraint yields predictions about what kinds of words are possible and what kinds are impossible. For example, the ordering makes it possible to derive *Darwinianism* or *Darwinianisms* but not *Darwinsian*, *Darwinsism*, *Darwinismian*, and so on.

Within this theory, irregular inflectional rules, such as the one that relates *mouse* to *mice*, belong to level 1, whereas regular inflectional rules, such as the one that relates *rat* to *rats*, belong to level 3. Compounding, the rule that produces *Darwin-lover* and *mousetrap*, is a level 2 rule. This predicts that *rat-eater* and *mouse-eater* are possible words, as is *mice-eater*, since the rule forming *mice* comes before the rule combining it with *eater*. However, *rats-eater*, even though it is cognitively quite similar to *mice-*

eater, sounds strange, at least to adult ears, as the theory predicts. Gordon carried out an elicited-production experiment with children between the ages of 3 and 5 in which he said, "Here is a puppet who likes to eat ____. What would you call him?" He provided a response for several singular nouns beforehand, so that the children were aware of the existence of the "*x*-eater" compound form. Almost always, children behaved just like adults: a puppet who likes to eat a mouse was called a *mouse-eater,* a puppet who likes to eat a rat was called a *rat-eater,* a puppet who likes to eat mice was called a *mouse-eater* or a *mice-eater,* but a puppet who likes to eat rats was called a *rat-eater,* never a *rats-eater.* Interestingly, children treated their own overregularizations, such as *mouses,* exactly as they treated legitimate regular plurals: they would never call the puppet a *mouses-eater,* even though they used *mouses* in their own speech.

Even more interestingly, Gordon examined how children could have acquired the constraint. Perhaps, he reasoned, they had learned the fact that compounds can contain either singulars or irregular plurals, never regular plurals. It turns out, though, that they would have no way of learning that fact. Although there is no grammatical reason why compounds would not contain irregular plurals, in fact the speech that children hear probably does not contain any. Compounds like *toothbrush* abound (there is no word *teethbrush,* though there could be); compounds like *people-mover* or *teeth-marks* containing irregular plurals are extremely rare, according to the standardized frequency data that Gordon examined, and he found none that was likely to occur in the speech children hear. Therefore, children were willing to say *mice-eater* and unwilling to say *rats-eater* with no good evidence from the input that that is the pattern required in English. Gordon suggests that this shows that the constraints on level ordering may be innate.

8.2.4   Biological Mechanisms

Human language is made possible by human biology. Unfortunately, understanding the biology of language is particularly hard because only humans have language and because many experiments with living humans are out of the question for obvious reasons. However, a variety of circuitous methods have been devised, and they have uncovered some fascinating facts pointing to some of the neural and anatomical adaptations that have given us language (Lenneberg 1967).

For example, the shape of the human vocal tract is specially adapted for speech: the low larynx and right angle bend create two independently modifiable resonant cavities ideal for the production of a large range of vowel sounds but at a considerable sacrifice in efficiency for breathing, swallowing, and chewing (Lieberman 1984). In fact, choking on food is a surprisingly common cause of accidental death in humans; this shows how powerful the evolutionary selective advantage for language use must have been.

As discussed in chapter 7, the brain appears to have circuits, mostly in the left hemisphere, that are specific to aspects of language (though exactly how their internal wiring gives rise to rules of language is unknown). It appears that the development of these circuits may be a driving force underlying the course of language acquisition. Cerebral metabolic rate and synaptic density attain a peak around the age of 2, then undergo a steep decline between the ages of 10 and 15 (Huttenlocher 1979). Perhaps as a consequence (no one is sure), children's word combinations begin during the second year. Furthermore, the ability to learn a language appears to decline beginning around early adolescence: acquisition of a second language without an accent is virtually impossible by late adolescence, and mastery of fine points of syntax that are second nature even to uneducated native speakers is difficult for adults to attain. This kind of evidence points to a neurologically determined "critical period" for language acquisition, analogous to the critical periods documented in visual development in mammals (Hubel and Wiesel 1970) and in the acquisition of songs by some birds (Marler 1970). Demonstrating critical periods in humans is difficult because almost no human reaches adolescence without hearing a language. There is an exception, however: deaf children brought up in the "oralist" tradition are denied access to sign language, a full-fledged language that they would easily acquire, and are required to read lips and speak, which few of them master. Later in life they may come into contact with signing members of the deaf community and acquire their first language then. If it is in adulthood that they first come into contact with this language, they do not acquire it proficiently, even with decades of exposure and practice (Newport and Supalla, in press). Furthermore, immigrants learning English as a second language also do poorly if they begin learning in adulthood, even if they work at it for an equal or greater length of time than immigrants who begin to learn it as children (Johnson and Newport 1989).

It seems, too, that the brain mechanisms underlying language are not just those allowing us to be smart in general. Strokes often leave adults with catastrophic losses in language, though not necessarily impaired in intelligence (see chapter 7). The opposite pattern of dissociation can be seen in the phenomenon of "linguistic savants" (Cromer 1986; Curtiss, Yamada, and Fromkin 1979; Gardner 1983). For example, Cromer (1986) presented a videotape of a loquacious teenage girl whose pronunciation, intonation, syntax, and vocabulary are impeccable—she sounds like she should be broadcasting for the BBC. However, the girl is severely retarded, and the content of her otherwise plausible-sounding narrative was completely made up and mostly nonsense.

One of the most famous explorations in the biology of language acquisition has been the attempt to teach sign languages to chimpanzees and other primates (Gardner and Gardner 1969; Premack and Premack 1983). Though once heralded as a refutation of the species-specificity and modularity of language, these efforts have since been reinterpreted as showing exactly the opposite if they show anything at all (Terrace et al. 1979; Seidenberg and Petitto 1979; Seidenberg 1986). Many of the early studies were plagued by bad habits associated with many animal owners: reliance on anecdotes that seem to demonstrate intelligence but may have been selected after the fact from a huge pool of random responses, unconscious nonverbal cueing by the trainer, and overly charitable interpretations of simple responses. Careful analyses have documented that chimpanzees usually require massive regimented teaching sequences to acquire quite rudimentary linguistic abilities, mostly limited to a small number of signs, strung together in long, repetitive, quasi-random sequences, used with the intent of requesting something (food or tickling, most often). This contrasts sharply with human children, who pick up thousands of words spontaneously, combine them in structured sequences where every word has a determinate role, respect the word order of the adult language, and use sentences for a variety of purposes such as commenting on interesting objects. This is not to say that chimpanzees are not intelligent—such studies have shown that their cognitive sophistication is considerable (Premack and Premack 1983). But as Lila and Henry Gleitman have put it, "If any of our children learned language the way Washoe did, we would be terror-stricken and rush them to the nearest neurologist" (Gleitman and Gleitman 1981, 403).

8.3   Input to Language Acquisition

Children learn English because they hear English. To understand how they learn, we have to know what they hear. That is, we have to know the properties of the speech of parents or other caretakers who talk to children as they learn language—how reliable, informative, or transparent this input speech is with respect to the target language. The issue, essentially, is whether language is learned or taught. Oscar Wilde once noted that nothing worth learning can be taught, and it is not a bad idea to keep this quip in mind when thinking about the effects of parental speech on language learning. Language acquisition is a robust process; there is virtually no way to prevent it from happening short of raising a child in a barrel. It is doubtful that any subtle aspect of parental speech makes much of a difference. In this section we will consider some of the important aspects of the input to language acquisition, namely, positive evidence, negative evidence, "Motherese," prosodic information, and contextual and semantic information.

First, however, a note of warning: in considering the input to language acquisition, we must especially be aware of possible prejudices. Many parents like to think that their special efforts give their children a leg up in cognitive and linguistic development. But the effects of these efforts might be trivial, in a scientific sense, compared to the sophisticated learning that children do on their own. Worse is a class prejudice that makes working-class speech sound coarse and unsophisticated to the ears of those who hold that prejudice, a supposed "deficit" that they attribute to what they consider to be more haphazard interactions between parent and child. Indeed, the speech of different socioeconomic groups differs in vocabulary, pronunciation, inflection, and syntax, but these are differences in *dialects*. Scientifically speaking, the grammar of working-class speech—indeed, every human language system that has been studied—is intricately complex, though each system is complex in a different way, and none is "simpler" or "more primitive" than another. An instructive example comes from a dialect, called Black English, spoken in many urban American low-income black communities (see Labov 1970). A speaker of Standard English might think that the omission of *be* in Black English (*He wild; They calling*) is due to some kind of unsystematic simplified or sloppy version of Standard English. However, this is completely false. There are some grammatical constructions in Black English in which *be* is never omitted: elliptical sentences such as *He is!*, past tense forms such as *She was likin' me*, imperative and infinitival forms such as *Be cool!* or *You got to be good*, forms with traces of movement (see chapter 1) such as *I don't care what you are* or *Who is it?*, and others. Interestingly, these are exactly the contexts in which speakers of Standard English refuse to contract *is* to *'s*: no one says *I don't care what you're*, *Who's it?*, *Yesterday she's liking me*, and so on. The rules for omission of *be* in Black English are the same as the rules for contraction in Standard English. In other cases Black English is in fact more precise than Standard English. *He be working* indicates that he generally works, perhaps that he has a regular job; *He working* only means that he is working at the moment that the sentence is uttered. In Standard English *He is working* fails to make that distinction.

8.3.1 Positive Evidence

We can use the term *positive evidence* in an informal way to refer to the information available to the child about which strings of words are grammatical sentences of the target language. (As always in linguistics and psycholinguistics, "grammatical" sentences are those that sound natural in colloquial speech, though not necessarily those that would be deemed "proper English" in formal written prose. Thus, split infinitives, dangling participles, slang, and so on, are "grammatical" in this sense.) Is parents' speech "positive evidence"? That is, when a parent uses a sentence, can the child assume that it is part of the language to be learned, or do parents use so many random fragments, slips of the tongue, hesitations, and false starts that children would have to take much of it with a grain of salt? Fortunately for children almost all of the speech they hear during the language-learning years is fluent, complete, and grammatically well formed: 99.93 percent, according to one estimate (Newport, Gleitman, and Gleitman 1977). This assumes that "elliptical" utterances count as being "well formed," as, for example, when the question *Where are you going?* is answered with *To the store*. Since rules of ellipsis are part of the grammar of one's language or dialect and not just random snippings from sentences, this is the right way to count (for example, the grammar of casual British English allows the question *Will he go?* to be answered with *He might do*, whereas the grammar of American English does not).

8.3.2   Negative Evidence

Negative evidence refers to information about which strings of words are not grammatical sentences in the language, such as corrections or other forms of feedback from a parent that tell the child that an utterance is ungrammatical. Whether children get and need negative evidence is of crucial importance: in the absence of negative evidence, children who hypothesize a rule that generates a superset of the language will have no way of knowing that they are wrong (Baker 1979; Gold 1967). If children do not get (or do not use) negative evidence, their brain must contain some mechanism that either avoids generating too large a language or can recover from such overgeneration.

Brown and Hanlon (1970) attempted to test Skinner's behaviorist claim that language learning depends on parents' reinforcement of children's grammatical behaviors. Using transcripts of naturalistic parent-child dialogue, they divided children's sentences into ones that were grammatically well formed and ones that contained grammatical errors, and they divided adults' responses to those sentences into ones that expressed some kind of approval (for example, "Yes, that's good") and ones that expressed some kind of disapproval. They looked for a correlation but failed to find one: parents did not express approval or disapproval to their children contingent on whether the child's prior utterance was well formed or not (approval depended instead on whether the child's utterance was true). Brown and Hanlon also looked at children's well-formed and badly formed questions, and whether parents seemed to answer them appropriately (as if they understood them) or with non sequiturs. They found that parents do not understand their children's well-formed questions better than their badly formed ones. Other studies (for example, Hirsh-Pasek, Treiman, and Schneiderman 1984; Demetras, Post, and Snow 1986) have replicated that result, and they have found that when parents are sensitive to the grammaticality of their children's speech at all, the contingency between their behavior and that of their children is noisy, indiscriminate, and inconsistent from child to child and age to age. Thus, it appears that children do not receive negative evidence.

These results, though of profound importance, should not be too surprising. Every speaker of English judges sentences such as *I dribbled the floor with paint* or *Ten pounds was weighed by the boy* or *I murmured John the answer* or *I rejoiced the audience* to be ungrammatical. But it is unlikely that every speaker has at some point uttered these verbs in such sentences and benefited from negative feedback. The child must have some mental mechanisms that rule out vast numbers of "reasonable" strings of words without any outside intervention at all.

8.3.3 "Motherese"

Parents and caretakers in many parts of the world modify their speech when talking to young children, one example of how people in general use several "registers" in different social settings. Speech to children is slower, shorter, in some ways (but not all) simpler, higher-pitched, more exaggerated in intonation, more fluent and grammatically well formed, and more directed in content to the present situation, compared to speech among adults (Snow and Ferguson 1977). Many parents also expand their children's utterances into full sentences or offer sequences of paraphrases of a given sentence. However, one should not consider this speech register, sometimes called *Motherese*, to be a set of "language lessons." Though it may seem simple at first glance, in many ways it is not. For example, speech directed to children is full of questions—indeed, sometimes a majority of the sentences consist of questions. If you think questions are simple, just try to write a set of phrase structure and transformational rules that generates the following sentences and nonsentences exactly:

(6)   He can go somewhere.
      Where can he go?
      *Where can he go somewhere?
      *Where he can go?
      *Where did he can go?

(7)   He went somewhere.
      Where did he go?
      He went WHERE?

*Where went he?
*Where did he went?
*Where he went?
*He did go WHERE?

(8)   He went home.
Why did he go home?
How come he went home?
*Why he went home?
*How come did he go home?

Linguists struggle over these facts—some of the most puzzling in the English language—with the techniques of syntactic analysis (see chapter 1); but these are the constructions that infants are bombarded with and that they master by their early school years.

Another reason for doubting that Motherese is really a set of language lessons is that children whose mothers use it more do not develop language any faster (Newport, Gleitman, and Gleitman 1977). Furthermore, communities' ideas about children's proper place in society differ radically —for example, in some societies people tacitly assume that children aren't worth speaking to and don't have anything to say that is worth listening to. Such children learn to speak by overhearing streams of adult-to-adult speech. In other communities mothers consciously try to teach their children language, but not in the American style of talking to them indulgently. Rather, they wait until a third party is present and then coach their children in the proper, adultlike sentences they should use (Schieffelin and Eisenberg 1981). Nonetheless, those children, like all children, grow up to be fluent speakers. It surely does not hurt children when their parents speak slowly, clearly, and succinctly to them, but their success at learning cannot be explained by the properties of their parents' use of baby talk.

8.3.4   Prosodic Information

In English, syntactic structure influences a number of the "prosodic" properties of the speech wave, such as lengthening, intonation, and pausing (Cooper and Paccia-Cooper 1980). To hear this, listen to youself say the word *likes* in the two sentences *The boy he likes slept* and *The boy likes sleds*. In the first sentence the word *likes* is at the boundary of a relative clause and is drawn out, exaggerated in intonation, and followed by a pause; in the second it is in the middle of a verb phrase and is pronounced more quickly, is given uniform intonation, and is run together with the following word *sleds*. Possibly the exaggerated intonations, slow rate, and clear demarcation of sentence boundaries in parental speech could be informative to a child in the effort to find significant units in it, such as major clause and phrase boundaries (Gleitman and Wanner 1984). Little is known precisely about how children use prosodic patterns in language learning, but it has been shown that parents tend to exaggerate their prosodic patterns when speaking to children (Morgan 1986) and that children prefer to listen to speech that displays correlations between prosody and syntax than to speech that violates them (Fernald 1984; Hirsh-Pasek et al. 1987).

8.3.5   Contextual and Semantic Information

Mere exposure to sentences from a language is not enough for language learning to occur. Ervin-Tripp (1973) studied hearing children of deaf parents whose only access to English was through radio or television broadcasts. The children did not learn any speech from that input. The language input that children do seem to process consists of speech uttered in nonlinguistic contexts that they can encode via perception (Macnamara 1972; Schlesinger 1971). Furthermore, even before children have learned syntax, they know the meaning of many words and can make good guesses about what their parents might be saying based on their knowledge of how the referents of these words typically act (for example, people tend to eat apples, but not vice versa). In fact, parental speech to young children is so redundant with its context that a person with no knowledge of the order in which parents' words are spoken, only the words themselves, can infer from transcripts, with high accuracy, what was being said (Slobin 1977). Many models of language acquisition assume that the input to the child consists of a sentence and a full encoding of the meaning of that sentence, inferred from context and from the child's knowledge of the meanings of individual words (see, for example, Anderson 1977; Berwick 1986; Pinker 1982, 1984; Wexler and Culicover 1980). Although no one believes that this is literally true—children do not hear every word of every sentence and surely do not, at the outset, perceive the entire meaning of a sentence from context—it is a reasonable first idealization that can later be complicated once we understand how mechanisms that learn grammars from input might work at all.

This assumption seems reasonable as a first approximation, but of course it still leaves many problems unsolved. For one thing, blind children, whose access to the nonlinguistic world is obviously severely limited, learn language without many problems: at some stages they are no worse at naming the colors of familiar objects than sighted children are (Landau and Gleitman 1985). Furthermore, although children can perceive the *referents* of a sentence, they cannot literally perceive its *meaning*: in many cases semantic representations must themselves be learned as part of the language. For example, when a parent fills a glass with water from a pitcher, no perceptual information can tell the child whether the verb the parent is using means 'pour' or 'fill'.

8.4   How Does the Child Use the Information in the Input?

The input to language acquisition consists of sounds and situations; the output is a formal grammar specifying, for that language, the order and arrangement of abstract entities and relations such as nouns, verbs, subjects, phrase structures, c-command. Somehow the child must discover these entities to learn the language; we know that even preschool children have managed to do an analysis of this sort because of the results of the experiments on structure-dependence discussed in section 8.2.3. But how does the child go from sounds and situations to syntactic structure? Innate knowledge of grammar itself is not sufficient. It does no good simply to have the information "There exist nouns" written down in the child's brain; the child must have some way of *finding* nouns in parents' speech, in order to be able to determine, among other things, whether subject nouns come before the verb, as in English, or after, as in Irish. Once the child finds a word that can positively be identified as a noun in subject position, any innate knowledge would immediately be helpful, because the child could then deduce all kinds of implications about how it be used. But identifying examples of grammatical entities like nouns is the crucial first step, and it is not a trivial one. In English, nouns can be identified as those words that come after articles, take the suffix -s in the plural, and so on. But the infant obviously doesn't know that yet. Nouns do not occur in the same sentence positions in all the languages of the world, and they are not spoken with any particular tone of voice. Nor do they have a constant meaning—they often refer to physical things, like dogs, but they need not (witness *the playing of music* or *the redness of the sun*). The same is true for other linguistic entities: verbs, subjects, objects, auxiliaries, tense markers, and so on. Since children must somehow "lift themselves up by their bootstraps" to get started in formulating a grammar for their native language, this is sometimes called the *bootstrapping problem* (see Pinker 1982, 1984, 1989). Several solutions can be envisioned.

8.4.1   Extracting Simple Correlations

One possibility is that the child sets up a massive correlation matrix, noticing which words appear in which positions, which words appear next to which other words, which words take which prefixes and suffixes in which circumstances, and so on. On this theory, syntactic categories arise as the child discovers that certain sets of properties are correlated in large sets of words. For example, many words occur sentence-initially, are inflected with -s when referring to plural entities, and occur after words such as *a* and *the*. This set of words would be grouped together as the equivalent of the "noun" category (Maratsos and Chalkley 1981). The problem with the proposal is that there are an astronomical number of possible correlations among linguistic properties for the child to test. To take just two, the child would have to determine whether a sentence containing the word *cat* in third position must have a plural word at the end, or whether sentences ending in words ending in *d* are invariably preceded by words referring to plural entities. Most of these correlations never occur in any natural language to begin with. It would be a mystery, then, why children would be born with complex machinery designed to test for them, or to put it another way, it would be mystery why there are no languages exhibiting certain kinds of correlations given that children are capable of finding them. Confining the search to the simpler contingencies will not work either, because some of the common correlations among words in languages—such as the behavior of *where, can,* and *do* in examples (6)–(8)—depend on complex high-order combinations of words and positions. The child should look for correlations only where they might be relevant to grammar, such as whether auxiliaries come before or after subjects when a *wh*-word (*which, when, why,* and so on) is in the sentence. But knowing where the subjects and auxiliaries are in a sentence, a prerequisite to seeing how their positions might correlate with one another, is not something the child can do before language learning has begun. It is exactly the kind to ability we are trying to explain in the first place! Somehow, the child must break into this circle.

8.4.2   Using Prosody

A second way in which the child could begin learning syntax would be to attend to the prosodic properties of input sentences and to posit phrase boundaries at points in the acoustic stream marked by lengthening, pausing, and drops in fundamental frequency. But using this information is by no means straightforward. Careful experiments can detect the influence of syntactic boundaries in spoken speech, but in real life a multiplicity of factors other than phrase structure influence the prosodic contour of a sentence (syllabic structure of individual words, emotional state of the speaker, intent of the speaker, word frequency, contrastive stress). Somehow the child must subtract these influences from the input before attempting to derive phrase boundaries. Furthermore, these syntax-prosody correlations would have to hold for all languages, not just English; it is important then to find out whether in fact they do.

8.4.3   Using Semantics

A third possibility exploits the fact that there is a one-way correlation between syntax and semantics in the basic sentences of most of the world's languages (see Pinker 1982, 1984; Macnamara 1982; Grimshaw 1981;

Wexler and Culicover 1980). Though not all nouns are physical objects, all physical objects are expressed using nouns. Similarly, if a verb has an argument playing the semantic role (also called a "theta role"; see chapter 1) of "agent," then that argument will be expressed as the subject of basic sentences in language after language. (Again, this does not work in reverse: the subject is not necessarily an agent. In *John liked Mary* the subject is an "experiencer"; in *John pleased Mary* it is an object of experience; in *John received a package* it is a goal or recipient; in *John underwent an operation* it is a patient.) Similarly, entities directly affected by an action are expressed as objects (but not all objects are entities affected by an action); actions themselves are expressed as verbs (though not all verbs express actions). Even phrase structure configurations have semantic correlates: an argument of a verb reliably appears as its phrase-mate inside the verb phrase in the sentence's phrase structure tree (see chapter 1). If children assumed that semantic and syntactic categories are correlated in restricted ways in the early input, then they could use semantic properties of words and phrases (inferred from context; see section 2.5) as evidence that they belong to certain syntactic categories. For example, they could infer that a word that designated a person, place, or thing was a noun, that a word designating an action was a verb, that a word expressing the agent argument of an action predicate was the subject of its sentence, and so on. For example, upon hearing the sentence *The cat chased the rat*, they could deduce that in English the subject comes before the verb, that the object comes after the verb, and so on. This would give them the basis for creating the phrase structure trees that allow them to analyze the rules of the language, such as the ones involved in the experiments on structure-dependence.

Of course, children could not literally create a grammar that contained rules like "Agent words come before action words." This would leave them no way of knowing how to order the words in sentences such as *Apples appeal to Mary* or *John received a package*. But once an initial set of rules was learned, items that are more abstract or that do not follow the usual patterns relating syntax and semantics could be learned via their distribution in already learned structures. That is, children could now infer that *apples* is the subject of *appeal* and that *John* is the subject of *receive* because they are in subject position, a fact they now know thanks to the earlier *cat-chased-rat* sentences. Similarly, they could infer that *appeal* is a verb to begin with because it is in the "verb" position.

The use of semantics to get language acquisition started predicts that early child speech should have a "semantic look": children's very first nouns should be names of people and things; their first verbs should refer to actions; their first subjects should refer to agents of actions. By and large, this is true, as we will see in the next section (Brown 1973; Slobin

1985b). However, it is only true up to a point: especially with more "peripheral" aspects of language, children can be quite good at acquiring purely grammatical distinctions with little or no semantic influence. For example, children learning languages with grammatical gender seldom use feminine gender when using a masculine noun referring to a female person; they seem to realize right away that gender is an abstract grammatical feature, not a symbol for biological sex (Karmiloff-Smith 1979; Levy 1983.)

Most likely, children use some combination of semantic, correlational, and prosodic input cues, perhaps combined in such a way that they arrive at the grammatical analysis of the input that is most consistent with all of them (see Pinker 1987).

8.5   The Course of Language Acquisition

The course of language acquisition has been documented in great detail (see, for example, Brown 1973; MacWhinney 1982; Maratsos 1983; Menyuk 1969; Slobin 1985a,b; Wanner and Gleitman 1982). However, beyond the earliest word combinations, children's speech becomes so complex so quickly that no general characterization of their grammatical abilities has been offered. Furthermore, the *causes* of change in children's abilities over time have remained obscure; we will consider some of the possibilities in a later section.

8.5.1   Early Development

Children's early language development shows considerable variation in terms of the absolute ages at which different skills are attained, but far more uniformity in terms of the order in which they are attained and the kinds of errors that are made at different stages (Brown 1973).

Children typically begin to utter single words in a "holophrastic" stage beginning around their first birthday. However, another common pattern is for children to latch onto larger chunks of speech, often demarcated within a prosodic contour, and use them as memorized wholes for a period of time before breaking them down into their constituents (Nelson 1981; Peters 1983).

The transition to the first word combinations and sentences takes place around the age of 18 months. Children usually pass through a stage in which they combine words into strings no more than two items long, typically expressing one of a dozen or so semantic relations, including agent-action (*Mommy fix*), agent-object (*Mommy pumpkin*), action-object (*Hit ball*), object-location (*Sweater chair*), possessor-object (*Mommy sock*), recurring object or event (*More doggy*), disappearing or absent object or event

(*Allgone milk*), and notice of an object or event (*There doggie*) (Brown 1973; Braine 1976; Bloom, Lightbown, and Hood 1975). Children's two-word utterances often consist of correctly ordered two-word subsets of a three-item relation (for example, agent-action, action-object, and agent-object, drawn from the hypothetical full sequence agent-action-object; Bloom 1970). Though one might expect children to be sloppy about word order, this is the exception rather than the rule; early word sequences almost always exhibit one of the orders that would be correct in the adult language (Brown 1973; Braine 1976). Often when a pattern first appears, only a small number of words—rather than just any word in the child's vocabulary—is used to fill one of the roles (Braine 1976); for example, a child may use *big, hot,* and *cold* as the only modifiers appearing before a noun. Unstressed morphemes are usually absent entirely; in many languages, such as English, this has the effect of making this stage and later ones sound like the prose of telegrams, lacking closed classed morphemes such as prepositions, auxiliaries, and complementizers (for example, *Mommy put shirt chair*).

Though children often go through a one-word stage and a two-word stage, there is no three-word stage; at a certain point children begin to use sentences ranging from three to eight words, and the mean length of their utterances increases steadily until well into the fourth year. These longer utterances begin with combinations that are similiar to the two-word combinations except that either three-term and longer sequences (such as agent-action-object) are uttered in toto or one of the terms is itself expanded into a two-word combination; thus, rather than simply saying *Doggie run* (agent-action), children at this stage might say *Big doggie run* (agent-action, where agent = (attribute-object); see Brown 1973; Bloom 1970).

Early speech is simplified in many ways. For example, early utterances contain no syntactic mechanism indicating questions or other semantic modifications of the entire proposition. In English, for instance, yes-no questions are created by inverting the subject and auxiliary: *The man is here* becomes *Is the man here?* But in early speech questions are indicated by rising intonation (Bowerman 1973b) even though inverted sentences are as common or more common in parental speech (Newport, Gleitman, and Gleitman 1977). Likewise, relativization (*the man that I like*) and coordination (*The dog and the cat ran*) are infrequent, generally not becoming common until the fourth year (Brown 1973).

8.5.2   Later Development

Shortly after children progress to three-word and longer utterances (usually sometime in the third year), their speech undergoes an explosion in complexity. It is virtually impossible to give a precise account of the kinds of constructions children can use—that is, it is virtually impossible to write a grammar for children's speech (especially since, unlike adults, young children cannot reliably tell us whether a string of words is or is not "well formed" in their language when asked). Instead, it is easier to catalogue the ways in which their speech differs from that of adults—their systematic error patterns.

Many errors arise from children's formulation of a general rule for which there are lexical exceptions or complex constraining conditions in the adult language. We have already seen the case of past inflections like *breaked*, plural inflections like *mouses*, and control in exceptional verbs like *promise*. Children also overgeneralize the syntactic and semantic properties of words. For example, there are rules for "alternations" among the argument structures of verbs in most languages. An example is the English "causative rule" that converts intransitive verbs standing for events into transitive verbs standing for the causation of such events—for example, *The glass broke* and *He broke the glass*. There are subtle constraints on how this rule may apply. It works for causation of change of state (*The ice melted/I melted the ice*) and for causation of particular manners of moving (*The ball bounced/I bounced the ball*). However, it does not apply to causation of actions, such as *giggle*, or to causation of motion in a particular direction, such as *rise, fall, go,* or *come*. Apparently children do not apply these restrictions instantaneously; they first formulate a rule that applies to any kind of causation. Thus, they produce striking errors such as *Don't giggle me!* or *I come it closer,* meaning "Don't make me giggle!" or "I made it come closer" (Bowerman 1974, 1982a,b).

Children seem to like to keep clauses as self-contained, unmodifiable wholes. For example, children learning English often fail to invert the subject and auxiliary in questions beginning with *wh*-words, leading to errors such as *Why he can go?* for *Why can he go?* (Brown 1968; Kuczaj and Brannick 1979). In other languages, too, children fail to permute or deform the constituent orders of main clauses to signal "sentence modalities" such as questions, negations, and conditionals (Slobin 1973, 1985b).

Some errors seem to betray the overapplication of general linkages between syntax and semantics, perhaps reflecting a universal core of notions that children expect to be expressed in consistent grammatical fashion. For example, children may "expect" their language, whatever it is, to give them a standard grammatical way of expressing basic concepts such as objects moving to locations, agents acting upon objects, and the distinction between bounded events and states with no clear beginning or end points (Slobin 1985b). Thus, Russian has accusative case markers (suffixes on nouns indicating that they are direct objects) that must be used for all direct objects. But very young children use them to refer to objects affected by actions alone; in other words, they use them with verbs like *hit* or *move* but omit them with verbs like *read* or *like*. In other cases children may use a morpheme in a semantic class that is *broader* than the one used in the language. For example, some languages use one marker to signal the goal of a physical transfer (*go TO$_1$ the store*) and another to signal the goal of a transfer of possession (*give it TO$_2$ Bill*). Children, however, lump the two kinds of goal together and use the first one in the second kind of situation as well (Slobin 1985b), as if they saw transfer of possession as a kind of physical movement of an object. Similar overextensions can be heard in English, when children fail to select the proper preposition to accompany a verb, using one that fits some general conceptualization of a type of event. Children occasionally say things like *The ice cream was melted FROM the sun*, as though causality "flowed from" the sun, or *Can I have any reading BEHIND dinner?*, as though time were spread out in space like a line (Maratsos and Abramovitch 1975; Bowerman 1982a). In other words, these errors seem to show the use of a spatial metaphor to represent non-spatial events such as causation, transfer of possession, change of state, and passage of time, the causal force or object that undergoes the change being depicted as though it were moving from one location to another.

8.6   Causes of Developmental Changes

It is far easier to document change in children than to explain it. Several kinds of mechanism are presumably at work. *Maturational changes* in the brain after birth may affect language development in a number of ways. They may govern the onset of language, the differences in rate of language development among children, and the decline beginning in late childhood or early adolescence of the ability to attain native proficiency.

More indirectly, *changes in the child's general information-processing abilities* (attention, memory, short-term buffers for acoustic input and articulatory output) could leave their mark on a number of features of child language. For example, children selectively pick up information at the ends of words (Slobin 1973) and at the beginnings and ends of sentences (Newport, Gleitman, and Gleitman 1977), presumably because these are the parts of strings that are best retained in short-term memory. Similarly, the fact that early word combinations are two words long but seem to be subsets drawn from underlying patterns containing three or four elements (Bloom 1970; Brown 1973) appears to indicate that children can keep three-word sequences in mind but must pass them through an information-processing bottleneck with only two slots before they can pronounce them. *Conceptual development* might affect language development, in that if children have not yet mastered a difficult semantic distinction, such as the complex temporal relations involved in *John will have gone*, they may be unable to master the syntax of the construction dedicated to expressing it. *Complexity*, too, has a demonstrable role. Simpler rules and forms appear in speech before more complex ones: for example, the plural marker *-s* in English, which requires knowing only whether the number of referents is singular or plural, is used consistently before the present tense marker *-s*, which requires knowing whether the subject is singular or plural *and* whether it is first, second, or third person *and* that the event is to be expressed in the present tense (Brown 1973). Similarly, complex forms are first applied in simpler approximations. Russian contains one case marker for masculine nominative (a suffix on a masculine noun indicating that it is the subject of the sentence), one for feminine nominative, one for masculine accusative (indicating that the noun is a direct object), and one for feminine accusative. Children often use each marker with the correct case, never using a nominative marker for accusative nouns or vice versa, but do not properly use the masculine and feminine variants with masculine and feminine nouns (Slobin 1985b).

Though these four factors affect the course of development, they are global trends that do not have much to do with how the child picks up those aspects of parental speech that are relevant to acquiring that language—that is, with learning itself. Let us consider, in more detail, some processes that work to increase the child's mastery of the particular target language.

8.6.1   Extracting Patterns and Generalizations

Children clearly must notice similarities holding across many pairs of related items and abstract such similarities out as general rules. For example, *jog/jogged*, *play/played*, *turn/turned*, acquired as six independent verbs, eventually lead to the rule "past $(x) = x + $ d." When the pattern is extracted and applied to new inputs, productive regularization and possibly overregularization (*breaked*) are the result. As one might expect, variables that affect rates of pattern learning in adults also affect language development: more frequent verbs are learned correctly first, and more consistent patterns are learned before less consistent ones, all things being equal. For example, a group of English irregular verbs, all ending in *t* or *d*, do not change in the past tense form; *Yesterday I hit the ball* (also *put, cut, shut, split,* and so on). Children learn the past tense forms of these verbs faster than the past tense forms of other subclasses where the pattern of sound change relating the stem and the past tense form is less consistent from verb to verb, such as *give/gave, sit/sat, eat/ate,* which involve a vowel change that is roughly similar but not exactly consistent from verb to verb.

One might then suppose that with a detailed enough analysis of the input statistics, one could predict when children would begin to generalize, and how far they would extend their generalizations. It turns out that this is often not the case. One of the most dramatic demonstrations of the limitations of statistical factors comes from an examination of a computer simulation model designed to extract in parallel any combination of over 200,000 regularities relating phonological properties of English verb stems and phonological properties of their past tense forms (Rumelhart and McClelland 1986). The model is representative of a theory (*parallel distributed processing* or *connectionism*) that tries to explain changes in cognitive development in terms of the extraction of statistical regularities in the input. Rumelhart and McClelland have proposed a very different explanation for the phenomenon of past tense overregularization errors such as *breaked* than the one discussed here. In their model, no words are stored, and no rules are coined. Rather, the child records the input frequency of any of a huge number of possible mappings between phonological patterns in the stem and phonological patterns in the past tense version. Regularities are extended to new stems on the basis of their similarity to these phonological patterns. The differences between these two models have engendered an important controversy in psycholinguistics and cognitive science in general (see Rumelhart and McClelland 1986; Pinker and Prince 1988).

At first glance the model appears to duplicate the behavior of children, progressing from a stage at which irregular past tenses such as *broke* are used correctly, to a stage at which they are overregularized (*breaked*). This performance was a direct consequence of the statistics of the input verbs fed to the model. In written English high-frequency verbs tend to be irregular and vice versa. Children, Rumelhart and McClelland reasoned, are likely to learn a few high-frequency verbs first, then a large number of verbs, of which an increasing proportion would probably be regular. Therefore, they first fed their model a few high-frequency verbs, almost all of them irregular. The model, lacking widespread evidence for the regular pattern, reproduced the past tense forms of all the verbs correctly. Then they fed it a much larger collection of high-to-medium frequency verbs, the majority of them regular. The model, picking up this overwhelming patten, began to overregularize.

However, a change in input statistics cannot be the explanation for the onset of regularization in children—the ratio of irregular to regular verbs in parents' speech and in children's own vocabularies does not change during the period in development where overregularization errors such as *breaked* begin to appear, and it does not contain a huge preponderance of regular verbs at any point in this developmental sequence (Pinker and Prince 1988). The key event is not in the environment but in the child's head. At some point the child seems to use a productive rule in addition to having memorized forms from the input.

Most important, the key factor in the explanation of how children extract patterns must be which patterns they are capable of extracting. For language acquisition to succeed, these "patterns" must be surprisingly subtle and abstract, even for something seemingly as simple as the past tense alternations in English (see Pinker and Prince 1988). At first it might appear that the relevant patterns are correlations between phonological properties of the stem and phonological patterns of the past tense form. For example, *sting* goes to *stung*, *fling* goes to *flung*, and so on, so the rule might be: *ing* goes to *ung*. However, such patterns cannot be recorded and then applied willy-nilly. Two verbs can sound the same but have different past tense forms: *ring the bell/rang the bell, ring the table with flowers/ringed the table with flowers, wring the shirt out/wrung the shirt out*. Thus, the rule cannot just convert sound to sound; an abstract "mental dictionary entry" must intervene, specifying for each verb whether it is regular or irregular, and if it is irregular, which of the possible irregular patterns it takes.

Furthermore, irregularity must be listed for word *roots*, not for words themselves. This is a subtle distinction, but an important one. If a verb is transparently derived from a noun, it is still a verb, but it has a noun "root." Nouns obviously can't be marked in the mental lexicon as having an irregular past tense, because nouns don't have past tenses to begin with. Thus, verbs that intuitively sound like nouns that were converted into verbs also can't be marked in the mental dictionary as having an "irregular past tense," and they are automatically regular, no matter how similar they are in sound to a verb that has an irregular past tense form. (The same is true of verbs derived from adjectives.) This is why speakers of English say *braked the car*, not *broke the car* (the verb *brake* is, of course, derived from the noun *brake*), and *kinged the checker piece* (made it into a "king"), not *kung the checker piece*. (Baseball fans among you now know why Yaz *flied* out to right field, not *flew* out; hockey fans now know why Lemieux *high-sticked* Middleton, not *high-stuck* him.) On the other hand, when one verb is derived from another, it is a verb with a verb root, and if that verb root is irregular, the whole derived verb will be, too: thus, if *come* has the past tense *came*, then *become* must have the past tense *became*, and *overcome* must have the past tense *overcame* (though *succumb* does not have the past tense *succame*—the verb root must combine with a legitimate, independently occurring prefix to "count" as the root of the larger word, even if the prefix is itself meaningless). Meaning has nothing to do with any of this: *come, become, overcome, come around, come into some money* have different meanings but the same past tense form; whereas *hit/hit, slap/slapped*, and *strike/struck* have similar meanings but different past tense forms. The crucial property is not a verb's meaning but its root—an abstract linguistic property.

To master this system, children must be sensitive to "patterns" such as whether a verb is derived from a noun root or a verb root and whether it bears the label "regular" or "irregular." These patterns are invisible, odorless, and tasteless; children do not really "extract" them so much as they impose them. Gordon's experiment on "mouse-eaters" is one example of how the imposition of these patterns can be observed in the laboratory.

8.6.2   Parameter Setting and the Subset Principle

A striking discovery of modern generative grammar is that natural languages all seem to be built on the same basic plan. Many differences among languages are not radical differences in basic structure but different settings of a few "parameters" that allow languages to vary, or different choices of rule types from a fairly small inventory of possibilities. The notion of a "parameter" is borrowed from mathematics. For example, all of the equations of the form "$y = 3x + b$," when graphed, correspond to a family of parallel lines with a slope of 3; the parameter b takes on a different value for each line and corresponds to how high or low it is on the graph. Similarly, languages may have parameters. For example, all languages in some sense have subjects, but there is a parameter that can vary among languages corresponding to whether or not a given language allows the speaker to omit the subject in a tensed sentence with an inflected verb. This "null subject" parameter is set to "off" in English and "on" in Spanish and Italian (Chomsky 1981); a English speaker cannot say *Goes to the store*, but a Spanish speaker can say the equivalent. The reason this difference is thought of as a "parameter" rather than an isolated fact is that it corresponds not only to the presence or absence of overt subjects but also to a variety of more subtle linguistic facts that are all present in languages with null subjects and absent in languages that require the subject to be overt. For example, speakers of null subject languages can also use sentences corresponding to *Who do you think that left?* This is ungrammatical in English because *who* has been moved from its original position after *that*, leaving behind a silent "trace" symbol in a position where the presence of a trace automatically makes the sentence ungrammatical. In Spanish the trace can be deleted, just like any subject can, and the sentence is rendered grammatical. Thus, the rules of a grammar interact tightly; a single change will have a series of cascading effects throughout the grammar. On this view, the child only has to set these parameters on the basis of parental input, and the full richness of grammar will ensue when those parameterized rules interact with one another and with universal principles. The parameter-setting view can help explain the universality and rapidity of language acquisition: when the child learns one fact about her language, she can deduce that other facts are also true of it without having to learn them one by one.

This raises the question of how children set the parameters. One suggestion is that parameter settings are ordered and that children assume a particular setting as the default case, moving to other parameter settings on an ordered list as the input evidence forces them to (Chomsky 1981). But how would the parameter settings be ordered? One very general rationale comes from the fact that children have no systematic access to negative evidence. Thus, for every case in which parameter setting A generates a subset of the sentences generated by setting B (as in diagrams (c) and (d) of figure 8.1), the child would first hypothesize A, then abandon it for B only if a sentence generated by B but not by A was encountered in the input (Pinker 1986; Berwick 1986; Osherson, Stob, and Weinstein 1985). Children would then have no need for negative evidence; they would never guess too large a language. (For settings that generate languages that intersect or are disjoint, as in diagrams (a) and (b) of figure 8.1, either setting can be discarded if incorrect, because it will fail to generate sentences that will eventually turn up in parental speech.)

Much interesting research hinges on whether children do guess the smallest subset among a set of nested possible languages first. In some cases this seems to be true (Pinker 1984). We know that some languages, such as English, mandate strict word orders; others, such as Russian or Japanese, list a small set of admissible orders; still others, such as the Australian aborigine language Warlpiri, allow almost total scrambling of word order within a clause. Word order freedom thus seems to be a parameter of variation across languages, and the setting generating the smallest language would obviously be the one for fixed word order. Thus, if children are following this Subset Principle, they should assume that in the default circumstance languages have a fixed constituent order. They would back off from that prediction if they heard alternative word orders, indicating that the language did permit constituent order freedom. Fixed order in general would be the default case, though not any particular fixed order such as that of English or any other language. The alternative is that children could assume that the default case was constituent order freedom.

Consider the possible developmental predictions made by these accounts, starting with the "fixed order = default" theory. For fixed constituent order languages like English, the child's grammar should not generate constituent orders not permitted by the adult grammar; one should thus expect no overgeneration of constituent order by children learning languages like English. However, for free constituent order languages, it is possible that children could pass through a stage in which they had recorded some subset of the adult orders that they had heard or attended to

Table 8.1
Predictions of two hypotheses about children's default assumptions about word order freedom.

	Fixed constituent order language	Free constituent order language
Fixed order as default	No overgeneration	Undergeneration possible
Free order as default	Overgeneration possible	No undergeneration

but that they had not yet appreciated the full diversity of the language and had not yet set the parameter to word order freedom. If so, it is possible (though not necessary) that children acquiring free constituent order languages would pass through a stage in which they would fail to exploit all the ordering possibilities permitted by the adult language. In other words, children learning such a language could undergenerate constituent orders.

The other theory, "free order = default," makes very different predictions. Children learning free constituent order languages would immediately hypothesize correct rules permitting constituent order freedom and therefore would not undergenerate. On the other hand, for fixed constituent order languages, it is possible that children could first pass through a stage in which they had not yet recorded the particular fixed orders of the language; the parameter would thus remain at the default setting of "free order." With this strategy, then, we are prepared for the possibility that a child learning fixed constituent orders might overgenerate and utter orders that the target language does not permit. The predictions are summarized in table 8.1.

To decide between the theories, it is necessary to consider the developmental evidence corresponding to each column. A number of psycholinguists have analyzed the speech of young children acquiring a variety of languages and have tabulated (1) the proportion of their utterances that do not correspond to any allowable order in the language they are acquiring and (2) whether they use all, or only some, of the allowable orders if the language allows more than one. The data are as follows. For fixed constituent order languages, children generally stick to the orders used by their parents (about 95% of the time; see Pinker 1984). As for free constituent order languages, there have indeed been reports of children using only a subset of the permissible orders in the acquisition of Korean, Russian, and Swedish (Brown 1973). Such undergeneration is not universal (it has not been reported for Finnish (Bowerman 1973b) or Turkish (Slobin 1982)), but it need not be under either hypothesis. The "fixed order = default" hypothesis for the parameter of constituent order freedom seems to be true, and this helps to explain how children learn such languages given that they cannot count on being corrected if they deviate from the right orders. In general, formulating hierarchies of parameter settings and testing them against the facts of development is an important topic of current research (see, for example, Wexler and Manzini 1987).

8.6.3 Eliminating Errors through the Application of Principles

The strictest version of the Subset Principle would predict that children would never generate an incorrect form and its correct counterpart simultaneously, because that would define a superset of the target language, which contains only the correct form. However, children do exactly that in several domains. For example, children use regularized and irregular past tense forms (*breaked, broke*) side by side for a number of years (Kuczaj 1977). They extend certain alternations between argument structures across the board rather than restricting them to certain subsets of verbs (Bowerman 1982b); a case in point is the causative alternation discussed earlier (*Don't giggle me!*). This rules out the strongest version of the Subset Principle but leaves it a mystery how the child recovers from the error patterns in the absence of negative evidence. There must be some combination of positive data and a mental process that uses the positive data as evidence that some rule should be constrained or some form discarded.

One possibility is that some general principle applies to rule out a form in the adult grammar but that the child's grammar lacks some crucial piece of information allowing that principle to apply. As the child's knowledge increases, the relevance of the principle to the errant form manifests itself, and the form can be ruled out so as to make the grammar as a whole simpler or more consistent with the principle. One example of such a principle is the Uniqueness Principle in morphology, which would state that any inflectional category of a given stem takes just one form (for example, a single past tense form; a single masculine plural). Thus, when the child hears *broke* and matches it up with *break*, realizing that it is the past tense form of *break*, that would be sufficient for the child to discard *breaked* even in the absence of negative evidence (Pinker 1984). But then why do children persist in using the correct and incorrect forms side by side, sometimes for a year or more? One hypothesis is that the child has not yet realized that the irregular form is the past version of its stem; the child might misconstrue it as an independently existing verb. Is there any other evidence that children misconstrue irregular pasts as being independent verbs? Indeed, such evidence exists. First, children have been heard to use irregular pasts as though they were separate stems—for example, *to broke* (*Did he broke it?, They were broking it, She broked it*) side by side with *to break* (*Did he break it?, They were breaking it, She breaked it*) (Kuczaj 1977, 1981). Second, the transparency of the morphological relation between stem and past tense has been found to affect the amount of overregularization: verbs with dissimilar present and past tenses (*go/went*) are overregularized more than verbs with similar present and past tenses (*hit/hit*) (Bybee and Slobin 1982).

Another kind of principle is one that enforces some kind of consistency between different components of linguistic ability, so that the acquisition of knowledge in one component can lead to the reorganization of knowledge in another. Pinker (1989) suggests an example that might help explain the elimination of overgeneral alternations of argument structure, such as when children overextend the "locative alternation" (*load the wagon with hay/load hay into the wagon*), uttering forms like *Fill salt into the bear* (Bowerman 1982a). A general principle of argument structure is that the direct object is the argument that is affected in some way specified by the verb. The "container" argument is the direct object in *Fill the glass with water*, because the mental definition of the verb *fill* says that the glass becomes full. However, it is the "content" argument that is the object in *Pour water into the glass*, because the mental definition of the verb *pour* says that the water must move in a certain manner. If children mistakenly think that *fill* refers to a manner of motion (presumably, some kind of tipping or pouring) instead of an end state of fullness, that would be one reason for their being able to say *fill x into y*. (Indeed, it is a common strategy for children to focus on the manner of an action when learning verb meanings, often at the expense of acquiring information about the end state that the verb specifies; see Gentner 1978.) When children observe the verb *fill* in enough contexts to realize that it actually encodes the end state of fullness, not a manner of pouring or any other particular manner (for example, eventually they may hear someone talking about *filling* a glass by leaving it on a window sill during a storm), they can change their mental entries for *fill*. As a result, they would no longer consider it eligible to take the argument structure with the "content" as direct object, on the grounds that it violates the constraint that "direct object = specifically affected entity." The principle could have existed all along but only been deemed relevant to the verb *fill* when more information about its definition had been accumulated (Pinker 1989; Gropen 1989). There is some circumstantial evidence that the process might work that way. Gropen, Pinker, and Goldberg (1987) asked preschool children to select which picture corresponded to the sentence *She filled the glass with water*. Most children chose any picture showing water pouring; they did not care whether the glass ended up full. In a separate task they were asked to describe in their own words what was happening in a picture showing a glass being filled. Many of these children used incorrect sentences like *He's filling water into the glass*. Older children tended to make fewer errors of both verb meaning and verb syntax, and children who got the verb meaning right were less likely to make syntax errors and vice versa. This does not prove that improvements in verb meaning automatically lead to the elimination of syntactic errors, but it simply illustrates how one might begin to try to show how principles of correspondence between one component of linguistic knowledge and another might allow increases of knowledge in one to lead to the elimination of errors in another.

The topic of language acquisition is an intriguing mixture: language and thought, nature and nurture, biological hardware and abstract rule systems, absorption of regularities and imposition of constraints. On a more humanistic level, its concrete subject matter, the speech of children, is endlessly fascinating. However, any attempt to understand it scientifically is guaranteed to bring on a certain degree of frustration. Languages are complex combinations of elegant principles and historical accidents. We cannot design new ones with independent orthogonal variables; we are stuck with the ones entrenched in communities. Children, too, were not designed for the benefit of psychologists: their cognitive, social, perceptual, and motor skills are all developing at the same time as their linguistic systems are maturing and their knowledge of a particular language is increasing, and none of their behavior reflects one of these components acting in isolation. And of course, no two children are exactly alike. Given these inherent problems, it may be surprising that we have learned anything about language acquisition at all, but we have. The importance of the topic and the glimpses of elegance in the phenomena will always inspire ingenious hypotheses and tests; the complexity and richness in the data will always keep them honest.

Suggestions for Further Reading

There are several textbooks on child language acquisition that are excellent introductions to the literature in developmental psycholinguistics, though most are weak in their coverage of the acquisition of linguistic structure. Dale 1976 and de Villiers and de Villiers 1978 are good but a bit dated; Reich 1986 and Gleitman and Gleitman 1981 are more up to date.

Representative surveys of current research in language acquisition can be found in Wanner and Gleitman 1982, MacWhinney 1987, Fletcher and Garman 1979, and Demopoulos and Marras 1986. A comprehensive summary of cross-linguistic research can be found in Slobin 1985a. Studies with more explicit ties to linguistic theory can be found in Tavakolian 1981 and Roeper and Williams 1987. A comprehensive theory of language acquisition, reviewing a large amount of empirical work, is presented in Pinker 1984. Another comprehensive theory, supported with a mathematical proof and extensive discussions of implications for linguistic theory, can be found in Wexler and Culicover 1980.

For an informal introduction to formal learnability theory, see Pinker 1979; for a rigorous introduction, see Osherson, Stob, and Weinstein 1985. Some of the implications for linguistic theory are discussed in Baker and McCarthy 1981.

There are several classic articles on language acquisition that anyone going on in the field should read: Chomsky 1959, Lenneberg 1964a, Miller 1964, Ervin 1964, Brown and Bellugi; 1964, Brown and Hanlon 1970, and Slobin 1973.

Questions

8.1   Design three hypothetical empirical studies. One should determine whether children have access to negative evidence. The second should determine whether children ever use negative evidence. The third should determine whether children *need* negative evidence to learn a given construction.

8.2   Design a set of steps (that is, an algorithm, or recipe, or set of instructions) that would start off with no knowledge of English, would take the stem-past pairs in (i) as input, and would then know enough to be able to supply the correct past tense forms for those 10 verbs and for the ones in (ii) as well.

    (i)   walk—walked
          pick—picked
          sip—sipped
          tap—tapped
          sting—stung
          string—strung
          fling—flung
          bring—brought
          ping—pinged
          ring—rang

   (ii)   stop
          flip
          pack
          swing

8.3   Consider three languages. One of them is English, in which every sentence must contain a grammatical subject: *He ate the apple* is grammatical; *Ate the apple* is ungrammatical. In the second language the subject is optional, but the verb always has a suffix that agrees with the subject (whether it is physically present or only "understood") in person, number, and gender. Thus, *He ate-3MS the apple* is grammatical (assume that *3MS* is a suffix, like *-o* or *-ik*, that is used only when the subject is 3rd person masculine singular), as is *Ate-3MS the apple* (those who speak Spanish or Italian will see that this hypothetical language is similar to those languages). The third language has no inflection on the verb but allows the subject to be omitted: *He ate the apple* and *Ate the apple* are both grammatical.

Assume that a child has no access to negative evidence but knows that the language to be learned is one of these three. Does the child have to entertain these hypotheses in any fixed order? If so, what is it? What learning strategy would guarantee that the child would arrive at the correct language? (Show why.)

References

Anderson, J. R. (1977). Induction of augmented transition networks. *Cognitive Science* 1, 125–157.

Anderson, J. R. (1983). *The architecture of cognition.* Cambridge, MA: Harvard University Press.

Baker, C. L. (1979). Syntactic theory and the projection problem. *Linguistic Inquiry* 10, 533–581.

Baker, C. L., and J. McCarthy, eds. (1981). *The logical problem of language acquisition.* Cambridge, MA: MIT Press.

Berko, J. (1958). The child's learning of English morphology. *Word* 14, 150–177.

Berwick, R. C. (1986). *The acquisition of syntactic knowledge.* Cambridge, MA: MIT Press.

Bloom, L. (1970). *Language development: Form and function in emerging grammars.* Cambridge, MA: MIT Press.

Bloom, L., P. Lightbown, and M. Hood (1975). Structure and variation in child language. *Monographs of the Society for Research in Child Development,* 40.

Bowerman, M. (1973a). Structural relationships in children's utterances: Syntactic or semantic? In T. E. Moore, ed., *Cognitive development and the acquisition of language.* New York: Academic Press.

Bowerman, M. (1973b). *Early syntactic development: A cross-linguistic study with special reference to Finnish.* Cambridge: Cambridge University Press.

Bowerman, M. (1974). Learning the structure of causative verbs: A study in the relationship of cognitive, semantic and syntactic development. In E. Clark, ed., *Papers and reports on child language development,* no. 8. Stanford University Committee on Linguistics, Stanford University, Stanford, CA.

Bowerman, M. (1982a). Reorganizational processes in lexical and syntactic development. In Wanner and Gleitman 1982.

Bowerman, M. (1982b). Evaluating competing linguistic models with language acquisition data: Implications of developmental errors with causative verbs. *Quaderni di Semantica* 3, 5–66.

Braine, M. D. S. (1976). Children's first word combinations. *Monographs of the Society for Research in Child Development,* 41.

Brown, R. (1968). The development of *wh* questions in child speech. *Journal of Verbal Learning and Verbal Behavior* 7, 279–290.

Brown, R. (1973). *A first language: The early stages.* Cambridge, MA: Harvard University Press.

Brown, R., and U. Bellugi (1964). Three processes in the child's acquisition of syntax. In Lenneberg 1964b.

Brown, R., and C. Hanlon (1970). Derivational complexity and order of acquisition in child speech. In J. R. Hayes, ed., *Cognition and the development of language.* New York: Wiley.

Bybee, J. L., and D. I. Slobin (1982). Rules and schemas in the development and use of the English past tense. *Language* 58, 265–289.

Chomsky, C. (1969). *The acquisition of syntax in children from 5 to 10.* Cambridge, MA: MIT Press.

Chomsky, N. (1959). A review of B. F. Skinner's *Verbal behavior. Language* 35, 26–58.

Chomsky, N. (1965). *Aspects of the theory of syntax.* Cambridge, MA: MIT Press.

Chomsky, N. (1975). *Reflections on language.* New York: Random House.

Chomsky, N. (1981). *Lectures on government and binding.* Dordrecht, Holland: Foris.

Chomsky, N. (1986). *Knowledge of language: Its nature, origin, and use.* New York: Praeger.

Comrie, B. (1981). *Language universals and linguistic typology.* Chicago: University of Chicago Press.

Cooper, W. E., and J. Paccia-Cooper (1980). *Syntax and speech.* Cambridge, MA: Harvard University Press.

Crain, S., and M. Nakayama (1986). Structure dependence in children's language. *Language* 63, 522–543.

Cromer, R. (1986). Case studies of dissociations between language and cognition. Paper presented at the Eleventh Annual Boston University Conference on Language Development, October 17–19.

Curtiss, S., J. Yamada, and V. Fromkin (1979). How independent is language? On the question of formal parallels between grammar and action. In *UCLA Working Papers in Cognitive Linguistics* 1, UCLA, Los Angeles, CA.

Dale, P. (1976). *Language development.* New York: Holt, Rinehart and Winston.

de Villiers, J., and P. de Villiers (1978). *Language acquisition.* Cambridge, MA: Harvard University Press.

Demetras, M. J., K. N. Post, and C. E. Snow (1986). Feedback to first language learners: The role of repetitions and clarification questions. *Journal of Child Language* 13, 275–292.

Demopoulos, W., and A. Marras, eds. (1986). *Language learning and concept acquisition.* Norwood, NJ: Ablex.

Ervin, S. (1964). Imitation and structural change in children's language. In Lenneberg 1964b.

Ervin-Tripp, S. (1973). Some strategies for the first two years. In T. E. Moore, ed., *Cognitive development and the acquisition of language.* New York: Academic Press.

Fernald, A. (1984). The perceptual and affective salience of mothers' speech to infants. In L. Feagans, C. Garvey, and R. Golinkoff, eds., *The origins and growth of communication.* Norwood, NJ: Ablex.

Fletcher, P., and M. Garman, eds. (1979). *Language acquisition.* Cambridge: Cambridge University Press.

Fodor, J. A. (1975). *The language of thought.* New York: T. Y. Crowell.

Fodor, J. A. (1983). *The modularity of mind.* Cambridge, MA: MIT Press.

Gardner, H. (1983). *Frames of mind: The theory of multiple intelligences.* New York: Basic Books.

Gardner, R. A., and B. T. Gardner (1969). Teaching sign language to a chimpanzee. *Science* 165, 664–672.

Gentner, D. (1978). On relational meaning: The acquisition of verb meaning. *Child Development* 49: 988–998.

Gleitman, L. R., and H. Gleitman (1981). Language. In H. Gleitman, *Psychology.* New York: Norton.

Gleitman, L. R., and E. Wanner (1982). Language acquisition: The state of the state of the art. In Wanner and Gleitman 1982.

Gleitman, L. R., and E. Wanner (1984) Richly specified input to language learning. In O. Selfridge, E. L. Rissland, and M. Arbib, eds., *Adaptive control of ill-defined systems.* New York: Plenum.

Gold, E. (1967). Language identification in the limit. *Information and Control* 10, 447–474.

Gordon, P. (1985). Level ordering in lexical development. *Cognition* 21, 73–93.

Greenberg, J., ed. (1978). *Universals of human language.* Vol. 4, *Syntax.* Stanford, CA: Stanford University Press.

Grimshaw, J. (1981). Form, function, and the language acquisition device. In Baker and McCarthy 1981.

Gropen, J. (1989). Learning locative verbs: How universal linking rules constrain productivity. Doctoral dissertation, MIT.

Gropen, J., S. Pinker, and R. Goldberg (1987). Constrained productivity in the acquisition of locative forms. Paper presented at the Twelfth Annual Boston University Conference on Language Development, October 23–25.

Hirsh-Pasek, K., D. G. N. Nelson, P. W. Jusczyk, K. W. Cassidy, B. Druss, and L. Kennedy (1987). Clauses are perceptual units for young infants. *Cognition* 26, 269–286.

Hirsh-Pasek, K., R. Treiman, and M. Schneiderman (1984). Brown and Hanlon revisited: Mothers' sensitivity to ungrammatical forms. *Journal of Child Language* 11, 81–88.

Hubel, D. H., and T. N. Wiesel (1970). The period of susceptibility to the physiological effects of unilateral eye closure in kittens. *Journal of Physiology* 206, 419–436.

Huttenlocher, P. R. (1979). Synaptic density in human frontal cortex during developmental changes and the effects of aging. *Brain Research* 163, 195.

Johnson, J. S., and E. L. Newport (1989). Critical period effects in second language learning: The influence of maturational state on the acquisition of English as a second language. *Cognitive Psychology* 21.

Karmiloff-Smith, A. (1979). *A functional approach to child language: A study of determiners and reference.* Cambridge: Cambridge University Press.

Kiparsky, P. (1982). From cyclical to lexical phonology. In H. van der Hulst and N. Smith, eds., *The structure of phonological representations.* Dordrecht, Holland: Foris.

Kuczaj, S. A., II (1977). The acquisition of regular and irregular past tense forms. *Journal of Verbal Learning and Verbal Behavior* 16, 589–600.

Kuczaj, S. A., II (1981). More on children's initial failure to relate specific acquisitions. *Journal of Child Language* 8, 485–487.

Kuczaj, S. A., II, and N. Brannick (1979). Children's use of the *wh* question modal auxiliary placement rule. *Journal of Experimental Child Psychology* 28, 43–67.

Labov, W. (1970). *The study of nonstandard English.* Urbana, IL: National Council of Teachers of English.

Landau, B. and L. R. Gleitman (1985). *Language and experience.* Cambridge, MA: Harvard University Press.

Lenneberg, E. H. (1964a). A biological perspective of language. In Lenneberg 1964b.

Lenneberg, E. H., ed. (1964b). *New directions in the study of language.* Cambridge, MA: MIT Press.

Lenneberg, E. H. (1967). *Biological foundations of language.* New York: Wiley.

Levy, Y. (1983). It's frogs all the way down. *Cognition* 15, 75–93.

Lieberman, P. (1984). *The biology and evolution of language.* Cambridge, MA: Harvard University Press.

Macnamara, J. (1972). Cognitive basis of language learning in infants. *Psychological Review* 79, 1–13.

240   Pinker

Macnamara, J. (1982). *Names for things: A study of child language*. Cambridge, MA: MIT Press.

MacWhinney, B. (1982). Basic processes in syntactic acquisition. In S. A. Kuczaj II, ed., *Language development*. Vol. 1, *Syntax and semantics*. Hillsdale, NJ: L. Erlbaum Associates.

MacWhinney, B., ed. (1987). *Mechanisms of language acquisition*. Hillsdale, NJ: L. Erlbaum Associates.

MacWhinney, B., and C. Snow (1985). The Child Language Data Exchange System. *Journal of Child Language* 12, 271–296.

Maratsos, M. P. (1974). How preschool children understand missing complement subjects. *Child Development* 45, 700–706.

Maratsos, M. P. (1983). Some current issues in the study of the acquisition of grammar. In P. Mussen, ed., *Carmichael's manual of child psychology*. 4th ed. New York: Wiley.

Maratsos, M. P., and R. Abramovitch (1975). How children understand full, truncated and anomalous passives. *Journal of Verbal Learning and Verbal Behavior* 14, 145–157.

Maratsos, M. P., and M. Chalkley (1981). The internal language of children's syntax: The ontogenesis and representation of syntactic categories. In K. Nelson, ed., *Children's language*, vol. 2. New York: Gardner Press.

Marler, P. R. (1970). A comparative approach to vocal learning: Song development in white-crowned sparrows. *Journal of Comparative and Physiological Psychology Monographs* 71 (No. 2, Part 2), 1–25.

Menyuk, P. (1969). *Sentences children use*. Cambridge, MA: MIT Press.

Miller, G. A. (1964). Language and psychology. In Lenneberg 1964b.

Minsky, M. (1975). A framework for representing knowledge. In P. H. Winston, ed., *The psychology of computer vision*. New York: McGraw-Hill.

Morgan, J. L. (1986). *From simple input to complex grammar*. Cambridge, MA: MIT Press.

Nelson, K. E. (1981). Individual differences in language development: Implications for development and language. *Developmental Psychology* 17, 170–187.

Newport, E. L., H. R. Gleitman, and L. Gleitman (1977). Mother I'd rather do it myself: Some effects and noneffects of maternal speech style. In Snow and Ferguson 1977.

Newport, E. L., and T. Supalla (in press). A critical period effect in the acquisition of a primary language. *Science*.

Osherson, D. N., M. Stob, and S. Weinstein (1985). *Systems that learn*. Cambridge, MA: MIT Press.

Peters, A. (1983). *The units of language acquisition*. New York: Cambridge University Press.

Piaget, J. (1926). *The language and thought of the child*. New York: Routledge and Kegan Paul.

Pinker, S. (1979). Formal models of language learning. *Cognition* 7, 217–283.

Pinker, S. (1982). A theory of the acquisition of lexical interpretive grammars. In J. Bresnan, ed., *The mental representation of grammatical relations*. Cambridge, MA: MIT Press.

Pinker, S. (1984). *Language learnability and language development*. Cambridge, MA: Harvard University Press.

Pinker, S. (1986). Productivity and conservatism in language acquisition. In Demopoulos and Marras 1986.

Pinker, S. (1987). The bootstrapping problem in language acquisition. In MacWhinney 1987.

Pinker, S. (1989). *Learnability and cognition: The acquisition of argument structure*. Cambridge, MA: MIT Press.

Pinker, S., D. S. Lebeaux, and L. A. Frost (1987). Productivity and constraints in the acquisition of the passive. *Cognition* 26, 195–267.

Pinker, S., and A. Prince (1988). On language and connectionism: Analysis of a Parallel Distributed Processing model of language acquisition. *Cognition* 28, 73–193.

Premack, D., and A. J. Premack (1983). *The mind of an ape*. New York: Norton.

Reich, P. A. (1986). *Language development*. Englewood Cliffs, NJ: Prentice-Hall.

Roeper, T., and E. Williams, eds. (1987). *Parameter-setting and language acquisition*. Dordrecht, Holland: Reidel.

Rosch, E. (1973). Natural categories. *Cognitive Psychology* 4, 328-350.

Rumelhart, D. E., and J. L. McClelland (1986). On learning the past tenses of English verbs. In J. L. McClelland, D. E. Rumelhart, and the PDP Research Group, *Parallel distributed processing: Explorations in the microstructure of cognition*. Vol. 2, *Psychological and biological models*. Cambridge, MA: MIT Press.

Schieffelin, B., and A. R. Eisenberg (1981). Cultural variation in children's conversations. In R. L. Schiefelbusch and D. D. Bricker, eds., *Early language: Acquisition and intervention*. Baltimore, MD: University Park Press.

Schlesinger, I. M. (1971). Production of utterances and language acquisition. In D. I. Slobin, ed., *The ontogenesis of grammar*. New York: Academic Press.

Seidenberg, M. S. (1986). Evidence from great apes concerning the biological bases of language. In Demopoulos and Marras 1987.

Seidenberg, M. S., and L. A. Petitto (1979). Signing behavior in apes: A critical review. *Cognition* 7, 177-215.

Shepard, R. N., and L. A. Cooper (1982). *Mental images and their transformations*. Cambridge, MA: MIT Press.

Shopen, T., ed. (1985). *Language typology and syntactic description*. Vol. 2, *Complex constructions*. New York: Cambridge University Press.

Skinner, B. F. (1957). *Verbal behavior*. New York: Appleton-Century-Crofts.

Slobin, D. (1973). Cognitive prerequisites for the development of grammar. In C. A. Ferguson and D. I. Slobin, eds., *Studies in child language development*. New York: Holt, Rinehart and Winston.

Slobin, D. I. (1977). Language change in childhood and in history. In J. Macnamara, ed., *Language learning and thought*. New York: Academic Press.

Slobin, D. I. (1982). Universal and particular in the acquisition of language. In Wanner and Gleitman 1982.

Slobin, D. I. (1985a). *The crosslinguistic study of language acquisition*. Vol. 1, *The data*. Hillsdale, NJ: L. Erlbaum Associates.

Slobin, D. I. (1985b). Crosslinguistic evidence for the language-making capacity. In D. I. Slobin, ed., *The crosslinguistic study of language acquisition*. Vol. 2, *Theoretical issues*. Hillsdale, NJ: L. Erlbaum Associates.

Snow, C. E., and C. A. Ferguson, eds. (1977). *Talking to children: Language input and acquisition*. Cambridge: Cambridge University Press.

Tavakolian, S., ed. (1981). *Language acquisition and linguistic theory*. Cambridge, MA: MIT Press.

Terrace, H., L. A. Petitto, R. J. Sanders, and T. G. Bever (1979). Can an ape create a sentence? *Science* 206, 891-902.

Wanner, E., and L. Gleitman, eds. (1982). *Language acquisition: The state of the art*. Cambridge: Cambridge University Press.

Wexler, K., and P. Culicover (1980). *Formal principles of language acquisition*. Cambridge, MA: MIT Press.

Wexler, K., and R. Manzini (1987). Parameters and learnability in binding theory. In T. Roeper and E. Williams, eds., *Parameters and linguistic theory*. Dordrecht, Holland: Reidel.

Whorf, B. (1956). *Language, thought, and reality*. Cambridge, MA: MIT Press.

9

Philosophical Issues in the Study of Language

James Higginbotham

Previous chapters have explored some of the major areas of linguistic research within cognitive science, research that has contributed to philosophical issues about structure and meaning in language and has in turn raised many philosophical questions about linguistics itself. In this concluding chapter we will consider a few of these: (1) the nature of the rules of language and their involvement in our linguistic activities; (2) the characteristics of evidence for linguistic principles, and the explanation of linguistic data; and (3) the links between linguistic analysis and our understanding of the structure of thought expressed in language.

9.1   Rules of Language

We have seen several examples of rules and principles that govern linguistic form, or the relation of form to meaning. But what is a rule of language? Are the rules of language like the general statements in science, or the rules of common life? Of course, the correct use of the word *rule* is not important; what is important is how linguistics understands this notion and how it should be distinguished from some other interpretations.

First, the rules of language are different from the rules of customary behavior, in that they are in general not consciously or explicitly known. For this reason, it is often said that the rules of a language are *tacitly* known to its speakers. For instance, as speakers of English we are said to know tacitly that a nominal predicate must agree with its subject in number. Our judgments about sentences like (1) and (2) support this conclusion:

(1)   They *is/are traitors.

(2)   I consider them traitors/*a traitor.

We all observe the rule, but only some of us are aware of it.

Contrast the rule of number agreement with a rule of ordinary life, such as the rule about stopping at red lights. This rule is consciously known and explicitly taught. It is even a matter of public law, although that is not necessary to its status as a rule (the rules of polite behavior, for example, are not imposed by law). Furthermore, we conform our behavior to the rule with the intention of so conforming it. This link between our actions and our intentions is one factor that distinguishes following a rule from merely showing regular behavior.

An example may help to make the distinction clear. Suppose that, whenever Sam is out in a beautiful sunset, he stops to admire it. He might do this, not because of any general intention to stop and look at sunsets, but simply because, on seeing a sunset, he feels the urge to stop. He does not make a rule to himself, "Whenever I see a sunset, I will stop," but his behavior is as regular as though he did. By contrast, when he stops at a red light, he does so because he generally intends to stop at red lights.

Is the rule of number agreement one that we follow because of our intention to do so? We are not introspectively aware of any such intention. But when we speak, we speak *in* a language, and its rules apply generally to our speech and to our interpretations of what others say. The rules guide us at best tacitly, and not explicitly.

Given that the rules of language are to be distinguished from those of common behavior, a distinctively philosophical question arises concerning the place of rules of this sort in the guidance of our actions. How are the rules of language, rules of which we are not in general aware, related to our thoughts and intentions? We can approach this question indirectly, by asking how language is learned and used, and what the study of the empirical problems found there seems to suggest. First, let us consider some possible answers to our question:

> 1. The rules of language are not rules in the sense of ones like "Stop at red lights" but are more in the nature of habits, such as the habit imagined above of stopping to admire a beautiful sunset. Conforming one's actions to a rule calls for awareness of the rule, whereas

habits do not require awareness (we have all had the experience of being surprised when it was pointed out to us that we had a certain habit). The statement that we as speakers of English follow the rule of number agreement means only that we habitually make predicates conform to the number of their subjects.

2. The rules of language are not conscious or explicit, but they are at least potentially so. Anthropologists have noticed rules to which people conform of which they are not aware. For instance, human societies differ in what they regard as the "comfortable distance" for friends or business associates to stand apart from one another when conversing. In general, "too close" connotes excessive intimacy, and "too distant" connotes hostility; but where the line is drawn varies from culture to culture. People are surprised when rules like this are brought to their attention, but they can recognize themselves as having followed them all along, once they are pointed out. A rule like number agreement might be of this kind.

3. The rules of language are not rules at all in any ordinary sense but describe a mechanism or mechanisms that we use in speaking and attending to language. Linguistic rules would be like the algorithms for vision (see "Visual Cognition" in the companion volume Osherson, Hollerbach, and Kosslyn 1990). In this case they would not be habits, and we might not even be potentially aware of them, just as we are not even potentially aware of the algorithms that our visual systems use in figuring out what objects are present to us.

4. The rules of language are like the rules that we consciously follow, except that they are not conscious, and possibly not even potentially conscious.

These views are to be found, with much elaboration and refinement, in the existing literature (see the Suggestions for Further Reading). Among them, the one that is most distant from what we might have expected is the last, which is the view most closely identified with Noam Chomsky's work. Because of its affinity with Descartes's doctrine that the activities of the mind are not reducible to more familiar physical operations or to simply mental activities shared by animals both with and without language, it may be called *Cartesian*. The Cartesian view in various forms is characteristic of much work in cognitive science. The other three views might be called *reductionist*, in that each attempts to interpret the notion "rule of language" by assimilating it to a more familiar paradigm, of habit, of unexpressed thought, or of psychological (and potentially physical) mechanism. Perhaps one of these reductionist views, or some combination of them, will in time be vindicated; however, as we will see, it is difficult at present to maintain any combination of them as exhausting the notion "rule of language." For this reason, the nature of tacit knowledge has been a subject of recurrent interest in cognitive science and philosophy.

Some information about rules of language can be gained from what is empirically known about language learning and language use. First, the rules of language are not ordained down to the last detail by the laws of nature: so much is already shown by the existence of different languages. There must be some process of linguistic acculturation, in which humans pick up the language around them. The simplest such process would be drill. If language fit this paradigm, then it would be under the control of the stimuli that occasioned it, and it would be inculcated by explicit training, relying only on the learner's ability to discern the salient features of the scene. But neither part of the paradigm holds. Normal language use is appropriate to its setting but is not controlled by it; nor do children receive much formal training as they learn to speak (see chapter 8). The process of linguistic acculturation must therefore be more complex.

Second, a striking feature of language, which any general theory of its acquisition and mastery must account for, is its *unboundedness*. The stock of sentences (and even of potential words) of a human language is unlimited, and it is in fact easy to construct infinite sets of sentences, infinitely many of whose members will exceed any given finite length. For example, recursive rules of phrase structure allow language users to embed complex NPs indefinitely (see chapter 1). Such a sequence might begin as follows:

(3)   [The man whom you saw] is here.

[The woman who met [the man whom you saw]] is here.

[The person who likes [the woman who met [the man whom you saw]]] is here.

And so on.

Evidently, we are not trained in sentences one at a time, or even in finite batches however large, since such training or teaching would not begin to approximate an unbounded output. Moreover, language is not the only unbounded system available to us. Prominent among such systems are the numbers, the distinct shapes and arrangements of geometrical figures, and musical melodies. How are such systems made available? In each case a natural hypothesis is that we grasp them through the iterative deployment of a finite stock of devices. Iteration is already illustrated in our ways of building up complex numerical expressions and in the number system itself, where we start from zero or one and "go on adding one."

If we reject drill as the means of learning language, we might instead conceive of language mastery as consisting in a speaker's having in some way grasped a complex theory, governing the formal conditions on the nature of constructions and their meanings. Our early experience guides us to the theory to construct. Somehow, from hearing such rules as number agreement observed—in the sense that we hear the grammatical examples in (1) and (2) and do not hear the ungrammatical examples—we construct a theory that permits the grammatical ones and excludes the others. Similarly, our evidence for meaning can be expected to come from a combination of our linguistic and perceptual experience.

In supposing that speakers acquire language from linguistic and perceptual evidence, we have made the substantive assumption that other features of a sufficiently normal environment are not relevant. What language we have acquired is assumed not to have varied with our carbohydrate intake as children, for instance, or how often our parents smiled at us. Malnutrition, emotional deprivation, and other ills certainly impair cognitive abilities. We are assuming, however, that language does not depend on any other features of life than the linguistic, across a broad normal range.

Assuming now that the rules of language are part of a theory that speakers tacitly possess, it would not be appropriate to think of these rules as reflecting habits of speech or the effects of drill. As we will now see, it follows that an otherwise natural way of understanding the relations of linguistic rules to our thoughts and intentions cannot be accepted as it stands.

If an account of the rules of language cannot be based on habits, we might still regard the rules as potentially conscious, or as guiding our activities beneath the surface of consciousness, as in the second possibility sketched earlier. For simple rules like number agreement, this is a plausible position. Consider, however, the complex rule for pronominal coreference discussed in chapter 1. This rule involved the notion of *c-command* in syntactic structures, a concept that is fairly remote from what speakers would know without an explicit study of grammatical theory. Similarly, the rules governing the distribution of negative polarity items like *any*, discussed in chapter 2, could be stated only with reference to abstract concepts from logical theory, such as downward entailingness. Of course, these rules are potentially conscious in the sense that theoretical investigation can discover them and linguists can explicitly know them. But their theoretical character sets them apart from rules of customary behavior to which participants in the activities covered by the rules simply have not attended.

The third view seeks to explain the absence from consciousness of linguistic rules by locating them in a distinctive faculty of the mind, or *module* in the sense of Fodor (1983). Some of the evidence that supports this point of view has been presented in chapters 4–6, where it was stressed that language processing involves elaborate rules of which we are not aware. Let us review some of the evidence that syntax and semantics are modular in nature.

Part of the evidence that language involves rules, and not merely habits, is that a person's grammar exhibits a certain *autonomy*, or independence of conditions of use, both by that speaker and by others. It is a striking fact that sentences that have virtually no likelihood of utterance are at once understood and that ambiguities can be perceived even where it is obvious that the speaker would have intended only one of a family of possible meanings. Examples of expressions perceived as sentences even though they are nonsensical include Chomsky's famous case (4):

(4)   Colorless green ideas sleep furiously.

The independence of meaning from use is seen in examples like (5):

(5)   I almost had my wallet stolen.

(4) is grammatical, although nonsensical. (5) is normally perceived as meaning 'I almost suffered the theft of my wallet'. On reflection, however, it is also found to have the meanings 'I almost succeeded in stealing my wallet' (compare *I almost had the tournament won*) and 'I almost arranged (was on the point of arranging) for my wallet to be stolen' (compare *They almost had a man shot*).

It seems, then, that the view that linguistic rules reflect the operation of abstract mechanisms is supported by the autonomy of the principles of grammar. It is not to be denied that there are strong analogies between visual algorithms and the mechanisms of hearing and speech. But there are limits to the analogy, because language is not just a perceptual and motor faculty. The limits are basically two: language serves us also when we think without saying anything; and some of the properties of language are perceived only on reflection. Example (5) illustrates the second point, showing that the cognition of language goes beyond perception. The first point is introspectively obvious, although it is controversial what moral might be drawn from it. If the view can be defended that much of thinking is "silent speech," then perhaps it is not so telling against the abstract-mechanisms view.

Because it is not committed to reducing the rules of language to something else, the fourth, Cartesian, view of linguistic rules is compatible with the known phenomena that we have reviewed, including the complexity of the rules of grammar, their inaccessibility to consciousness, and their autonomous character. Another aspect of Descartes's conception of the mind is generally rejected as a research assumption, however—namely, his thesis that the mind was a *separable substance* and in particular not a physical thing. Contrary to Descartes, cognitive scientists who otherwise adopt his views consider that the study of the mind is the study of the brain and nervous system, conducted at some level of abstraction that we would like to clarify. Even if the current reductionist proposals for linguistic rules cannot be accepted, we may hope that empirical and conceptual research will bring us closer to understanding the relations between states and operations of the brain and the rules of language.

9.2 Types of Explanation

Science is responsive to evidence and aims to explain phenomena, including physical, social, and psychological facts. Here we will consider the types of explanation found in linguistic theory and the evidence on which it is generally based. The chief point will be that explanations of different types must be distinguished and that each has a role to play in linguistic theory.

Explanations answer the question "Why?" in theoretical terms proposed on the basis of the evidence. An explanation may be very long and complicated, or very simple; it may be mathematical or formal, or relatively informal; and it may be more or less general.

For example, why is it possible to skate on ice, and not on other smooth surfaces, like glass? The answer is that the pressure of the skater's weight partly melts the ice, reducing friction so that a force in the direction of the skates' runners results in motion. That is a simple, informal explanation of a familiar fact. The sciences abound in more complicated explanations, covering general classes of phenomena.

Some explanations account for particular events, such as why a particular eclipse of the moon occurred or why a certain bridge collapsed on a certain occasion. These explanations often depend on accounts of when a certain *kind* of event will occur, such as an eclipse, or the collapse of a bridge, or (to use an example from chapter 6) the systematic misperception of "garden path" sentences. A particular eclipse of the moon might be explained by showing that an eclipse will occur whenever three bodies are aligned in such and such a way and then pointing out that the earth, moon, and sun were indeed so aligned, as shown by independent astronomical measurements. Similarly, the collapse of a particular bridge might be explained in virtue of laws that apply to all nearly rigid bodies constructed of a certain material when subject to stress. Finally, misperception of garden path sentences is held to follow from the internal system for sentence perception, which applies to normal sentences as well as to the misperceived ones.

Other types of things that may be explained, which are neither particular events nor kinds of events, are *capacities* and *abilities*. For instance, if the engineers who designed a certain bridge tell us that it can carry a thousand cars without collapsing, they make a statement about a capacity (or capability) of the bridge; if we say that Sonja can skate, we make a statement about her abilities. Explanations of capacities and abilities are as important in cognitive science as they are elsewhere.

The explanation of a capacity or ability can be broken into two major components, which we will call the *state component* and the *conditions component*. The bridge that can hold a thousand cars is in a certain *state* that is responsible for its having that capacity. The capacity will be exercised when a thousand cars are on the bridge and when in addition the proper *conditions* are in effect. These conditions often "go without saying," but they are important in bringing out the scope of an explanation. In the bridge example, for instance, the engineers would not be regarded as having spoken falsely if terrorists were busy undermining the bridge as the cars drove across it. If we say that Sonja can skate, but she is now making many slips and falls because she is grieving or distracted, we have still spoken truly about Sonja, for she still has her ability to skate, although something is interfering with its exercise.

Let us take stock of the above distinctions. We have discriminated among

1. Explanation of a particular event (why Sonja skated without falling at 12 noon);
2. Explanation of a kind of event (why Sonja will skate without falling when she is on the ice);
3. Explanation of a capacity or ability (why Sonja can skate under certain conditions);
4. Explanation of the state component of an ability (what it is about Sonja's limbs and sense of coordination that enables her to skate).

These distinctions can usefully be applied to explanation in linguistics. Again, we can discriminate among

1. Explanation of a particular linguistic event (why Sonja said such and such yesterday; why Sonja heard a certain utterance in a certain way);
2. Explanation of a kind of linguistic event (why Sonja will hear sentences of a certain kind as having a certain meaning);
3. Explanation of a capacity or ability with respect to language (why Sonja could learn a language; why she is able to speak and understand a language under favorable conditions);
4. Explanation of the state component of linguistic ability (what it was about Sonja as a neonate that put her in a position to learn language; what it is about her brain now that enables her to speak and understand a language).

Since it deals with specific perceptual events and kinds of events, research in perceptual psycholinguistics seeks explanations of the first two kinds. Developmental studies focus on explaining the growth of a capacity and the conditions under which it will be exercised; most explanations in that field are of the third kind. The fourth kind is the province of the more abstract parts of linguistic theory, phonology, syntax, and semantics, usually studied as the theory of linguistic *competence*. Because explanations of this kind are to be carefully distinguished from the others, let us look at a simple example of an abstract explanation.

Why do the grammaticality judgments in (1) and (2) come out as they do? The explanation given earlier was that a predicate must agree in number with its subject. But for this explanation to be satisfactory, we will have to characterize the notions "subject" and "predicate" themselves. We can do this in terms of the concept of phrase structure, as follows. Suppose that a clause (C) consists of two immediate constituents, a noun phrase (NP) and a predicate phrase (PredP). Then we say that the *subject* of the clause is the NP that is an immediate constituent of C, and its *predicate* is its sister constituent, also an immediate constituent of C. Recognizing also the grammatical feature *number*, which may be set at singular or plural and which attaches to both subjects and predicates, we would propose generally that structures like (6) are grammatical and those like (7) are not:

(6) $[_C [_{NP} +$ singular$] [_{PredP} +$ singular$]]$

(7) $[_C [_{NP} +$ singular$] [_{PredP} -$ singular$]]$

Suppose that this explanation is correct, and consider a person—say, Mary—to whom it applies. What has been explained about Mary is an aspect of the state that she is in that enables her to speak and understand English. The evidence that she is in this state may be that she judges the expressions in (1) and (2) in certain ways—say, rejecting the starred ones and accepting the others. As noted in chapters 1–3, much of the evidence in linguistic theory derives from the judgments that native speakers make about the grammaticality or ungrammaticality of utterances in their language. Thus, people who makes linguistic judgments are like the subjects of a psychological experiment; and if they are investigating their own native language, they may be both the experimental subjects and the experimenters.

The types of facts to be explained in linguistic theory differ at least in the ways distinguished above. Particular *phenomena* in language might be the effect of any of a number of factors, of which linguistic competence is only one. Suppose, for instance, that a person suffers from a language disability, of one of the sorts considered in chapter 7. As noted there, it is possible that the disability stems from a deficiency in linguistic competence; but it is also possible that competence is intact, although the conditions required for its proper exercise have been disrupted. Inversely, a person to whom a language is not native can often speak it and understand it quite well, although such a person's underlying competence does not approach that of a native speaker. The distinctions made here should help you to appreciate the complexity of the problems linguistic phenomena pose and in the assessment of philosophical views about linguistic competence listed in the Suggestions for Further Reading.

9.3   Linguistic Structures and Structures of Thoughts

The analysis of the structure of our thoughts has two components, the *structural* and the *conceptual*. The first is concerned with explaining how thoughts are put together out of the concepts that make them up, and the second with the nature of the primitive concepts themselves. This division in the realm of thoughts is parallel to the linguistic division between syntax and morphology, on the one hand, and the nature of primitive lexical items, on the other. The correspondence is not exact, because there are syntactically complex expressions, called *idioms*, that express single concepts (for instance, the idiom *kick the bucket* simply means 'die') and because apparently simple words may contain a kind of analytical complexity (for instance, the word *kill* involves the concept of death, since a person who is killed dies). However, it is fair to say that the properties of language, in which our thoughts are embodied, are indispensable for understanding the properties of thoughts and the relations among them. We will consider some points on the structural, and then on the conceptual, side of the investigation.

9.3.1   The Structural Component of Thoughts

Reasoning goes forward in language, and the properties of arguments that exhibit correct or incorrect reasoning have been a traditional subject of both philosophical and linguistic interest. The analysis of arguments in language is much advanced by an exact understanding of how language works. Logical investigation brings to light puzzles and problems that show that sentences that at first glance seem parallel in structure may have very different logical properties. The solution of these puzzles turns out to be particularly revealing of how we put our thoughts into words.

Here is a fairly simple and typical illustration. Consider the pattern of inference shown in (8), where a and b are names or other definite NPs like *the president* and C represents a context in which they occur:

(8)   C (a);
       a is b; therefore:
       C (b).

This pattern, which shows the *substitutivity of identity*, is shown to be correct by the countless inferences that conform to it, as for instance (9):

(9)   The president is in California;
       Ronald Reagan is the president; therefore:
       Ronald Reagan is in California.

(This pattern is often called *Leibniz's law*, having been enunciated by that philosopher as a property of the concept of strict equality or identity.) However, the following inference is obviously fallacious:

(10)   The president is elected every four years;
       Ronald Reagan is the president; therefore:
       Ronald Reagan is elected every four years.

The fallacy cannot be dismissed as a quirk, on pain of abandoning Leibniz's law or leaving its context of application uncertain. How do we know that, although (9) is a correct inference, (10) is not? And what general classification can we give of both the correct and the incorrect cases?

An answer suggests itself when we reflect that the reference of the expression *the president* varies with the time of its use, in a way that the reference of a proper name, such as *Ronald Reagan*, does not. If we make such relativity explicit, then we should understand the first premise of (10) as in (11):

(11)   Every fourth year is a time t such that
       The person who is to become president at t is elected at t.

Fixing some time t_0 as the time for evaluating the second premise, it would be rendered as in (12):

(12)   Ronald Reagan is the president at t_0.

The conclusion of the argument is then as in (13):

(13)   Every fourth year is a time t such that
       Ronald Reagan is elected at t.

But now the inference is plainly fallacious. The term *the president* is not just functioning as a name, because the generalization *every fourth year* binds a variable within it. In fact, (9) exhibits the same error as the absurd inference (14):

(14)   For every whole number x, $x^2 \geq x$;
       4 is 2^2; therefore:
       For every whole number x, $4 \geq x$.

We can immediately see the absurdity of (14), but the absurdity of (9) has to be revealed by analysis.

The literature on syntax and semantics provides many puzzles of this sort. They are not all as easy as this one; in fact, it is fair to say that many have never been insightfully resolved and that more are waiting to be discovered as research deepens.

9.3.2   The Conceptual Component of Thoughts

Research on human concepts starts with the recognition that the concepts that we have, or that we find in language after language, constitute only a small number of the concepts that are potentially available. Let us call concepts that are commonly attested, easily learned, and generally expressed by single words in natural languages the *natural* concepts. According to this definition, the natural concepts include "green," "snow," "tree," "squirrel," and the like. These concepts pick out certain regions of space and time as the region that is green, the region where snow is to be found, and the regions for each point in time occupied at that point by a tree or a squirrel. However, not all of our concepts are spatiotemporal; for instance, the concept expressed by *every* is an abstract concept that applies to any realm of things (see chapter 2). Numbers and geometrical shapes are other examples of abstract concepts.

That there are other concepts besides the natural ones is most easily shown with reference to abstract concepts. The shapes of bodies are innumerable, but only a few of them have names. We have words like *ellipse* and *spiral* but no word for, say, a closed figure that is partly curved and partly straight. The *concept* expressed by *partly curved and partly straight closed figure* is a perfectly respectable concept (in fact, we have just expressed it), but it is for us not a natural one. To take another example from chapter 2, the quantifier concepts of natural languages possess a peculiar property, conservativity, that is not shared by all such concepts; in fact, it belongs to very few.

The study of natural concepts is therefore a critical part of the study of our cognitive makeup. In research on human concepts it is important to note that natural and nonnatural concepts—like natural human languages and "bizarre," nonnatural, or artificial languages—are equally "reasonable," considered in themselves. Consider the nonnatural concept, call it "X," which applies to any ensemble made up of the top half of a human and the bottom half of a building. This concept is as determinate as the more ordinary concepts with whose aid it was characterized: we would have no more difficulty in telling how many Xs there are in a city than in telling how many people and buildings there are in it. But we have every reason to expect, from the fact that there is no known language in which there is a simple word for "X," and from the fact that humans do not project X-like concepts as the meanings of words to which they are exposed, that the concept "X" is not a natural one. More precisely, X-like concepts are not natural for *us*, although they might be natural for some other creature. Our bias toward concepts like "person" and "building" and against concepts like "X" is something that we contribute.

The issue of natural concepts arises for vocabulary items of all sorts. The philosophical point made here is that the objects that fulfill our natural concepts constitute our system of "things," the common world in which human beings live. In probing the basis for our knowledge and use of language, we investigate our largely untaught and highly structured conception of that world.

Suggestions for Further Reading

Chapter 4 of Chomsky 1986 contains a discussion of issues surrounding the notion of rule-following in the methodology of linguistics and responds especially to a form of skepticism about rule-following presented as an interpretation of the later views of the philosopher Ludwig Wittgenstein in Kripke 1982. For a defense of the thesis that the rules of language constitute a set of mechanisms, or a "module" of the mind, see Fodor 1983. Higginbotham 1987 considers whether Fodor's account of modularity exhausts the sense of that term as applied to language. Similar questions are brought up in Peacocke 1986 and in the discussion in Peacocke et al. 1986. A classic statement of skepticism about linguistic methodology is Quine 1970a; Chomsky responds at length in chapter 4 of Chomsky 1975.

Hornstein and Lightfoot 1981 contains an excellent introductory essay on linguistic explanation and several detailed contributions on the subject by other authors. A classical view of scientific explanation is found in Hempel and Oppenheim 1948. A distinction among types of explanation comparable to that used here is made in chapter 1 of Chomsky 1978, where alternative views are also discussed.

The issues of language and thought, involving questions of logical and grammatical form and natural concepts, form a central part of modern analytic philosophy. Quine 1970b contains an important and influential view of the enterprise. Chierchia and McConnell-Ginet, forthcoming, is an introduction to contemporary linguistic and philosophical problems.

Questions

9.1   In the text it was suggested that knowledge of numbers, geometry, and music is comparable to knowledge of language in terms of its unbounded nature (there is an infinite number of possible numbers, geometrical shapes, and melodies). Are there further analogies, as some have thought? Taking numbers, geometry, or music as an example, explore to what extent it is a cognitive ability like language: Is it known explicitly or tacitly? Is it a matter of habit, or is there, for instance, numerical, geometrical, or musical competence similar to grammatical competence? Does it have a special relation to perception?

9.2   What hypotheses might explain why the sentence *I almost had my wallet stolen* (1) is not immediately perceived to be ambiguous and (2) is seen on reflection to be three ways ambiguous? Do these hypotheses have consequences for the nature of linguistic competence or for the nature of our practical abilities? What investigations might be undertaken to further support or disconfirm these hypotheses?

9.3   The following inference is generally understood as correct in one sense, not correct in another:

That train is the 5:15;
The 5:15 is often late; therefore:
That train is often late.

Explain both senses as carefully as you can. In what way is your analysis similar to the analysis of the fallacious inference about Ronald Reagan in the text?

References

Chierchia, G., and S. McConnell-Ginet (forthcoming). *Introduction to semantics: Meaning and linguistic structure.* Cambridge, MA: MIT Press.

Chomsky, N. (1975). *Reflections on language.* New York: Pantheon.

Chomsky, N. (1978). *Rules and representations.* New York: Columbia University Press.

Chomsky, N. (1986). *Knowledge of language: Its nature, origin, and use.* New York: Praeger.

Fodor, J. (1983). *The modularity of mind.* Cambridge, MA: MIT Press.

Hempel, C., and P. Oppenheim (1948). The logic of explanation. Reprinted in H. Feigl and M. Brodbeck, eds. (1953). *Readings in the philosophy of science.* New York: Appleton-Century-Crofts.

Higginbotham, J. (1987). The autonomy of syntax and semantics. In J. Garfield, ed., *Modularity in knowledge representation and natural-language understanding.* Cambridge, MA: MIT Press.

Hornstein, N., and D. Lightfoot, eds. (1981). *Explanation in linguistics.* London: Longman.

Kripke, S. (1982). *Wittgenstein on rules and private language.* Cambridge, MA: Harvard University Press.

Osherson, D. N., J. M. Hollerbach, and S. M. Kosslyn, eds. (1990). *Visual cognition and action: An invitation to cognitive science, vol. 2.* Cambridge, MA: MIT Press.

Peacocke, C. (1986). Explanation in computational psychology: Language, perception, and level 1.5. *Language and Mind* 1, 101–123.

Peacocke, C., G. Humphreys, P. Quinlan, J. Higginbotham, S. Schiffer, and S. Soames

(1986). Discussion of "Explanation in computational psychology." *Language and Mind* 1, 355–402.

Quine, W. V. O. (1970a). Methodological reflections on current linguistic theory. In D. Davidson and G. Harman, eds., *Semantics of natural language*. Dordrecht, Holland: Reidel.

Quine, W. V. O. (1970b). *Philosophy of logic*. 2nd ed., 1986. Cambridge, MA: Harvard University Press.

Contents of Volume 2

Visual Cognition and Action: An Invitation to Cognitive Science
*edited by Daniel N. Osherson, Stephen Michael Kosslyn, and
John M. Hollerbach*

Contents of Volume 3

Thinking: An Invitation to Cognitive Science
edited by Daniel N. Osherson and Edward E. Smith

Index

DATE DUE